W9-BQM-466

# A Brief History *of the* Paradox

# A Brief History *of the* Paradox

## Philosophy and the Labyrinths of the Mind

*Roy Sorensen*



OXFORD
UNIVERSITY PRESS
2003

OXFORD
UNIVERSITY PRESS

Oxford New York
Auckland Bangkok Buenos Aires Cape Town Chennai
Dar es Salaam Delhi Hong Kong Istanbul Karachi Kolkata
Kuala Lumpur Madrid Melbourne Mexico City Mumbai Nairobi
São Paulo Shanghai Taipei Tokyo Toronto



Published by Oxford University Press, Inc.
198 Madison Avenue, New York, New York 10016
www.oup.com



Library of Congress Cataloging-in-Publication Data
Sorensen, Roy. A.
A brief history of the paradox: philosophy and the labyrinths of the mind/ Roy Sorensen.
p. cm.
Includes bibliographical references and index.
ISBN 0-19-515903-9
1. Paradox. 2. Paradoxes. I. Title.

BC199.P2S67 2003
165—dc21 2003048631

Permission to print V. Alan White's "Antimony" kindly granted by the author.

Book design by planettheo.com

9 8 7 6 5 4 3 2 1
Printed in the United States of America
on acid-free paper

*To*

*those who never*

*have a book dedicated to them.*

There are two famous labyrinths where our reason very often goes astray: one concerns the great question of the Free and the Necessary, above all in the production and the origin of Evil; the other consists in the discussion of continuity and of the indivisibles which appear to be the elements thereof, and where the consideration of the infinite must enter in. The first perplexes almost all the human race, the other exercises philosophers only.

—Gottfried Leibniz, *Theodicy*

Here and elsewhere we shall not obtain the best insight into things until we actually see them growing from the beginning . . .

—Aristotle, *Politics*

# Contents

# List of Figures

# Preface

Mathematicians characterize prime numbers as their atoms because all numbers can be analyzed as products of the primes. I regard paradoxes as the atoms of philosophy because they constitute the basic points of departure for disciplined speculation.

Philosophy is held together by its questions rather than by its answers. The basic philosophical questions come from troubles within our ordinary conceptual scheme. These paradoxes bind generations together with common problems and an accumulating reservoir of responses.

Philosophy is generally presented in terms of its issues or in terms of its history. A study of the history of paradoxes provides an opportunity to practice both approaches simultaneously.

This book is guided by an anthropological hypothesis: paradoxes developed from the riddles of Greek folklore (as did the oracles of Delphi, Christian catechisms, and the game of charades). Accordingly, I begin classically with the Greek philosophers. They refined informal verbal dueling into "dialectic," the procedure best known through Plato's dialogues. The efforts of the Greeks were improved in turn, yielding contemporary logic and dialectical conceptions of history and science.

Paradoxes are questions (or in some cases, pseudoquestions) that suspend us between *too many* good answers. When an amoeba divides in two, does it go out of existence? On the one hand, organisms can survive the loss of half of their bodies. The only problem with the mother amoeba is that she has been too successful; instead of losing half her body as a dead tissue, she has created a second healthy amoeba. On the other hand, amoeba reproduction seems like suicide because there is nothing to survive *as*. It would be arbitrary to identify the mother amoeba with just one of her daughters. And to say that the mother amoeba continues as the pair of daughters conflicts with the idea that organisms are unified individuals.

Typically, the case for one solution to a paradox looks compelling in isolation. The question is kept alive by the tug of war between evenly matched contestants. The Greeks were intrigued by surprising, enduring oppositions such as these.

Common sense may seem like a seamless, timeless whole. But it really resembles the earth's surface; a jigsaw puzzle of giant plates that slowly collide and rub against each other. The stability of terra firma is the result of great forces and counterforces. The equilibrium is imperfect; there is constant underlying tension and, occasionally, sudden slippage. Paradoxes mark fault lines in our common-sense world.

Do these fissures reach into reason itself? Many philosophers urge us to follow the argument wherever it leads; in the case of Socrates, even to death. But what do we do when compelling arguments lead us in *conflicting* directions?

One radical response, pioneered by Heraclitus, is to accept the reality of contradictions. He thinks the paradoxes are out there. This line of thought has been extended by

Hegel, Marx, and nowadays, by the dialethic logicians of Australia.

At the other extreme are those who trace our inconsistency to reliance on our senses. Parmenides dismisses the appearance of there being many things that are changing and moving. He conceived of reality as a single, unified whole. Zeno's paradoxes were intended to reinforce Parmenides's conclusion by extracting absurdities from common sense.

Most philosophers are moderates who try to reconcile perception with reason. Democritus's compromise was a changing universe of complex objects built up from unchanging, indivisible atoms moving about in the void. Rationalists pitch the negotiation in reason's favor. They trace paradoxes to shortages of a priori insights. With the rise of science, empiricists have driven a hard bargain in the opposite direction. They trace paradoxes to a glut of misinformation. If we could cleanse ourselves of superstition and subtler contaminants, we would gain the patience needed to answer what riddles can be answered and the maturity to admit ignorance when at the outer range of our senses. Paradoxes have both shaped and been shaped by the classic debate between rationalists and empiricists. A faithful portrayal of paradoxes situates them in their natural intellectual environments. Without this background, they take on the appearance of circus animals.

I concede that paradoxes *sometimes* ought to be studied in isolation. Logicians and mathematicians routinely assemble paradoxes in a clinical setting. Antinomies, paralogisms, and sophisms are stood before the reader like draftees at a mass medical screening. Much has been learned by analytical methods that ignore the bigger picture. But why *always* ignore the bigger picture?

In any case, I am interested in the developmental and antiquarian aspects of paradoxes. Consequently, my approach is more leisurely. Although I have my own theory of paradoxes, my general intent is to have the paradoxes enter at their own initiative and in their original order.

The deepest paradoxes are extroverts, naturally good at introducing themselves. These challenges to compulsory, universal beliefs are self-illuminating; they stimulate us to draw distinctions and formulate hypotheses that bear on the issue of how we ought to react to paradoxes. Is common sense ever mistaken? Are paradoxes symptoms of the frailties of human reason? Do they point to ineffable truths? When is it rational to ignore arguments?

When Aristotle's nephew Callisthenes volunteered to record the expedition of Alexander the Great, he had to follow the impetuous Alexander into situations that invited miscalculation. The discoverers of paradoxes expose their historians to a parallel danger. From what appears to be a safe distance, I see the inquirer crane his head for a better look, eventually placing one foot on one solid-looking principle and the other foot on a second principle that is actually incompatible with the first. In my eagerness to document his insecure footing, I risk misstep myself. In the following pages, I take this chance over and over, across two millennia. Sooner or later, I must share the fate of those I chronicle. I apologize for these errors but am grateful to those who led me up to a position to make them.

I also have more specific acknowledgments. I thank the editor of *Mind* for permission to reprint, in chapter one, a portion of "The Egg Came Before the Chicken," *Mind* 101/403 (July 1992): 541-42. I am grateful to V. Alan White for permission to quote "Antinomy" from his website devoted to philosophy songs at www.manitowoc.uwc.edu/staff/awhite/phisong.htm. Finally, I thank colleagues and my students at Dartmouth College for their comments and suggestions on earlier drafts of this book.

# A Brief History
*of the*
# Paradox

ONE

# Anaximander and the Riddle of Origin

"*. . . 5, 1, 4, 1, 3—Done!*" exclaims a haggard old man.

"You look exhausted, what have you been doing?"

"*Reciting the complete decimal expansion of* π *backwards.*"

So goes one of Ludwig Wittgenstein's philosophical jokes. A beginningless individual borders on contradiction. Yet philosophy itself may have begun by embracing this absurdity. For this is Anaximander's (ca. 610 B.C.–585 B.C.) solution to the first paradox in recorded history.

## WHERE DO WE COME FROM?

People are interested in tracing their ancestral lines. Anaximander generalized this curiosity. He notes that each human being begins as a baby who survives only if nurtured. Anaximander infers that the first human beings were cared for by animals. The Greeks knew of sharks that gave birth to live, autonomous young. Anaximander conjectured that the first human beings were born from aquatic creatures who then reared them.

But where did our animal ancestors come from? Here again, Anaximander seems ahead of his time. He infers that these creatures had inanimate precursors.

What were the precursors of *those* precursors? However long we continue the series, it makes sense to ask, what happened before that? Yet it seems impossible for history to be without a beginning. Isn't that the point of Wittgenstein's joke?

Perhaps some of Anaximander's contemporaries tried to precisely formulate the absurdity as an impossible wait: If there is an infinite past, then an infinite amount of time would have had to elapse to reach the present moment. An infinite wait is endless. But here we are at the present moment! Therefore, the past must have a beginning.

Unlike Anaximander, readers of this book are at home with negative numbers. We can model an infinite past by letting 0 represent the present moment, -1 represent yesterday, -2 the day before yesterday, and so on. For us, the fact that there are infinitely many numbers before 0 does not raise a mystery about how 0 can be reached. Why should an infinite past be any more puzzling than the infinite sequence of negative integers?

This mathematical model seems apt for an infinite future. +1 could be tomorrow, +2 could represent the day after tomorrow, and so on. You can imagine encountering an immortal destined to count forever. Each positive integer will be counted by this number god.

But negative numbers are not enough to solve the paradox of origin. There is a "something from nothing" feel about the claim to have recited infinitely many digits.

## WHAT IS A PARADOX?

When discussing whether the barbarians originated philosophy, Diogenes Laertius reports, "As to the Gymnosophists and Druids we are told that they uttered their philosophy in riddles . . . " I take paradoxes to be a species of riddle. The oldest philosophical questions evolved from folklore and show vestiges of the verbal games that generated them.

Seduction riddles are constructed to make a bad answer appear as a good answer. How much dirt is in a hole two meters wide, two meters long, and two meters deep? This question entices us to answer, eight cubic meters of dirt. The riddler then reminds us that no dirt is in a *hole*.

Mystery riddles, in contrast, appear to have no answer. One way to achieve this aura of insolubility is by describing an object in an apparently contradictory way. As a boy, Anaximander must have been asked the ancient Greek riddle, "What has a mouth but never eats, a bed but never sleeps?" (Answer: A river.) Literary riddles elaborate the genres found in folklore. Anaximander probably learned of the riddle of the Sphinx from Hesiod's *Theogony*. We know it best from Sophocles' play *Oedipus the King*. The Sphinx is a monster who challenges travelers with a riddle she learned from the Muses: "What goes on four legs in the morning, two legs in the afternoon, three legs in the evening?" She wants her victims to remain ignorant of the underlying metaphors.

Oedipus answers by *decoding* the question: At the dawn of life, a baby begins life on all fours, then learns to walk upright on two legs, and finally spends his twilight years hobbling around with a cane. Tragically, Oedipus fails to solve deeper question of his own origin (continuously posed by the blind prophet Tiresias in his "riddling speech").

With most mystery riddles, there is little hope of understanding the question until after the answer is revealed. Two weeks before flying a plane into one of the World Trade Center's towers, Mohammed Atta phoned Ramzi Binalshibh asking help with a riddle: Two sticks, a dash and a cake with a stick down—what is it? Binalshibh was baffled. After the attack on September 11, he realized that two sticks stand for 11, a dash is a dash and a cake with a stick down signifies 9.

Sometimes the riddler himself is in the dark. When the Mad Hatter asks Alice, "Why is a raven like a writing desk?," he has no idea of what the answer is. Neither did the creator of the Mad Hatter, the logician Lewis Carroll.

The poser of a paradox need not drape its meaning behind ambiguities and metaphor. He can afford to be open because the riddle works by overburdening the audience with too many good answers. Consider the folk paradox, "Which came first, the chicken or the egg?" The egg answer is backed by an apparently compelling principle: Every chicken comes from an egg. The trouble is that there is an equally compelling principle supporting the opposite answer: Every egg comes from a chicken.

Bodies of conflicting evidence are usually unstable. Our ambivalence gets washed away by further witnesses, new measurements, and recalculations. In contrast, paradoxes are exceptionally bouyant. Whenever one side seems to prevail, balance is restored by a counterdevelopment. From engineering, we know that this kind of dynamic equilibrium is most simply achieved by symmetry. When two boards are propped up against each other (like this: /\), their equal but opposed forces keep the pair standing. This symmetry is evident in the chicken or egg riddle. But we will also encounter more complex configurations.

The Greeks were fascinated by antagonistic struggle. They admired questions that are sustained by a balance of power between rival answers. Their playwrights became adept at smelting the ore of paradoxes.

The paradox lover delights in an unexpectedly even match—especially when his audience can foretell the rightful outcome. Children know the answers to Zeno's paradoxes of motion: Can you walk out of a room? Can an arrow travel through the air? If a slow tortoise is given a small head start, can the fleet-footed Achilles overtake the tortoise? Zeno confounds his audience by arguing logically for a *no* answer to each of these questions. Like Lewis Carroll's Alice, children know "there is a mistake somewhere"—but they cannot quite put their fingers on it.

Paradoxes can often be "dissolved" by showing that a precondition for a solution fails to hold. Developers of the logic of questions define a *direct answer* as an answer that offers exactly as much information as the questioner requested, neither more nor less. When I ask, "Was Anaximander or his teacher Thales the first Greek to map the stars?" I present you with two direct answers and request that you pick the correct answer (or *a* correct answer). You completely comply with my request by asserting, "Anaximander was the first Greek to map the stars." In a fill-in-the-blank question, such as "What is the ratio of the earth's height to its diameter?" you are presented with an infinite range of values. Anaximander chose "The ratio of the earth's height to its diameter is 1:3." (Anaximander thought that the earth had the shape of a dog's water bowl; a cylinder, curved in at the top to prevent spillage.) If none of the direct answers to the question are true, you can only truthfully respond by challenging the presupposition that one of the direct answers is correct.

Parts of a riddle are sometimes identified as *the* paradox: the most surprising possible *answer* or the *support* for that answer or even the whole *set* of possible answers.

Gareth Matthews, for instance, defines a paradox as a statement that conflicts with a conceptual truth. His example is the Stoic doctrine that those and only those are free who know that they are not free.

Most philosophers agree arguments play an essential role in paradox. R. M. Sainsbury identifies the paradox with the unacceptable *conclusion* of an argument that has acceptable premises and an acceptable inference pattern. J. L. Mackie says the paradox is the whole *argument.*

The remaining philosophers say a paradox is a *set* of individually plausible but jointly inconsistent propositions. According to Nicholas Rescher, philosophical positions can be classified as different ways of solving the paradox by rejecting a member of the set. This set could be considered as the answer set of a tidier paradox whose form is, Which, if any, of the following propositions is true? This useful format has no presuppositions and so limits the respondent's options to direct answers. The Greeks invented this tool and I regularly employ it in this book.

Although I think paradoxes are riddles, I also think parts of a paradox can be called paradoxes in the same spirit that parts of a rose can be called a rose. A rose is a shrub of the

Fig. 1.1

*Rosa* genus. But it is pedantic to deny that the cut flowers of the shrub are roses.

The rose analogy puts me in mind of an exchange between Bertrand Russell and Wittgenstein. As a student, Wittgenstein would think ferociously about a problem and then just proclaim his solution, rather like an edict from the czar. Russell chided him for not including the reasoning behind his conclusions. Wittgenstein wondered aloud whether, when he gave Russell a rose, he should give him the roots as well.

Philosophers read arguments into an amazing variety of phenomena: explanations, predictions, thought experiments, even history itself (as if war were just a heated stretch of a great debate). I would not be surprised if it was a philosopher who first pointed out that the Canadian flag (fig. 1.1) harbors a hidden argument. Look at the white area at the top left and the top right. By reversing figure and ground, you can see these two regions as a pair of contentious heads tilted down at a 45-degree angle.

My account does not require that any of the good answers to a paradox be based on arguments. A good answer might

Fig. 1.2

rest on what you see or on common sense. Is the moon closer to the earth when near the earth's horizon? Aristotle's eyes said yes, but his astronomical theory said no. After gazing at a waterfall, Aristotle saw the bank of a river apparently moving—while simultaneously appearing stationary! Here, an inconsistency seems to occur *within* a single perception. Argument-based definitions of paradox go against the psychologist's description of such illusions as "visual paradoxes," such as Roger Penrose's triangle (fig. 1.2). The triangle has three equal sides and therefore three equal angles. Yet if asked how big the angles are, you just "see" that each is bigger than 60 degrees. Since the angles of a triangle must add up to 180 degrees, you only half-believe the angles are bigger than 60 degrees. But you cannot shake the visual impression. Psychologists think the dissonance is irresolvable because our visual systems are compartmentalized. Each mental module contains, as it were, a little man (a homunculus) who makes rudimentary judgments. How does the homunculus make judgments? Well, each little man is composed of yet littler men (who are even less sophisticated). The hierarchy reaches bottom when we reach behavior that can be explained mechanically. The little man dedicated to judging angles cannot communicate with the other little men who specialize in judging lengths. The angle-judging homunculus always gives the same verdict even after you measure the angles with a protractor. For the sake of speed, the judgments of homunculi are based on a small number of criteria and a few simple rules for processing the limited data. There is no time for communication and deliberation. Consequently, homunculi are dogmatic. They often lock into disagreement. Illusion is the price that must be paid to evolve perceptions that can keep up with a dynamic environment.

When all the good answers to a riddle are the verdicts of a system composed of homunculi (such as the ones undergirding vision and speech), then the conflict is not rationally resolvable. The paradox might go away because something *causes* the conflicting homunculi to stop judging. Some perceptual illusions disappear as we age. A paradox might also be tolerable because we can hold an irrational tendency in check (as when a self-controlled air traveler ignores his fear of falling) or because we come to embrace it (as when a lover embraces his jealousy). But there is no *reasoning* with homunculi.

To be resolvable, a paradox must have a cognitive element. So philosophers are attracted to paradoxes that have answers that can be believed or disbelieved on the basis of reasons. Further, they relativize *paradox* to the best available reasoners. What counts is what stymies those in the best position to answer.

Although I think philosophers exaggerate the role of arguments in paradoxes, I have personally found their argument-based definitions of paradox to be educational. Philosophy only became comprehensible to me after I got into the habit of casting issues in logical molds. Instead of approaching great thinkers with diffuse curiosity, I could study them with a specific agenda. The history of philosophy became visible through the prism of paradox.

## THE OLDEST RECORDED PARADOX

Anaximander's paradox is, Does each thing have an origin? He answers *no*: there is an infinite being that sustains everything else but which is not grounded in any other thing. Anaximander's reasoning can be reconstructed as an escape from an infinite regress: There are some things that now exist but have not always existed. Anything which has a beginning owes its existence to another thing that existed before it. Therefore, there is something that lacks an origin.

Until Christianity, there was consensus that the universe cannot have a beginning. The only worry was whether there was a loophole in Anaximander's argument for an uncaused cause. For instance, some philosophers wondered whether there could instead be an infinite sequence of finite things. Each negative integer is finitely far from 0 and "comes from" a predecessor that is itself only finitely far from 0: -1 is preceded by -2, -2 is preceded by -3, . . . Every member of this infinite sequence has an origin (its predecessor) and is only finitely far from the present (zero) even though there is no starting point for the sequence as a whole.

This suggests an alternate solution to the problem of the origin of man. Instead of following Anaximander's postulation of an infinite *thing*, assume an infinite *relationship* between finite things. In particular, if there is an infinite sequence of parents and children, a parent could care for each child and there is no need to postulate an animal origin for human beings. Aristotle favored this dissolution. He believed that each species is infinitely old. Thus, Aristotle believes that the riddle "Which came first, the chicken or the egg?" rests on a false presupposition. Neither came first because each chicken comes from an egg and each egg comes from a chicken.

Charles Darwin eventually vindicated Anaximander's presupposition; chickens and eggs have only been around for a finite amount of time. Therefore, eggs must have preceded chickens or vice versa.

Anaximander's views on the origin of man apply equally to the origin of chickens. Eggs need to be hatched and chicks need to be reared. Therefore, some nonchicken must have served as a parent. Consequently, there was a chicken egg before there were any adult chickens.

Anaximander thought some aquatic creature reared human babies. Relative to modern biology, that is silly. But I think contemporary evolutionary theory concurs with Anaximander on the priority of the egg. Given Gregor Mendel's theory of inheritance, the transition to chickenhood can only take place between an egg-layer and its egg. For a particular organism cannot change its species membership during its lifetime. It is genetically fixed. However, evolutionary theory assures us that organisms can fail to breed true. So, although it is indeterminate as to which particular egg was the first chicken egg, we can know that whichever egg that may be, it precedes the first chicken—whichever that may be. The egg's precedence is a biological rather than a logical necessity. Given Jean Lamarck's theory of acquired traits, the chicken could have come first.

Since Anaximander did not know the necessary biology, his solution to the chicken or egg riddle was a lucky guess.

But he deserves much credit for creating a rational basis for his conjecture.

## IMPLICATIONS OF THE UNCAUSED CAUSE

Anaximander's infinite being tells us something about the past. But what about the future? Does each thing end? That seems impossible because we can always ask, What is next? An endless future is also vaguely dissatisfying because of its incompleteness. We are shaky with all species of indeterminacy: infinity, vagueness, randomness. These concepts are particularly paradox-prone. But sometimes there is no avoiding them. Having accepted the "boundless" apeiron as the universal origin of everything, Anaximander also accepts it as universal destiny. Our finite world is sandwiched between two infinities.

According to Anaximander, our present environment emerged from the infinite source through a process of separation. If you take a tube, and blow earth, sand, and fine particles into a body of water, the bubbling solution is initially an undifferentiated mixture. But then the air rises out of the water. The coarsest particles sink to the bottom. These particles are followed by finer elements. The finest are left on top. Like has gone to like. Similarly, the earth arose from watery beginnings through a process of sedimentation. As the water receded, land was exposed.

Anaximander drew the first world map of these land masses. Herodotus describes the map in such detail that scholars have redrawn it. Anaximander invokes balance to explain why the earth does not fall endlessly into space. The nature of this equilibrium has received several interpretations. Aristotle says that Anaximander appealed to the symmetry of forces that are acting upon the earth. Since there is no more reason for it to move in one direction rather than another, it stays where it is.

## WHEN DOES A PARADOX BECOME A FALLACY?

Anaximander explained changes in our present epoch as a battle between opposites. The heat of the day gives way to the cold of night. The moist dew in the morning gives way to the dryness of the midday sun. Winter must give way to summer and then summer to winter. Everything evens out. This is the point of the single sentence that is preserved from Anaximander's book *The Nature of Things*: "In to those things from which existing things have their coming into being, their passing away, too, takes place, according to what must be; for they make a reparation to one another for their injustice according to the ordinance of time." Unlike contemporary physicists who strike a posture of value-neutrality, Anaximander frames his law normatively: Opposites *ought* to balance out. Health is a balancing of the bitter and sweet, the hot and the cold, and so on. All change involves righting a previous wrong. If one opposite were able to permanently prevail, there would be a destruction of the world order.

People of Anaximander's era believed that good fortune and bad fortune balanced out. Herodotus reports that in 540 B.C., Polycrates seized power in Samos with the help of his brothers. After securing his position by murdering one brother and sending the other into exile, Polycrates made a pact with the Egyptian ruler Amasis. Polycrates then embarked on a phenomenally successful policy of conquest.

Amasis became worried: He wrote Polycrates a friendly warning:

> It is pleasant to learn that a friend and ally is doing well. But I do not like these great successes of yours; for I know the gods, how jealous they are, and I desire somehow that both I and those for whom I care succeed in some affairs, fail in others, and thus pass life faring differently by turns, rather than succeed at everything. For from all I have heard I know of no man whom continual good fortune did not bring in the end to evil, and utter destruction. Therefore if you will be ruled by me do this regarding your successes: consider what you hold most precious and what you will be sorriest to lose, and cast it away so that it shall never again be seen among men; then, if after this the successes that come to you are not mixed with mischances, strive to mend the matter as I have counselled you.
>
> (Herodotus 1920, iii, 40)

Polycrates felt that the loss of his signet ring would cause him the greatest grief. So he summoned a galley and set out to sea. Before the whole crew, Polycrates threw the ring into water. Five or six days later, a fisherman caught a large fish. It was such a fine fish that he offered it to Polycrates. Polycrates accepted the gift and invited the fisherman to dine on the fish with him. When Polycrates's servants cut open the fish, they discovered the lost ring and returned it to him. When Amasis learned of this amazing turn of events, he concluded that it was impossible to save a man from his destiny and predicted that Polycrates would soon fall into grave misfortune. And indeed, when Polycrates sailed to Magnesia at the invitation of the Persian governor, he was brutally murdered.

Did Amasis commit the gambler's fallacy? This is the mistake of assuming that the law of averages works by compensation rather than by swamping. A fair coin should land heads 50 percent of the tosses and tails 50 percent of the tosses. If the coin lands heads five times in a row, is it more likely to land tails on the sixth toss? If the law of averages works by compensation, then the answer is yes. The surplus of heads needs to be evened out by a surplus of tails. But chance has no memory. The law of averages actually works by swamping. In the long run, the percentage of heads and tails tends toward 50 percent because lucky stretches become dwarfed by the large number of cases.

Fallacies differ from paradoxes in being clearly diagnosed errors. By "clear" I mean clear to the experts. Modern casinos are filled with people who still commit the gambler's fallacy. Surprisingly, this confusion about the law of averages was only straightened out in the seventeenth century. It is hard to avoid anachronism when analyzing Anaximander's mix-up between swamping and compensation. The label "compensation paradox" better fits his era. Our reexplanation of his "cosmic justice" as the effects of mindless swamping would have struck Anaximander as a radical extension of his own demythologizing methodology.

We understand Anaximander's error because we are still tempted to commit it ourselves. Even experts commit statistical fallacies when caught off guard. New learning does not erase old approaches. We are compartmentalized. The modern compartment for refined probability techniques exists side by side with the ancient compartment of rules of thumb for coping with chance. When the new compartment is not cued into performance, the old compartment springs into action. Consequently, experts will think like novices when not on their toes.

Anaximander's physics of opposites is a monument to the compensation paradox. A natural quantity such as mass or energy is conserved. But it is a mistake to think that luck is conserved. We care about whether years are dry or wet, hot or cold, and so on. Thus, if we believe that the law of averages works by compensation, then we will think the privation that goes with a dry year will be balanced by the bounty afforded by a wet year. Our preferences will be projected onto nature. We will think that the fundamental forces (not just luck) work by compensation.

Anyone looking for regularities in nature will notice that some things balance out. Human beings achieve equality by monitoring the quantities and then periodically adding or subtracting. They read this balancing act onto the world. Thus we find the Chinese preoccupation with yin and yang and the attention to karma in India. Some people notice that fortunes really do not balance in this life. Their commitment to compensation is so algebraically firm that they solve the inequality by postulating a preexistence or an afterlife.

Compensation requires memory of past transactions. Memory has a function only if inferences can be drawn from what is remembered. Those memories must get their content from earlier perceptions. And that content must be sensitive to my desires if my bad fortunes will be balanced by good fortunes. Thus, Anaximander's law of compensation requires the operation of at least one metaphysical overseer.

True, Anaximander's primary emphasis is on secular explanations. He played down the role of the gods. While his compatriots regarded thunderbolts as Zeus's divine spears, Anaximander says that thunder and lightning are caused by the wind. Nevertheless, Anaximander does ultimately attribute intelligence to the infinite. Given the law of compensation, fortune must have a memory. A good event makes a bad event more likely and vice versa. What goes around comes around. The infinite steers all things in directions we are obliged to follow.

I suspect that Anaximander's unusually small anthropomorphic tendency was nursed into action by the eerie character of a beginningless process. Infinity is humbling. In the course of growing up, we overwrite new tricks on the basic repertoire that all children are allotted. When these grown-up techniques fail us, we revert to this more basic repertoire—we crave parental protection and guidance. Despite extraordinary resistance to anthropomorphism, Anaximander ultimately reads in intentions where there are none.

People still put a human face on infinity. I learned the cosmological argument for God's existence from an older boy on my block. The gist of it was: "Everything has a cause. Something exists. Therefore, something caused everything without itself being caused." Later, also on the street, I heard the objection that the conclusion contradicts the first premise. This inconsistency can be avoided by interpreting the first premise as governing only things that are contingent on the existence of other things. The "first cause" cannot be just another contingent thing. For then its existence would depend on something and so not stop the backward regress. The first cause must be a being that depends on nothing else. Therefore, it is a necessary being upon which everything else ultimately bases its existence. This first cause is commonly nominated for the office of creator.

Indeed, this candidate would win a majority vote in a popular election. The electorate would include luminaries such as the fourth-century philosopher Augustine. He realized that this basic line of reasoning raises many questions.

And many were asked. When young Augustine asked what God was doing before He made the world, he was told: “Preparing hell for people who ask questions like that.”

There have been gentler answers. When asked what God was doing before He created the world, the mathematician J. E. Littlewood replied: “Millions of words must have been written: but he was doing Pure Mathematics and thought it would be a pleasant change to do some Applied.” (1953, 136)

TWO

# Pythagoras's Search for the Common Denominator

*Son:* Dad, will you help me find the least common denominator in this problem?

*Dad:* Good heavens, son, don't tell me that hasn't been found. They were looking for it when I was a kid!

Anaximander set an example of how to frame a paradox and how to respond to it. His followers understood that solutions require disciplined reason-giving. But they had not yet developed the practices that constitute *proof* of a proposition. To some degree, astronomy and engineering gave the ancients a running start. But the strongest influence on proof practices came from mathematical lore.

## THE MATHEMATICAL SETTING

Anaximander's vision of the world was basically accepted by his successors. However, the Greeks never got comfortable with infinity. They associated reality with what is well formed. Infinity is boundless, limitless, and indefinite. How can what is real be based on what is ill defined?

Anaximander's successor, Anaximenes, tried to firm up infinity. Whereas Anaximander thought that the infinite was a mix of earth, air, fire, and water, Anaximenes believed air was the underlying basic element. Fire is dilated air. When air is compressed it becomes a cloud. Compressed further it becomes liquid water. Yet further compression yields earth, then stone. As air becomes compressed, it becomes colder, denser, heavier, and darker. Anaximander's opposites are just so much thinning and thickening of air. Quantitative changes account for qualitative differences.

If the underlying nature of reality is quantitative, then arithmetic and geometry become keys to the structure of reality. These keys had already been partly crafted by the Egyptians. Herodotus reports that the Egyptian interest in fractions and geometry sprang from the pharaoh's practice of taxing farmers in proportion to their arable land. When the Nile flooded part of a farmer's property, the farmer's tax liability would be scaled down to the amount of land remaining for farming.

Commentators on the history of mathematics characterize the Egyptian interest in mathematics as unrelentingly practical. However, any culture that develops mathematics develops *recreational* mathematics. A scroll known as the Rhind Papyrus contains the earliest recorded arithmetical and geometrical riddles. From this manual we learn that the Egyptians of the

Twelfth Dynasty (ca. 2000-1788 B.C.) had a close approximation to $\pi$ (they put it at 3.16) and that they knew the formula for the volume of a truncated pyramid: $V = (n/3)(a^2 + ab + b^2)$, where $a$ and $b$ are lengths of the sides of the base of the pyramid and $n$ is the height of the pyramid. Yet the Rhind Papyrus also makes it evident that the Egyptians relied heavily on trial and error in their calculations. They solved multiplication problems by repeated addition.

Many scholars, especially those who are mathematicians, are struck by the absence of proofs in Egyptian mathematics. But this is the rule rather than exception for ancient societies. The Babylonians and Mayans and Hindus only take a passing interest in verifying their results. The steps leading up to the discovery were a means to an end. They did not regard the process of reasoning as a supporting structure that should be publicly displayed. An architect does not use glass walls to assure everyone that the beams are sound. Early mathematicians are content to *report* their discoveries.

The Greeks changed mathematical thinking. Their descendants wanted to live in glass houses.

## THE PYTHAGOREANS

Pythagoras (ca. 582-500 B.C.) insisted that mathematical evidence be public in the sense that his colleagues should be able to survey the lines of reasoning. But Pythagoras actually forbade proofs (or even theorems) from being disseminated to outsiders. Pythagorean mathematics along with the rest of the cult's doctrines were sacred secrets.

This secrecy makes it difficult to divine the basis for Pythagoras's ritualistic insistence on proof. From what has been divulged, we can infer that the demand for strict deductive demonstration issued from spiritual perfectionism. Pythagoras taught that, as punishment, our souls are entombed in our bodies. Our souls yearn to join the divine celestial bodies from whence they originated. Death does not bring release for the immortal soul because it transmigrates into an animal that is just being born. After going through animals that dwell on land and in the sea and in the air, the soul once again enters the body of a human being. Eating meat is therefore cannibalism.

The purpose of life is to live in accordance with what is highest in us. We revere our divine origin by observing taboos, such as by abstaining from meat, alcohol, and intercourse. More positively, we express our desire for purity by pursuing wisdom. Pythagoras was the first to call himself a *philosopher* (a lover of wisdom).

The purest form of inquiry is mathematical. Here one frees oneself from reliance on the senses. One proceeds immaterially, deducing results from self-evident truths. The uncertainties of the empirical realm are transcended.

Pythagoras's mathematical approach to nature yielded stunning successes. He discovered musical intervals by inventing the monochord (a one-stringed instrument with movable bridges). The ratios responsible for these consonant sounds seemed to be repeated by the positions of heavenly bodies. In addition to the mathematical relationships discovered in natural phenomena, Pythagoras believed that they existed in ethics. Mathematics gains a foothold in morality through notions of reciprocity, equality, and balance.

Pythagoras used a geometrical representation of numbers that made it natural to think that the world is generated out of numbers. The Pythagoreans represented numbers by

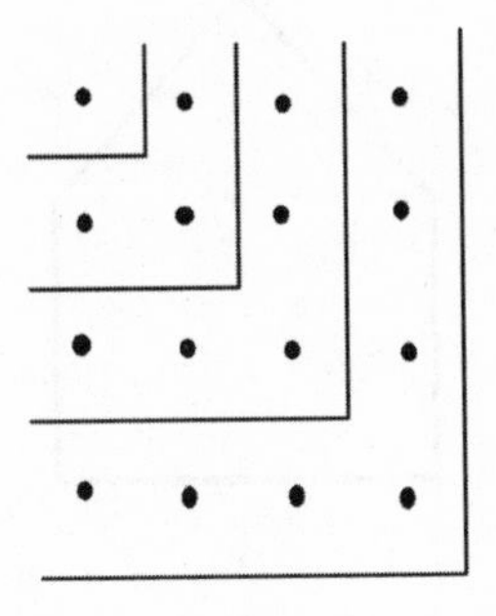

Fig. 2.1

means of pebbles arranged on a flat surface. Square numbers were constructed by surrounding one pebble with *gnomons.* A gnomon is a set of units that resembles a carpenter's square (fig. 2.1). This notation probably helped Pythagoras solve the arithmetical problem of finding triangles that have the square of one side equal to the sum of the squares of the other two. But it also suggests a way of bringing more and more of reality under the control of numbers. By adding larger and larger gnomons, one brings larger and larger regions into the space surrounding the original "one."

The numbers are the whole figure including the space as organized by the pebbles or dots. If there were no space between the dots, there would just be a single big dot. Pythagoras thought of big numbers as spatially bigger. Thus, all of reality is encompassed by the natural numbers.

Pythagoras's metaphysical mathematics embodied an aesthetic appreciation for beautiful arguments. Some of the Pythagoreans' lovely proofs are immortalized in Euclid's *Elements.*

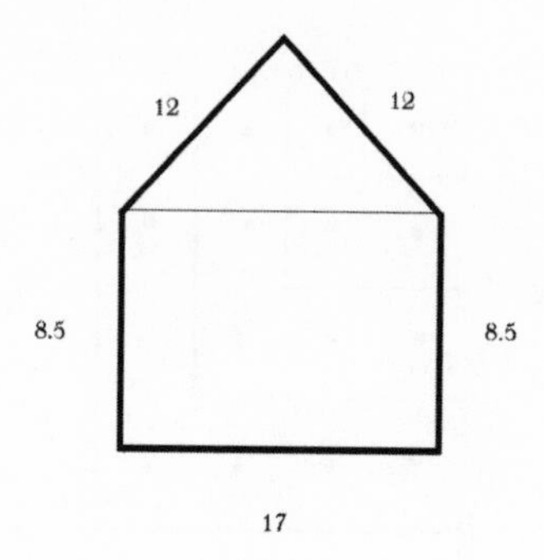


Fig. 2.2

The most famous result attributed to Pythagoras is the Pythagorean theorem. It is even mentioned at the end of *The Wizard of Oz*. After the Scarecrow discovers that he has a brain, he is presented with a diploma. To illustrate his newfound acumen, the Scarecrow states that the sum of the square roots of any two sides of an isosceles triangle is equal to the square root of the remaining side.

Well, the Scarecrow's heart is in the right place. The Pythagorean theorem actually states that in a *right* triangle the square on the hypotenuse is equal to the sum of the squares on the sides containing the right angle.

We more commonly come to grief with the Pythagorean theorem when precisely specifying the shapes of objects. For instance, the official rule book for Little League baseball defines home plate as an irregular pentagon (fig. 2.2). This figure is impossible because it requires the existence of a (12, 12, 17) right triangle (Bradley 1996). According to the Pythagorean theorem, the squares of the sides of a right triangle must add up to the square of the hypotenuse: $a^2 + b^2 = c^2$. But $12^2 + 12^2 = 288 \neq 289 = 17^2$.

Does the rule book make Little League baseball an impossible game? Many key terms of baseball (strike, run, etc.) are defined in terms of home plate. Children *appear* to be playing baseball. But if we stick with the official definition of home plate, then they are merely playing a game that resembles Little League baseball (in the way a rounded square resembles a round square).

We instead regard the rule book's definition as a flawed effort to tidy up a word that we already understand. The point of the definition was to achieve uniform playing conditions. What really makes something a home plate is its playing a certain role in baseball. This can and has been done without anyone defining the precise shape of home plate.

The Pythagorean theorem does not invalidate any Little League baseball games. However, the Pythagorean theorem did undermine Pythagoreanism. The trouble started when Hiappasus of Metapontum applied the Pythagorean theorem to a 1-1 right triangle. By the Pythagorean theorem, the hypotenuse equals $\sqrt{2}$. If there is a ratio that equals $\sqrt{2}$, then it is some fraction $p/q$ lying between 1 and 2. What could it be? Not $3/2$ because $(3/2)^2 = 9/4$ which is greater than 2. Not $5/4$ because $(5/4)^2 = 25/16$ which is less than 2. Hiappasus derived a contradiction from the supposition that there is a pair of numbers that works. Contrary to Pythagorean doctrine, some things are not commensurate with the natural numbers.

## THE RELIGION OF DEDUCTION

Hiappasus leaked his result to outsiders. He was expelled by the Pythagoreans and then drowned at sea. The Pythagoreans said this was punishment by the gods for his indiscretion.

Would the gods have backed a false theorem? The Pythagoreans pictured the gods as purely intellectual beings. As such, they should be logically perfect beings who believe all the logical consequences of what they believe. A logically perfect being sees how the Pythagorean theorem implies that the hypotenuse of a right isosceles triangle is incommensurable with its sides. So the gods could not be surprised by Hiappasus's proof.

The Pythagoreans were mistaken in viewing deduction as a divine activity. As perfectionists, they tried to emulate the gods when constructing mathematically rigorous proofs. But we reason only because of our imperfections. A being who believes all the logical consequences of what he believes has no need to reason.

The paradox posed by Hiappasus can be formulated as a set of four individually plausible but jointly inconsistent propositions.

1. Reality has a mathematical structure.
2. If reality has a mathematical structure, then all relationships can be represented by numbers.
3. The numbers are the natural numbers: 1, 2, 3, . . .
4. The hypotenuse of an isosceles right triangle is incommensurable with its sides.

The first proposition is fundamental to the Pythagorean outlook. The second proposition spells out their commitment to modeling the world in terms of ratios. The ratio was supposed to specify the essence of the thing. This implies that an isosceles right triangle lacks a specific nature. Yet a 1-1 right triangle has the same nature as a 2-2 right triangle.

What could they have in common if not the same mathematical relationship? The third proposition, which the Pythagoreans would have regarded as hardly worth stating, is a truism about what *number* means. The last proposition is Hiappasus's surprising theorem.

The Pythagoreans perceived the result as a serious threat to a core element of their philosophy, proposition 1. To us, this refutation does not seem as injurious to a mathematical picture of reality because we accept the existence of irrational numbers. But for many of Pythagoras's followers, mathematical metaphysics no longer added up.

There were two reactions to this predicament. Heraclitus renounced the assumption that reality must live up to our rational expectation. Reality goes its own way, embodying the very opposites that power riddles of the universe. Our senses reveal a world in chaos and flux, a world that overflows the dams and channels erected by reason. Real life throws us borderline cases, chance happenings, and developments without beginnings or endings.

Parmenides' reaction was to renounce the assumption that there could be a number of things. If there is only one thing, then there can be no problem of incommensurability. Everything will then square with reason. You just need to stick with reason and not get distracted by your senses. The next chapter is devoted to Parmenides' resolute approach.

THREE

# Parmenides on What Is Not

At about 515 B.C. Parmenides was born in Elea, a Greek colony on the southern coast of Italy. He discovered a paradox that was to make "Eleatic" denote a group of philosophers who believe reality is a changeless unity.

"All is one" sounds positive. But Parmenides reaches this positive conclusion by relentless negative thinking. He revolutionized philosophy by turning attention from what is to what is not.

Parmenides would object to this characterization. He argued that it is impossible to think about what is not the case. What is not the case is not there to be thought about. We can only think about what exists.

## THE PROBLEM OF NEGATIVE EXISTENTIALS

The business tycoon Heinrich Schliemann refuted the statement "Troy does not exist" by digging up the remains of a city that fits Homer's description of Troy in the *Iliad.* Walls were dynamited, tombs were pried open, officials were bribed.

Consider this tidier refutation: If "Troy does not exist" is about anything, it is about Troy. Just as an epitaph can be engraved only if there is a surface to be scratched, a statement can be about something only if there is something for that statement to be about. "Troy does not exist" is a self-defeating remark. It denies one of its preconditions for being meaningful. It is like saying "No one can refer to Athens."

Yes, this armchair archaeology seems ludicrous. Although scholars before Schliemann had been mistaken about Troy's nonexistence, they seem to have *correctly* asserted many other statements about what does not exist: "Atlantis does not exist," "Zeus does not exist," "Pegasus does not exist," etc. How can these denials be true given Parmenides' reasoning about *about*?

Twentieth-century philosophers dubbed this "the problem of negative existentials." A negative existential is a statement that denies the existence of something. How can such a statement be true given that there must be something for the statement to be about?

One tempting solution is to say that "Pegasus does not exist" is about the idea of Pegasus. But if Pegasus is the *idea* of Pegasus, then "Pegasus does not exist" is *false*. The *idea* of Pegasus does exist. Remember that the problem is to explain how a negative existential could be *true*. In any case, Pegasus is clearly not an idea. He is supposed to be the winged horse of Bellerophon. Ideas do not fly.

Alexius Meinong (1853-1920) suggested that there might be some things that have a kind of being other than existence. According to him, Pegasus *subsists*. Meinong's strategy is to challenge the step from "There is something which is Pegasus" to "Pegasus exists." A common objection to Meinong is that the difficulty would reappear for negative subsistence statements such as "Pegasus does not subsist." We would need a *new* explanation for how these statements could be true.

Even so, Meinong's solution enjoyed an initial period of popularity. Its fortunes plummeted when Bertrand Russell (1872-1970) presented a brilliantly detailed alternative in his classic article "On Denoting." According to Russell, "Pegasus" is a disguised description. "Pegasus exists" means that there is exactly one horse that has wings and is ridden by Bellerophon. This statement is false if there are two or more such horses or if there are no such horses. "Pegasus does not exist" specifies the second alternative and so means "Each thing is such that it is not a winged horse ridden by Bellerophon." This analysis frees us from referring to nonexistent objects.

Russell was proud of the way his theory of definite descriptions solved paradoxes. He advised his fellow logicians to collect paradoxes because they serve the same role as experiments in science. Just as we can test a theory by how well it answers observational questions, we can also test a logical theory by how well it resolves deductive riddles.

The problem-solving power of Russell's theory, coupled with Russell's polemical skills, shrank Meinong to an amusing footnote. When I was a student, Meinong was still regarded as a marginal transitional figure. I was therefore surprised to see a book on Meinong mentioned on a morning television program. The film reviewer, Gene Shalit, was exhibiting books with stranger and stranger titles. The climax was Terence Parsons' *Nonexistent Objects*. Shalit was incredulous that Parsons had written a whole book about things that do not exist.

## NEGATION AND TIME

Parmenides next considers whether things can come into existence or pass out of existence. He believes he has already shown that "nonexistent thing" is a contradiction in terms like "round square." Nothing can be both round and square because no square can have a perimeter that is everywhere equidistant from its center. It follows that nothing can *become* a round square. Nor could anything change from being a round square to being a more respectable figure. Similarly, no thing could become a nonexistent object or start out as a nonexistent thing and then become existent. Parmenides concludes that anything that exists has no beginning and no end.

Could something *not* have a property? If "Pythagoras is not fat" is true, then there is either a state of affairs in which Pythagoras is fat or not. If there is a state of affairs in which Pythagoras is fat, then "Pythagoras is not fat" is not true. If there is no such a state of affairs, then there is no state of affairs that could be referred to by "Pythagoras is not fat." Thus "$x$ is not $F$" statements have the same problem as "$x$ does not exist" statements.

One might suggest that a *negative* fact makes "Pythagoras is not fat" true. If there is a state of affairs consisting of Pythagoras not being fat, then "Pythagoras is not fat" could be made true by that fact. However, Parmenides would counter that reality is about what is the case rather than what is not the case. If you permit one negative fact, you open a floodgate to countless negative facts. These negative facts are hard to distinguish from one another. At this moment, there is no earthquake in Elea. Is that nonearthquake the same nonearthquake that is now transpiring in Ionia? There is no determinate answer to such a question. Reality must be *definite*.

If "Pythagoras is not fat" is meaningless, then we cannot make sense of Pythagoras changing from being fat to not being fat. Accordingly, Parmenides denies that any thing changes over time.

Can things change over space? According to geographical surveys, the island of Crete extends for 257 kilometers and then ends. But to have an ending, Crete would cease to be at a certain point in space. Ceasing to be is failing to exist. Parmenides concludes that no object can be limited in size.

Wouldn't this unlimited size make for intolerable crowding? No, because Parmenides denies that there is more than one thing! If there were two distinct things, then there would be a statement that is true about one but not about the other. A statement such as "Pythagoras is not Anaximander" cannot be true because nothing can be a non-Anaximander. A non-Anaximander is a nonexistent thing.

For Parmenides, an argument is not a cab that can be dismissed when it has taken you as far as you wished to go. You must go all the way. Parmenides concludes that there is exactly one changeless thing. For all its unity and simplicity, this oneness is difficult to picture. Parmenides tends to envisage it as a big, round sphere. The sphere is without gaps or variations in density or movement.

If reality were literally a sphere, then we could distinguish between the surface of the sphere and its core. Parmenides has already argued against there being objects with different parts. So the great unity which is reality cannot be a sphere or any other familiar object. Much of what Parmenides positively says about reality can only be consistently interpreted as metaphor.

## THE RULE OF REASON

The natural objection to Parmenides is that his reasoning is refuted by experience. Our senses tell us that there are *many* things. These things come in various sizes. They are sometimes in motion. They undergo qualitative changes such as when milk sours.

Those following in the footsteps of Anaximander did not question the authority of experience. Even Heraclitus, who is the first to emphasize perceptual illusions, pictures experience as a teacher. Heraclitus thinks our senses show every thing is in constant flux. But there is a unity in the change. When Heraclitus says "You cannot step into the same river twice," he only means that you cannot step twice into the same water of a river. There is one river but many distinct bodies of water flow through it. Heraclitus urges a balance between experience and reason. He says that the senses can instruct us only insofar as the intellect appraises their worth as witnesses.

Admittedly, the Pythagoreans did elevate the status of pure reasoning. But they viewed reason as a divine shortcut to results that can be triumphantly corroborated by the senses. Only with Parmenides do we see an attempt to completely veto the senses. Parmenides heartily agreed that his arguments conflicted with experience. But he insisted on the supremacy of the intellect over the senses.

Parmenides stresses the principle that one should follow the argument wherever it leads. Previous philosophers had assumed the senses place an important check on one's reasoning. But they had trouble resisting Parmenides' suggestion that reason is king. After all, the testimony of the senses must be judged by reason. What is the alternative? Any method that purports to be better than reason would have to be adopted and applied by reason. This gives reason an almost despotic dominion over all methods of inquiry.

Although Parmenides thinks the senses convey a grand illusion, he recognizes a practical necessity for dealing with this realm of appearances. To that end, he proposes a physical theory more or less in the tradition of Anaximander. He tidies up his predecessors by expunging references to voids and privations (such as the view that darkness is merely the absence of light). But even after purging nothingness from traditional physics, Parmenides only offers a theory that aims to be *like* the truth. His real truth is an uncompromising monism.

## REACTION TO PARMENIDES

Some dismissed Parmenides as an equivocal trickster. The Greeks were aware of how negations can trip us up into absurdity. In the *Odyssey* Homer describes how a giant, one-eyed Cyclops, Polyphemos, inadvertently trapped Odysseus and his overly inquisitive crew in his cave. Polyphemos controlled the entrance with a huge rock that only he could move. After Polyphemos discovered that he had blocked the escape of Odysseus's men, he ate two of them for dinner. The next morning Polyphemos had another pair for breakfast.

Odysseus, "man of many wiles," decided to ingratiate himself with the help of his large supply of strong wine. After Polyphemos devoured yet another pair of men, Odysseus offered him a cup of this delicious wine. Polyphemos eagerly accepted a second cup. Then another . . . In a contented stupor, Polyphemos asked Odysseus for his name so that he may receive a favor. Odysseus replied "Nobody." The Cyclops's reward to Nobody was a promise to eat him last. Polyphemos slipped off into sleep, gurgling up human remains as he slumbered. Odysseus and his remaining men then seized a stake and rammed it into Polyphemos's single eye. The blinded monster gave a horrible cry that brought all the neighboring Cyclops running to his blockaded cave. They called, asking whether Polyphemos was crying out because some human was leading away his flocks or whether someone was killing him by treachery or violence. From the cave, the mighty Polyphemos bellowed "Nobody is killing me by treachery or violence!" Upon hearing this, his Cyclops neighbors returned to their own caves, advising Polyphemos to bear what the gods send in patience. Odysseus and his men then escaped, taunting the blinded Cyclops as they rowed away.

The monist Parmenides drew his own taunts. "If Parmenides is right, dog is man and heaven is earth."

By Parmenides' reasoning, there is at most one meaningful statement. For if there were two, then one statement would have a meaning that the other statement does not have.

Parmenides is pioneering a semantic solution to paradoxes. Instead of trying to answer the riddle, he characterizes "Does Pegasus exist?" as covert nonsense. If you think that the meaning of a name is its bearer and you think "Pegasus" has no bearer, then you think "Pegasus exists" and "Pegasus does not exist" are equally meaningless. Since the conclusion of an argument must be a proposition, neither of these statements can be the conclusion of an argument. If you also believe that paradoxes are conclusions or arguments, then you will be committed to denying that there is any paradox of negative existentials.

The riddle theory of *paradox* allows for the possibility of meaningless paradoxes. Riddles need only appear to be genuine questions; they can instead be meaningless utterances that look like questions. Pseudoquestions need only appear to have answers and so need only appear to have an overabundance of good answers. Each pseudoanswer can score well on standard criteria for ranking responses without genuinely expressing a proposition. They can be good in the way that counterfeit currency is good.

Parmenides appears to accept the point that there is only one meaningful statement And he does not shy away from the conflicts with common sense that his critics allege. Parmenides would gain nothing by playing down conflicts with common sense. Critics were therefore at a loss as to how to object to Parmenides. How can you accuse Parmenides of something more absurd than what he explicitly professed?

The only response to Parmenides is an identification of an essential misstep in his reasoning. Since his premises are nonempirical, he can be refuted only on the basis of linguistics and logic. Neither of these fields existed in Parmenides' era, so little of merit could be said in response to Parmenides' revolutionary style of philosophical argument. No one could capitalize on the analogies that the Greeks perceived between Parmenides' reasoning and linguistic tricks such as Odysseus's use of "Nobody."

Contemporary philosophers and linguists agree that Odysseus's ruse turns on an equivocation between using

"Nobody" as a name and using it as a quantifier (a quantifier indicates how much: *some*, *most*, *all*). On the surface, names are the easiest words to understand because their meaning is whatever bears the name. All human beings have a strong tendency to apply the name model of meaning to all words, even when they cannot think of any reasonable referent. We should not picture "nobody" as *naming* anything at all. "Nobody" draws its meaning from how it functions in a whole sentence; it does not draw its meaning from what it names.

People have no more insight into how they speak than into how they see. For instance, parents try to teach their babies how to speak by asking them lots of questions. But interrogatives are the most sophisticated grammatical constructions, always mastered at the *end* of the child's linguistic maturation. Similarly, "Paradoxes are riddles" may seem too simple to be true. But actually I have helped myself to a rich explanatory entity. Questions are far more versatile and subtle than arguments or sets or any other entity that philosophers have used to define paradox. My objections to their definitions will almost always complain of them being too narrow.

In his day, Parmenides was invincible. The ancient Greeks were at an embryonic stage of linguistic self-consciousness, struggling to draw basic grammatical distinctions such as between verb and noun. They were not in a position to tackle "nobody."

Revolutionary progress in linguistics has not precluded persistent myths about the nature of language. In the early twentieth century, Germans were responsible for great advances in our understanding of language. However, they also had a weakness for the view that philosophizing is possible, if not only in German, then only in German and Greek! This linguistic nationalism is manifest as late as 1953 in Martin Heidegger's *Introduction to Metaphysics.*

Ironically, Greek is especially prone to equivocation on issues of being. English is nearly as bad. The word *is* is ambiguous between the *is* of predication as in "Cicero is eloquent" and the *is* of identity as in "Cicero is Tully." This is the basis for the deductive graffiti found in university lavatories: Homer is blind. Love is blind. Therefore, Homer is love. These premises treat the *is* of predication as if it were the *is* of identity.

There is also a rather peripheral *existential* sense of *is.* When people say "I am" is the shortest complete sentence of English, they intend the existential sense. In Greek, the existential sense is more central and so it is easier to slide to the existential sense from other senses of the Greek counterpart of *is.*

Finally, I should mention the *is* of mention. This is used to describe the word for a thing rather than the thing, as in: Athena loves Zeus. Zeus is a four-letter word. Therefore, Athena loves a four-letter word. The second premise involves the *is* of mention but the argument is valid only if *is* receives the identity reading.

Diogenes Laertius attributes the following sophistry to Chrysippus: "If you say something, it passes through your lips: now you say wagon, consequently a wagon passes through your lips." Sometimes there is genuine uncertainty about whether a word is being used or mentioned. Is *uncopyrightable* being used or mentioned in the sentence "The only 15 letter word that can be spelled without repeating a letter is uncopyrightable"? Normally, the difference between words and things seems too obvious to actually be confused. Yet the tendency to extend the properties of words to things and vice versa is culturally universal. The Egyptians believed they could survive after death by preserving their names after death. Accordingly, the controversial Egyptian leader Hatshepsut (the first female pharaoh) had her name written all over monuments in the Valley of the Kings. When she died, her bitter stepson Thutmose III masterminded a massive erasing campaign. By rubbing out "Hatshepsut," he hoped to rub out Hatshepsut.

Such different concepts are marked by the little word *is*! Bertrand Russell characterized the ambiguity of *is* as a disgrace to the human race.

People judge the subtly of words by their size. They scoff at the suggestion that big issues can turn on little words. Recent political history illustrates this size principle. In 1997, Paula Jones was pursuing a sexual harassment case against President Bill Clinton. Various women were questioned about any sexual relationships with the president. Monica Lewinsky signed an affidavit saying that in her case, there is absolutely no sex of any kind in any manner, shape, or form, with President Clinton. Clinton's attorney Robert Bennett quoted Lewinsky's affidavit as part of his defense against Jones's allegations. The president later conceded he had improper contact with Lewinsky (although no contact that fit the definition of sexual relations imposed on Clinton for the purpose of his testimony). On August 17, 1998, Solomon Wisenberg cross-examined the President. He asked President Clinton whether he agreed that Lewinsky's statement was completely false.

*Clinton*: It depends on what the meaning of the word "is" is. If the—if he—if "is" means is and never has been, that is not—that is one thing. If it means there is none, that was a completely true statement . . .

*Wisenberg*: I just want to make sure I understand Mr. President. Do you mean today that because you were not engaging in sexual activity with Ms. Lewinsky during the deposition that the statement of Mr. Bennett might be literally true?

*Clinton*: No, sir. I mean that at the time of the deposition, it had been—that was well beyond any point of improper contact between me and Ms. Lewinsky. So that anyone generally speaking in the present tense, saying there is not an improper relationship, would be telling the truth if that person said there was not, in the present tense; the present tense encompassing many months. That what I meant by that . . .

Journalists cited this section of the testimony as an illustration of Clinton's sophistry. But Clinton is right about the flexibility of the present tense. Part of the philosophical puzzle about "Is it now, now?" turns on the fact that the present can be narrowed to an arbitrarily thin slice of time. As with many philosophical riddles, the answer to "Is it now, now?" is "It depends." If the riddler indexes *now* to the interval in which the whole sentence is uttered, then it is now, now. If the riddler restricts *now* to the time that the word *now* is uttered, then it is not now, now. We can resist the riddler's insinuation that there is a mistake in our normal usage of *now* by noting that *now* works like an accordion. We are free to compress *now* and we are free to stretch *n -o -w*.

Clinton is right that a period of months is commonly sufficient to cover the present tense. Of course, "There is no sex" is still misleading because there had been relevant "improper contact." The point of the affidavit was to provide evidence that the president was not engaged in a pattern of sexual impropriety. The improper contact had been recent enough to support Paula Jones's allegation. But in the adversarial setting of legal examination, witnesses are not obliged to prevent listeners from inferring falsehoods. That is the job of the lawyer asking the questions.

Am I being too soft on Clinton? I confess to an experience that has inclined me to keep out of his way. When Clinton was elected in 1992, a reporter learned that the official photographs of the president are taken *prior* to the inauguration—before the oath of office is administered, while he is not yet president. He wondered whether these really were photographs of the president. The reporter phoned the chairman of the New York University philosophy department—which was me. I told the reporter not to worry about it. The inaugural photographs really were photographs of President Clinton. Think of it this way. A photograph of Clinton does not need to be a photograph of the full spatial extent of his body. Just a representative part of his body will do. The same applies for temporal parts; a photograph of one stage of Clinton is a photograph of Clinton. Even a baby picture of Clinton is a picture of President Clinton. The reporter perked up at the mention of temporal parts. So I waxed on about Albert Einstein's pioneering work in modeling time as a fourth dimension. In this "block universe," Clinton is a space-time worm extending from his birth to his death, much as the Long Island Expressway extends from the western end of Long

Island to its eastern extreme. The reporter thanked me. I felt I had nipped the problem in the bud.

Later I heard back from a dissatisfied publicity officer. Why was the chairman of the philosophy department calling the president of the United States a "space-time worm"? When I obtained a copy of the newspaper, I was chagrined to learn that the philosophical community had been credited with the discovery of a new enigma about the inaugural photographs. We heirs of the glorious Greek tradition were whiling away our days in debates about the Great Inaugural Photograph Issue (apparently taking a break from our usual controversy about how many angels can dance on the head of a pin).

The reporter cast a shadow over my ambitions as an academic administrator. I knew how one of my fellow admirers of Parmenides must have felt. Pericles had been an effective Athenian statesman. Then he quarreled with his eldest son, Xanthippus. His angry son

> thought himself so ill used and disobliged, that he openly reviled his father; telling first, by way of ridicule, stories about his conversations at home, and the discourses he had with the sophists and scholars that came to his house. As for instance, how one who was a practiser of the five games of skill, having with a dart or javelin unawares against his will struck and killed Epitimus the Pharsalian, his father spent a whole day with Protagoras in a serious dispute, whether the javelin, or the man that threw it, or the masters of the games who appointed these sports, were to be accounted the cause of this mischance. (Plutarch 1880, 122)

Although Pericles was Athens's most famous democrat, his aristocratic background and his penchant for philosophical abstraction kept him under suspicion; most philosophers were aristocrats opposed to democracy. Fortunately, philosophers were also regarded as impractical dreamers and so tolerated. Even so, Pericles' political opponents trumped up charges of impiety against his teacher Anaxagoras. Anaxagoras had to be rescued from prison (probably by Pericles) and resettled in Lampsacus. He founded a school there. When Anaxagoras died, the citizens of Lampsacus erected in the marketplace an altar dedicated to Mind and Truth.

Parmenides also enjoyed a good reputation—despite all the ridicule. He was esteemed by his fellow citizens and attracted loyal students. It is to his most famous pupil that we next turn.

FOUR

# Sisyphus's Rock and Zeno's Paradoxes

Sisyphus was condemned to push a boulder uphill only to have it roll back under its own weight. Hades condemned him to do this over and over, for eternity in the underworld. Is the attempt to solve paradoxes equally futile? Most of the central paradoxes that philosophers now study were being discussed over two thousand years ago.

Albert Camus argues that Sisyphus is a heroic figure. Sisyphus gains victory in defeat; the very attempt to do the impossible ennobles him. Some philosophers justify the struggle with paradoxes in the same defiant way.

I do not think you can try to do what you believe to be impossible. You try by moving toward your goal. If you believe that nothing you do can bring you closer, nothing you do counts as trying.

Happily there is no need for heroism. History shows that most paradoxes are short-lived. Each generation's sample of paradoxes is biased toward leftovers that have resisted past efforts. Even these exceptionally hardy paradoxes are sometimes solved. The methodological point of this chapter is to substantiate this optimism by recounting Zeno's paradoxes.

## ZENO'S PARADOXES OF PLURALITY

Parmenides visited Athens in 450 B.C. He was accompanied by his favorite pupil Zeno. Young Socrates might have been a favorite of Zeno; Plato passes on gossip that the two were lovers. In any case, Zeno of Elea (ca. 490–ca. 430 B.C.) had written a well-regarded book in defense of his teacher. Whereas Parmenides' arguments spring from the semantics of negation, Zeno's arguments pull infinite rabbits from finite hats.

Some of Zeno's arguments bolster Parmenides' rejection of anything having size. If an object has a size, then it has parts. This collective is actually a conglomeration of things rather than a single thing. Therefore, the only genuine *individuals* must have no size. But if an object has no size, then it is nothing at all. Go ahead, add a sizeless object to another object. There is no increase in size. If thousands of sizeless objects were put together, they would still not add up to anything. Since sizeless things do not differ from nothing, they are nothing.

Zeno had a second argument against size. If a thing has size, it has an outer part. For example, the skin of an orange projects beyond the pulp. Each projecting part will itself have some parts that project beyond other parts. The

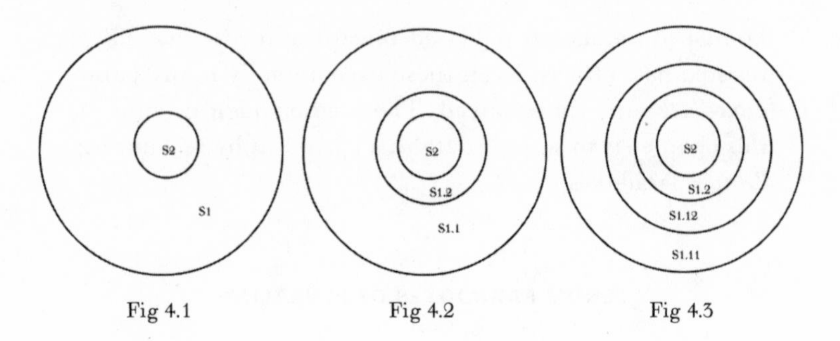


Fig 4.1 Fig 4.2 Fig 4.3

projection principle applies endlessly; so any object with a size must be infinitely large. In sphere S (fig. 4.1), part S1 projects beyond the core S2. This outer portion S1 can be divided again (fig. 4.2) into an "inner outer" portion, S1.2, and an outer portion, S1.1. The outer layer S1.1 can in turn be divided into an inner part S1.12 and an outer part S1.11 (fig. 4.3). We can go on to S1.111, then S1.1111, and so on. If there is some minimum size for each portion, then the sphere as a whole will be infinitely large.

Zeno advances a third argument against plurality. If there is more than one thing, then there is some particular number of them. This might be a huge number but it is still a finite number. This is the point of Archimedes' calculation in *The Sand Reckoner*. To counter the association of largeness with infinity, Archimedes patiently calculated that the number of grains of sand needed to fill a sphere as big as our universe is less than $10^{51}$.

Having persuaded us that there must be a finite number of things, Zeno turns around and argues that it equally follows from "There is more than one thing" that the number is infinite. For between any two things, there must be a third thing. If there are two separate things, some third thing must separate them. This third thing must itself be separated from its neighbors. Since there must be a further separator whenever one separator is postulated, the number of things is infinite.

Many witnesses to Zeno's *reductio ad absurdum* arguments believed he was showing off his debating skill. First, Zeno would prove one side of the case and then, in a turnabout, prove the other side. Thus the couplet by Timon of Philius: "Also the two-edged tongue of mighty Zeno, who, / Say what one would, could argue it untrue." But Zeno does not think that everyone can be refuted. Parmenides, for one, cannot be refuted.

Unlike Parmenides, Zeno does not offer direct arguments in favor of a particular truth. He always proceeds indirectly, reducing the competing doctrines to absurdity. Socrates tries to make sense of Zeno's book (from which Zeno has just read aloud):

> "Zeno, what do you mean by this? If existing things are a many, you say, then they must be both like and unlike. But this is impossible, since unlike things cannot be like or like things unlike. That's what you are saying, isn't it?"
>
> "Just so," Zeno replied.
>
> "Then if it is impossible for unlike things to be like, and for like things to be unlike, then it is impossible for things to be a many; for if there were a many, impossible consequences would follow. Is that the purpose of your argument—to maintain against all comers that there cannot be a many? And do you regard each of your arguments as proof of this, so that in your view the

> arguments put forward in your treatise are just so many proofs that there is not a many? Is that right, or have I misunderstood you?"
>
> "No," said Zeno, "you have grasped admirably the whole purpose of the work."
>
> (From Plato's *Parmenides* 127 D)

Many of the mathematicians and physicists who present Zeno's paradoxes assure their readers that Zeno is not crazy. They say he is just challenging us to clarify our ideas. But the above passage from Plato suggests that Zeno is not interested in prompting us to develop better theories of familiar phenomena. Zeno contends those phenomena do not exist. When an atheist asks, "Could God make a stone so big that he himself could not lift it?" he is not inviting the theist to develop a coherent theory of omnipotence. The atheist is using the stone paradox to refute the possibility of God. Zeno is equally destructive. Zeno wants to serve his teacher Parmenides by exposing the absurdity of all rival positions. He makes the point explicitly in his reply to Socrates:

> The truth is that these writings were meant as a kind of support to the arguments of Parmenides against those who try to ridicule him by saying that if the whole is one, many absurdities and contradictions follow. This treatise of mine is a reply to those who say that there is a many, and it pays them back with interest; for it shows that consequences still more ridiculous follow if what is is a many than if it is a one, if you pursue the matter far enough.
>
> (From Plato's *Parmenides* 127 D)

## ZENO'S PARADOXES OF MOTION

Zeno is more famous for his defense of Parmenides' claim that there is no motion. Plato does not mention any of these arguments. We learn about them principally through Aristotle.

The best known of these puzzles is the bisection paradox. Can you walk across a room? To reach the opposite side, you must first walk halfway across. After that, you must walk half of the remaining distance. And then half the new remainder. There are infinitely many of these halfway points. No one can perform infinitely many acts in a finite amount of time.

Zeno's second paradox of motion pits Achilles against a tortoise. Since Achilles is the faster runner, we give the tortoise a head start. Can Achilles overtake the tortoise? To pass the tortoise, Achilles must first make up for the head start. But by the time he has covered that distance, the tortoise has moved ahead further. Achilles must therefore make up for that distance. But once Achilles has done that, the tortoise has moved again. Although this new distance is shorter, Achilles must still make up for it. But the enterprise of making up this endless sequence of distance debts is futile. Achilles cannot pass the tortoise because he cannot catch up infinitely many times.

The third paradox asks whether a moving arrow is at rest. An arrow is at rest if it is in a place equal to itself. At any given moment, even a very speedy arrow cannot be where it is not. Therefore, it must be where it is, and so in a place equal to itself. So a flying arrow cannot move.

The final paradox of motion concerns opposite movement of objects in front of fixed observers in a stadium

**BEFORE**

A A A A

B B B B →

← C C C C

**AFTER**

A A A A

B B B B

C C C C

Fig. 4.4

(fig. 4.4). Let AAAA represent the fans. Let BBBB and CCCC represent two complex bodies that move in opposite directions at equal speed until they are aligned with the fans. Is this convergence possible? After moving, the first B has moved past two As. Yet the first C has passed *four* Bs. Therefore, the first C has moved twice as fast as the first B. This contradicts the opening assumption that the blocks were moving at equal speeds.

## ARISTOTLE'S SOLUTION

I remember having trouble understanding the stadium paradox. Doesn't Zeno realize that velocity is relative? BBBB and CCCC are moving equally fast with respect to AAAA but are moving twice as fast with respect to each other.

Aristotle's solution to the "paradox" simply draws the distinction we find so obvious. I thought this was uncharitable to Zeno; could such a brilliant philosopher be guilty of so obvious an equivocation?

Well, what is obvious varies with one's background. Lead cups are obvious hazards to us. But Zeno did not grow up with public health warnings about lead poisoning. Nowadays, we regularly travel in moving compartments that are themselves environments for moving things (such as a conductor walking down the aisle of a train). We take for granted the fact that the earth itself is moving much faster than any vehicle. We have gotten into a habit of relativizing motion. Perhaps Zeno and Aristotle never acquired this habit. Then, Zeno could have made the mistake and Aristotle would have needed to think carefully to correct Zeno.

Another possibility is that Zeno intended the stadium paradox as a refutation of the hypothesis that time consists of discrete, indivisible units. In this setting of atomic time, the rightmost B and the leftmost C have passed each other. Yet there is no moment at which they are aligned. Since the two moments are separated by the smallest possible time, there can be no moment between them—it would be a time smaller than the smallest time from the two moments we considered. The moral would then be that if time exists, there are no smallest units of time. Zeno could then couple this conditional conclusion with some other argument against the possibility of time being continuous. That would give him the result that time is unreal.

Aristotle's solution to Zeno's other three paradoxes of motion employs the distinction between actual infinity and potential infinity. After the immortal Apollo is born, he becomes older and older without limit. But he never reaches an infinite birthday. He is always younger than his father Zeus. Both of their ages are potentially infinite but never actually infinite. When Apollo strides across a room, his path can be divided endlessly in half. But contrary to the bisection paradox, this potential infinity does not mean that Apollo actually performs infinitely many journeys in a finite amount of time. When Achilles races the tortoise, there is no limit to the number of times he catches up to a position previously occupied by the tortoise. But this potential infinity of catch-ups does not mean Achilles actually caught up infinitely many times. Similarly, the flight of an arrow can be analyzed into an unlimited number of subflights. Whenever we divide its flight into $n$ parts we could have divided it into $n + 1$ parts. But this does not mean that the flight of the arrow is a collection of actual subflights.

## ZENO'S ARGUMENT AGAINST PLACE

Parmenides had already presented an argument against place. Common sense distinguishes between an object and the room it occupies. After all, an object can move from its place and another object can take its place. Indeed, the object can simply vacate the area, leaving an empty place. Since the object is what is and the place is what is not, Parmenides' objections to nonexistent things bear down on places.

One reply to Parmenides is that places are not mere nothings. The stalls in a stable are places but only come into being with the creation of the stable. Zeno's rejoinder is that if places exist and everything that exists has a place, then each place will have a place. There will be an infinite hierarchy of places.

In *A Room of One's Own*, the egalitarian Virginia Woolf argues that everyone should have their own room. Zeno shows us that Woolf can ill afford to extend the franchise to rooms themselves.

## ZENO AND THE MILLET SEED

Zeno amplified Parmenides' case against the senses by alleging perceptual inconsistencies. In a dialogue with Protagoras,

Zeno asks whether a single millet seed makes a sound when it falls. Protagoras answers no. Zeno continues: A bushel of millet does make a sound when it falls. A single millet seed makes up some fraction of the bushel. Therefore, the millet seed must make a little noise when it falls. For the sound of the bushel is just a composite of the sounds of the seeds that constitute it. Thus, our senses falsely indicate that the millet seed makes no sound.

This just seems like the fallacy of composition. The fact that the *parts* lack a property (audibility) does not imply that *whole* lacks the property.

To save Zeno from triviality, some suggest that the millet seed is a rudimentary version of the paradox of the heap. The underlying argument would then be a slippery slope: The fall of one seed does not make a sound. If $n$ seeds do not make a sound, then $n + 1$ seeds do not make a sound. Therefore, a bushel of seed does not make a sound.

If the millet seed counts as rudimentary sorites, then what about Democritus's (ca. 460–ca. 370 B.C.) dilemma about cones?

> If a cone were cut by a plane parallel to the base [by which is clearly meant a plane indefinitely near to the base], what must we think of the surfaces forming the sections? Are they equal or unequal? For, if they are unequal, they will make the cone irregular as having many indentations, like steps, and unevenessess; but, if they are equal, the sections will be equal, and the cone will appear to have the property of the cylinder and to be made of equal, not unequal, circles, which is very absurd.
>
> (Plutarch 1921, 179–80)

A cone is a pile of infinitely thin circular disks. If the disks get progressively smaller, then the "cone" will be a tiered structure, like a wedding cake. If the disks are equal, then the "cone" will be cylinder. One can interpret this dilemma as skepticism against the principle that insignificant differences can accumulate into a significant difference.

Attributing the sorites paradox to Democritus or Zeno is overly generous. Zeno is reported to have invented about forty paradoxes. It is natural for them to have varied in quality. Like the rest of us, Zeno may have owed his success to his large number of attempts.

## REACTION TO ZENO

Most philosophers now believe that Zeno's paradoxes have been solved by the transfinite arithmetic invented by Georg Cantor at the end of the nineteenth century. Since the theory is discussed in chapter 22 and rigorously presented elsewhere, I shall content myself with the simplest Cantorian reply: Zeno mistakenly assumes speed limits. People can go fast enough to perform a hypertask in which infinitely many acts are performed in a finite interval of time. You exit a room by acting more and more quickly. You move halfway in ten seconds, then next half in five seconds, the next half in 2.5 seconds, and so forth. In twenty busy seconds, you are across the room.

There have been challenges to the feasibility of hypertasks. J. F. Thomson (1970) tried to prove the logical impossibility of performing an infinite number of tasks. Consider a lamp that has a single button which turns the light on if it was off and off if it was on. Since the lamp starts in the off position, it will be on if the button is pressed an odd number of times and off if pressed an even number of times. Now suppose that Thomson manages to press the button an infinite number of times by making one jab in one minute, a second jab in the next half minute, a third in the next quarter minute, and so on. At the end of the two minutes of jabbing is the lamp on or off? It cannot be on because Thomson never turned it on without also turning it off. Nor can it be off: for after first turning it on, he never turned it off without also turning it on.

The appearance of contradiction is a mirage generated by the incompleteness of the supposition. Thomson's instructions only specify what happens at $2 - \frac{1}{2}^{n-1}$ minutes, not the second minute itself. Consider a man who tells us that every number less than 1 is either fair or foul. In the sequence ½, ¼, ⅛, . . . the first member is foul, the second fair, alternating so that $\frac{1}{2}^{n}$ is foul if *n* is odd and fair if *n* is even (Bennacerraf 1970). Now, is the limit of the sequence fair or foul? It cannot be foul because there is a fair after every foul. But neither can it be fair because there is a foul after every fair. The dilemma is spurious. The instructions only cover the sequence, so nothing is implied about a number outside the sequence.

Others suggest that the "paradox of the gods" cannot be handled by Cantor:

> A man decides to walk one mile from A to B. A god waits in readiness to throw up a wall blocking the man's further advance when the man has traveled ½ mile. A second god (unknown to the first) waits in readiness to throw up a wall of his own blocking the man's further advance when the man has traveled ¼ mile. A third god . . . & c. *ad infinitum*. It is clear that this infinite sequence of mere

> *intentions* (assuming the contrary to fact conditional that each god would succeed in executing his intentions if given the opportunity) logically entails . . . that the man will be arrested at point A; he will not be able to pass beyond it, even though not a single wall will in fact be thrown down in his path.
>
> (Bernardete 1964, 259-60)

If we add the assumption that the man will not stop unless a barrier is put in his way, we get a contradiction.

This paradox rests on an underestimate of the ways intentions can conflict (Yablo 2000). I am able to pick a number bigger than any number you pick. And you are able to pick a number bigger than any number that I can pick. But that does not mean we can exercise these abilities simultaneously.

Now suppose there is an infinite queue of demons who are calling off *yes* or *no* in reverse order. Each demon is interested in being the first to say *yes* but resolves to say *no* otherwise. At first blush, we expect that some demon will say *yes*. But this is logically impossible given that they all stick to their plan. For suppose one of the demons says *yes*. Then all of the demons behind him say *no*. But then his immediate predecessor would have said *yes* because all of *his* predecessors said *no*.

The wall gods are like the yes-no demons. Each god is able to block the traveler. But since a god blocks only if he is the first blocker, the traveler cannot be stopped.

Alfred North Whitehead remarked, "To be refuted in every century after you have written is the acme of triumph . . . No one ever touched Zeno without refuting him, and every century thinks it worth while to refute him." (1947, 114) I think this compliment will not be paid by future centuries. There are still paradoxes involving hypertasks. None of them overturns the verdict that all of Zeno's paradoxes were solved by Cantor a hundred years ago.

Cantor's triumph shows that some important paradoxes can be solved. We now have answers to Zeno's riddles that satisfy the exacting standard set by modern mathematics. Twenty-four hundred years is a long wait. But remember that the comparison was with Sisyphus, who labors for eternity.

FIVE

# Socrates: The Paradox of Inquiry

Ancient riddle sessions form the trunk of a tree with many branches: Hindu Vedic hymns, acrostic poetry, crossword puzzles. The Socratic method of questioning is another branch. A full understanding of what counts as solving a paradox requires an appreciation of the rules of the game Socrates defined.

## THE SEARCH FOR DEFINITIONS

The Delphic oracle said that no man is wiser than Socrates (ca. 470–399 B.C.). Socrates cited this as a license to question anyone who was reputed to be knowledgeable. If the esteemed individual had knowledge to impart, Socrates would help fulfill the oracle by becoming enlightened. If the wise man did not have knowledge, Socrates would help fulfill the oracle by showing that the examinee was no wiser than he.

Socrates approached the pundits of Athens as a student asking for instruction. In keeping with this humble status, Socrates appears to have written no treatises. What we know about Socrates comes chiefly from Plato's dialogues. His early dialogues are presented as a fairly accurate intellectual biography of Socrates. But as Plato's views mature, Socrates increasingly takes on the literary role of being a spokesman for Plato's philosophy.

Socrates professed to know nothing except that he was ignorant. It was natural that he ask the questions. Socrates asks short questions: "What is courage?", "What is piety?", "What is justice?" Until the *Meno*, he focuses on moral issues. Socrates had studied physics. But he had concluded that inquiry into physical causes cannot yield reasons for acting or thinking in one way rather than another. Only reasons justify actions. Only through reasons can we be influenced by the future (writing for posterity) or by ideals (designing a garden with the dimensions of a Golden rectangle) or by what does not exist (searching for the Fountain of Youth).

When Socrates asks you a question, he wants to know what you think. It's personal. You cannot satisfy him by reporting what the wise say. You cannot satisfy him by reporting what most people think. If your position is refuted, *you* will have discovered that your beliefs conflict with each other. The pain of contradiction will motivate you to revise *your* beliefs.

Socrates keeps the conversation simple. An uncluttered field of discussion helps him spot inconsistencies. If you begin a speech, Socrates cuts you off. If you change the topic, he herds you back. If you speak obscurely, he presses you to clarify.

If asked, "What is virtue?" you might answer that virtue is a trait such as fortitude, temperance, honesty. However,

Socrates rejects answers that consist of examples. He wants a definition. The kind of answer that would satisfy him states the essence of a thing, such as "Clay is earth mixed with water," and "A triangle is an enclosed three-sided figure." Socrates is not interested in merely learning how people use a word or how a term is officially defined.

Socrates demands a definition that reflects a reality independent of our wills. When you define $\pi$ as the ratio of a circle's circumference to its diameter, you arbitrarily label an interesting concept. The arbitrariness of the label does not make the concept arbitrary. The concept concerns an objective relationship. Essential facts about $\pi$ can be discovered but can never be invented or altered by a stipulation or vote.

In 1897, the Indiana House of Representatives considered House Bill No. 246 to establish a new value for $\pi$. The bill passed through the Committee on Canals and was recommended by the Committee on Education, plus the Committee on Temperance. A mathematician, Professor C. A. Waldo of Purdue University, happened to be at the capitol. He was surprised to hear a debate on $\pi$. After his intervention and some publicity from the *Indianapolis Sentinel*, the senators agreed to postpone consideration of the bill. It was never taken up again and so did not become law.

If House Bill No. 246 had passed, the senators may have succeeded in assigning the label $\pi$ to another (much less interesting) concept. But the ratio originally designated by $\pi$ would have still equalled 3.14159265 . . . Even in Indiana.

For a period, disciples of Pythagoras ruled the Greek settlement of Croton. But they could never have solved the problem of incommensurability by decreeing that $\sqrt{2}$ equals 3/2.

Socrates believes that words refer to forms that exist independently of human practices. A form (or "universal") is something held in common between separate things. The statement "Bucephalus and Dobbins are horses" is really about three things: Bucephalus, Dobbins, and horseness. Horseness would exist even if all the particular horses were destroyed. Forms have a higher degree of reality than the particular things that are related by that form.

## PROTAGOREAN ORIGINS OF SOCRATIC DIALOGUE

After Socrates' interlocutor proposes a definition, Socrates subjects it to searching examination. Frequently, the logic behind his questions does not emerge until Socrates rounds up his interlocutor's concessions as premises for some unsuspected conclusion. On other occasions, Socrates asks for clarification simply because there seems to be a trivial counterexample to the definition. In any case, what begins as a leisurely tutorial develops into a debate. Socrates assumes an increasingly dominant role in the conversation. His "teacher" is eventually buffeted from absurdity to absurdity.

The Greeks loved to see the lofty cut down to size. The spectacle was all the more amusing because Socrates was a squat, pop-eyed, snub-nosed character wearing a shabby toga.

The method of inquiry Socrates favored, eristic, or as he preferred to call it "dialectic," developed out of the formal debating games pioneered by Protagoras (though Socrates credits Zeno with its invention). An umpire arbitrarily assigns a proposition to be defended by one side against the questioning of the other. The interrogator wins if he forces the examinee into a contradiction. In especially restrictive formats, the respondent can only answer *yes*, *no*, or *don't know*. The interrogator also had to operate within limits. For instance, there was a prohibition against asking for a premise that is equivalent to the issue in question. This is the origin of strangely labeled fallacies such as "begging the question." The jargon was extended beyond the setting of debates to condemn informal reasoning such as Plato's circular defense of tradition in the *Timaeus*: "[W]e must accept the traditions of the men of old time who affirm themselves to be the offspring of the gods—that is what they say—and they must surely have known their own ancestors. How can we doubt the word of the children of the gods?"

Protagoras grew rich by charging coaching fees. Some of the men Protagoras trained went on to become coaches themselves. This was the economic basis of the Sophist movement. The Sophists sparred with men of repute to gain notoriety for their debating skills. The Sophists would travel from place to place staging exhibitions to drum up business. Then as now, people will pay for advice on how to make friends and influence people. Highly successful Sophists could settle down in one city. Some even hired assistant teachers and founded small schools. Aristocrats viewed these vocational instructors as money-grubbers. Philosophers from that class, such as Plato, took pride in never stooping to accept money for teaching.

In reality, upwardly mobile Athenians had little alternative to paying for skills that were now important. Oratory was valued in their increasingly litigious society. At times, there were so many legal suits that the losers began to sue their neighbors just to pay the victors.

Lawyers sued lawyers. Law students sued their teachers. Teachers sued students: Euathlus had contracted to pay Protagoras for his lessons when he had won his first case. After completing his studies, Euathlus never went to court. Determined to collect his fee, Protagoras threatened to sue. He pointed out that if he sued Euathlus, then Euathlus would be obliged to pay either way. If Protagoras won the suit, then Euathlus would be obliged to pay because that is what the court ordered. If Protagoras lost, then Euathlus would have won his first case and so would have to pay in virtue of his contract.

However, Euathlus had learned his lessons well. Euathlus countered that if he won, then, in accordance with the court's decision, he owes nothing to Protagoras. If Euathlus loses, then he has yet to win his first case and so is still under no obligation to pay.

The Sophists made a dramatic impact on Greek culture. Lawyers became favorite figures in plays. In *The Clouds*, Aristophanes portrays Socrates as an archetypal sophist. While receiving a tour of Sokrates's decrepit thinkery, Strepsiades is puzzled by some students who are bent over double, faces to the ground, behinds to the sky. The guide explains that these students major in geography and minor in astronomy. The ridicule rankled Socrates' followers because, in Plato's dialogues, Socrates sharply contrasts himself with the Sophists. Socrates denies that he ever taught for money. He always presents himself as a pure seeker of the truth.

## MENO'S PARADOX OF INQUIRY

Socrates espouses no doctrines until the *Meno*. This dialogue begins much as the earlier dialogues. Meno is reputed to know much about virtue and attempts to enlighten Socrates by reviewing the various kinds of virtue. Socrates interrupts this survey and asks for the general principle that enables Meno to distinguish virtues from other traits. When Meno attempts to define *virtue*, he receives the usual treatment by Socrates. The befuddled Meno makes a rueful comparison:

> Socrates, I used to hear before ever I met you that you do nothing but perplex yourself and other people. And now, it seems you are bewitching *me*—and drugging me and binding me completely with your spells, so that I have become saturated with perplexity. And if you will allow me to speak facetiously, you seem to me to resemble to a striking degree, both in appearance and in other respects, the flat electric ray that lives in the sea. For it numbs anyone who comes in contact with it, and you seem to have done something of the sort to me. For in truth, I feel a numbness both in my mind and on my lips, and I do not know what answer to make to you.
>
> (Plato's *Meno* 80 A)

Meno then acts on the maxim that the best defense is a good offense. He challenges Socrates with a dilemma: if you know the answer to the question you are asking, then nothing can be learned by asking. If you do not know the answer, then you cannot recognize a correct answer even if it is given to you. Therefore, one cannot learn anything by asking questions.

The natural solution to Meno's paradox of inquiry is that the inquirer has an intermediate amount of knowledge—enough to recognize a correct answer but not enough to answer on one's own. Consider a student confronted with a multiple choice question: "Whom did Socrates save in the campaign against Potidaeu? (*a*) Alcibiades (*b*) Xantippe (*c*) Euclides (*d*) Pericles." The student knows that at the battle of Delium a general with a name starting with *A* saved Socrates after Socrates had saved his life in the campaign against Potideau. From this shard of knowledge and the knowledge that exactly one of the test alternatives is correct, the student deduces that Socrates saved Alcibiades in the campaign against Potideau. Meno's paradox can be solved for cases in which the inquirer has some pieces of knowledge that he can bring together to identify the correct answer.

This solution does not apply to situations in which the inquirer has no knowledge with which to start. For instance, newborn babies seem perfectly ignorant. If an infant boy begins as a "blank slate," he has no clues to exploit.

Extreme skeptics deny that adults know any more than babies know. If these skeptics were to follow through by ending their questioning, then these self-professed know-nothings would be free of the inconsistency. But Socrates is trying to end his total ignorance by asking questions.

## THE DOCTRINE OF REMINISCENCE

Socrates salvages the Socratic method by scaling back Socratic ignorance. He concedes that there is a sense of *know* in which people know much—indeed everything! He demonstrates this sense by shepherding Meno's slave boy into the deduction of a geometrical truth. Although the slave boy has never been exposed to geometry, Socrates facilitates the boy's recognition of the theorem by asking him questions. The boy sometimes responds incorrectly but soon spots his mistake when Socrates draws attention to the consequences of his answers. Socrates concludes that the slave boy had dormant knowledge of the theorem before he was questioned. Instead of teaching him anything new, Socrates merely revives the boy's knowledge.

Where did the slave boy's knowledge come from? Socrates infers that the boy is remembering facts that he explicitly knew in a state before he was ever born. The boy had the knowledge because he dwelt among the forms. This knowledge was forgotten during the trauma of birth. But he recovered the knowledge when Socrates prompted the boy's memory.

Socrates generalizes: We never learn anything new. We relearn what we formerly knew by encountering objects that serve as reminders. The form of a horse comes back to mind when we see particular horses. A particular horse is an imperfect reflection of the form for horse and so is not the sort of thing that could give us knowledge of horses on its own.

Socrates denies that any one can teach any one anything. (Maybe this is why he will not teach for money!) All Socrates can do is prompt memories. Socrates' mother, Phaenarete, was a midwife and Socrates regards himself as continuing the family business: "The only difference is that my patients are men, not women, and my concern is not with the body but with the soul that is in travail of birth. And the highest point of my art is the power to prove by every test whether the offspring of a young man's thought is a false phantom or instinct with life and truth." (Plato's *Theaetetus* 150) The midwife does not produce the child on her own. Similarly, Socrates merely helps others reanimate knowledge that they must have first acquired in an earlier state of existence.

Mental midwifery is hazardous work. Most people do not question the ordinary world of appearances. They resent the suggestion that there is a further reality behind this realm of appearances. In Plato's *Republic*, Socrates dramatizes the perils of philosophy with the allegory of the cave. Men are

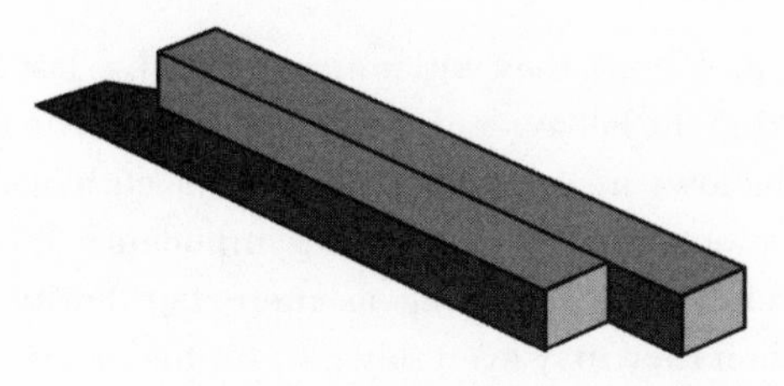

Fig. 5.1

shackled together in a way that keeps them facing a cave wall. Behind and above them is a fire and a walled walkway. The barrier conceals servants who stroll by with figurines above their heads. These figurines cast shadows on the cave wall. This shadow play is the only reality for the prisoners, who have never seen things under normal conditions. Shadows assume the status of objects (fig. 5.1).

Through regular traffic with the shadows, the prisoners become adept at predicting the patterns. What would happen if one of the unwitting prisoners were released from his shackles and permitted to turn around? Would he not be shocked by the scene behind him? Suppose he ventured out of the cave. He would ascend clumsily up unfamiliar steps. He would emerge into sunlight that would leave him painfully dazzled. If he overcame the impulse to withdraw back into the familiar darkness, he would eventually acclimate to the real world of objects. He would be delighted by the colors and richness of reality. He would marvel at the sun that illuminates everything and is the source and sustenance of all there is.

Eventually the liberated man would feel obliged to rescue his friends back in the cave. Reluctantly, he would return to the cave in the hope of freeing them from illusion. Since he would now be used to sunlit conditions, his descent back to the cave would be as clumsy as his earlier ascent. As he resumes his seat with his friends, they will notice that he has lost his knack for predicting the behavior of the shadows. When he tells them that the shadows are mere effects of real objects blocking light, his companions will be amazed by his impudence. If he persists in denigrating their learning as mere familiarity with an illusion, then they may even slay him for his heresy.

## FOLLOWING THE ARGUMENT WHEREVER IT LEADS

The allegory of the cave portends Socrates' own arrest and execution for heresy and corrupting the young men of Athens.

Socrates was unconventionally religious in his obedience to his "daimon"—a personal voice that warned against certain actions. Such introspectiveness was alien to Greek religious thinking.

Socrates interpreted the charge of corrupting the youth as an attack on his activities as "the gadfly of Athens." Most of his speech before the court was a defense of the Socratic method. Socrates eloquently made the case for inquiry unfettered by tradition or deference to authorities.

After Socrates was convicted, the prosecution proposed the death penalty. The custom was for defendants to suggest an alternative punishment. The jury chose between the two. Socrates proposed that the state provide him free room and board at the Prytaneum, a kind of state hotel used to reward those who had been of extraordinary service to the state. The jury chose its only consistent sentence: death.

Socrates disagreed with the verdict but accepted it. He had willingly accepted the benefits bestowed by the state. He had thereby consented to its laws and was obliged to follow the dictates of its judiciary.

Friends (and some foes) hoped Socrates would escape from prison and go into exile. He had practiced civil disobedience in the past. Socrates had said he would not obey a judicial order to cease philosophizing. (*Apology* 29 C-D) He had earlier disobeyed an edict that required citizens to expose enemies of the state. If civil disobedience was permissible then, why not now? Everybody knew Socrates had many influential allies in the Athenian aristocracy. Socrates' friend Crito actually did make arrangements for Socrates to escape. He beseeched Socrates to cooperate. Socrates replied:

> Dear Crito, your zeal is invaluable, if a right one; but if wrong, the greater the zeal the greater the danger; and therefore we ought to consider whether I shall or shall not do as you say. For I am and always have been one of those natures who must be guided by reason, whatever the reason may be which upon reflection appears to me to be the best; and now that this chance has befallen me, I cannot repudiate my own words: the principles which I have hitherto honored and revered I still honour, and unless we can at once find other and better principles, I am certain not to agree with you; no, not even if the power of the multiple could inflict many more imprisonments, confiscations, deaths, frightening us like children with hobgoblin terrors.
>
> (*Crito* 46-47)

Those under a death sentence were expected to take their own lives rather than put others through the ordeal of executing them. Accordingly, Socrates asked his jailer for hemlock and instructions on its use. The jailer explained that the poison is taken like a cup of medicine. You drink it down and circulate it through your body by walking about. When you feel your legs stiffen, you know that death is imminent. Socrates was bemused by the medical analogy. Ironic to the end, his last words were to the effect that he owed a debt to the god of medicine: "Crito, we ought to offer a cock to Asclepius. See to it, and don't forget."

SIX

# The Megarian Identity Crisis

Euclides and his friend Terspion are mentioned as among those who kept company with Socrates on the day he drank hemlock. After Socrates' death, Plato stayed with Euclides in Megara, which is a day's walk from Athens.

Euclides had learned the art of disputation from the writings of Parmenides. After hearing about Socrates, Euclides moved from Megara to Athens and became one of his most zealous disciples. When Athens and Megara fell into one of their periodic conflicts, the Athenians passed a decree forbidding any Megarian from entering Athens on pain of death. Euclides prudently returned to Megara. However, he still came frequently to Athens to visit Socrates. Euclides traveled at night concealed in a long female cloak and veil.

This subterfuge may have led Euclides to formulate the paradox of the veiled figure—also known as the unnoticed man, the hooded man, and the Electra: Socrates knew Euclides but did not know Euclides when disguised. How is this possible? If the veiled figure is identical to Euclides, then the veiled figure has every property that Euclides has: the same eye color, the same number of hairs, the same friends. Since Euclides has the property of being known to Socrates, the veiled figure must also have the property of being known to Socrates.

## THE *THEAETETUS* FROM A EUCLIDESEAN PERSPECTIVE

Paradoxes of knowledge and identity are intensively discussed in Plato's *Theaetetus*. Plato depicts Euclides as the chronicler of the philosophical exchange. Socrates' partners in dialogue are Theodorus, an old eminent mathematician and his gifted sixteen-year-old student Theaetetus. Terspion has been searching for Euclides at the Agora. Terspion finally finds his friend in the street near Euclides' house in Megara. A somber Euclides explains that earlier in the day he was going down to the harbor and saw Theaetetus. He was badly wounded and was being carried by the army from Corinth to Athens. Euclides advised Theaetetus to convalesce in Megara but Theaetetus was intent on returning home.

Euclides reminds Terspion of Socrates' prophecy concerning Theaetetus: he would be a great man if he lived. This prediction brings to mind a remarkable conversation between Socrates, Theaetetus, and his mathematics teacher, Theodorus. Euclides witnessed the dialogue and took notes. Subsequently he reconstructed the dialogue with the help of Socrates. Since Terspion is eager to hear the dialogue, Euclides invites him to his home so that they can rest while having the dialogue read to them by one of Euclides' servants.

Plato casts Euclides as the reconstructor of the dialogue because of Euclides' interests. Euclides was a strong believer in Socrates' thesis that all virtues are one thing: knowledge. This thesis stems from a principle of continence: people never wittingly pick an inferior alternative. If you are offered a choice between two figs and one fig, you choose two figs. Since we always aim for the best, people choose evil only when it is in the guise of the good.

Socrates acknowledges that the principle of continence precludes weakness of will. Those who drink wine to excess will sometimes sheepishly concede (between sips) that they know they would be better off abstaining. However, they continue drinking. Socrates takes the same attitude toward overimbibers as most present-day economists: Actions speak louder than words! We should not be misled by the drinker's lip service to the precepts of others. The drinker's real preference is revealed by his behavior. People imbibe because that is what they most want to do.

Socrates concedes that people sometimes choose a smaller good that can be immediately obtained over a larger good that would require a wait. He thinks this is due to illusions of perspective. In the late afternoon, your giant shadow appears to have a tiny head. But the head only looks ill proportioned because you are looking at it from the giant's feet.

Socrates suggests that there are also foreshortening illusions with respect to time. A child might prefer one fig *today* over two figs *tomorrow* because one fig now seems like the greater good. As people mature, their knowledge of this illusion weakens its effect. They thereby acquire the virtue of patience. Education reduces other vices. We become less cowardly with respect to snakes after learning that most of them are harmless. As we become more knowledgeable, our steady preference for what is best leads to objectively right choices. All vice is based on ignorance. All virtue is based on knowledge.

In *The Republic*, Socrates draws administrative corollaries of "virtue is knowledge." The best choice of a ruler is someone who is most virtuous. Philosophers are the most knowledgeable, therefore philosophers should be kings.

For Socrates, epistemology (the study of knowledge) interlocks with ethics and politics. Epistemology is also related to aesthetics (the study of beauty). Things are beautiful to the extent that they fit their form. A mutilated horse is ugly because it poorly matches the form for horses. A show horse is beautiful because of its fidelity to horsehood. By serving as exemplars, forms are ideals of beauty. Aesthetic appreciation is knowledge of how an object lives up to its form.

Much of *Theaetetus* is concerned with puzzles about the nature of knowledge in light of certain puzzles about identity. I follow Samuel Wheeler in conjecturing that these are variations of Euclides' veiled figure paradox. Just as Plato pays tribute to Theaetetus by having him review some of his important mathematical results in the dialogue, Plato pays tribute to Euclides by integrating his paradoxes into the analysis of knowledge.

There are also methodological themes that would have made for bittersweet reading by Euclides. Part of the dialogue summarizes Socrates' objection to Euclides' voracious appetite for controversy. Euclides was a contentious man who frequently litigated in civil courts. Socrates disapproved.

Socrates prefers dialectic debate in which both parties cooperate and follow the argument wherever it leads. There is no pressure to obtain a practical result. One has the leisure to linger on an interesting issue. If one side errs, the other side good-naturedly corrects the mistake in a constructive manner. The aim of both sides is a collaborative, sincere pursuit of truth.

Lawyers debate for the sake of persuasion. The truth is irrelevant. Each side in a legal contest is allocated a set amount of time to present his case (as measured by a water clock). So they are always in a hurry and are prevented from pursuing interesting digressions. A lawyer has no hope of nurturing a fresh idea because

> . . . his adversary is standing over him, enforcing his rights; the indictment, which in their phraseology is termed the affidavit, is recited at the time: and from this he must not deviate. He is a servant, and is continually disputing about a fellow-servant before his master, who is seated, and has the cause in his hands; the trial is never about some indifferent matter, but always concerns himself; and often the race is for his life. The consequence has been, that he has become keen and shrewd; he has learned how to flatter his master in word and indulge him in deed; but his soul is small and unrighteous.
>
> (*Theaetetus* 173)

To be persuasive, lawyers act as if they believe what they are asserting. Any lawyer who is ready to lie for his client is also prepared to deceptively argue for him. The obvious way that an argument can be deceitful is through the assertion of premises one does not believe. The more subtle way is to "infer" what one does not believe to follow from those premises (in the hope that the jury will join in the fallacy).

Socrates' harsh assessment of litigation offended Euclides. He founded his own school in Megara. Euclides does not appear to have toned down his wrangling. The intensity of debate led Timon to say that Euclides had carried the madness of contention from Athens to Megara.

Doctrinally, the Megarians were in close agreement with the Eleatics. Diogenes Laertius reports that Euclides studied the writings of Parmenides and "held that the supreme good is really one, though it has many names, wisdom, God, Mind, and so forth. He rejected all that is contradictory of the good, holding it to be nonexistent." (1925 ii. 120)

## HERACLITUS AND THE PARADOX OF CHANGE

Socrates shares Euclides' awe of Parmenides. At one point in *Theaetetus*, Socrates refuses to criticize father Parmenides. Socrates listens placidly to Theodorus's sour assessment of Parmenides' opposite, Heraclitus and his devotees:

> True to their own treatises, they are in perpetual motion. But their ability to keep to an argument or a question, quietly answering and asking in turn, amounts to less than nothing. Indeed, "less than nothing" fails to do justice to the absence of even the smallest particle of repose in these people. If you ask them a question, they pull from their quivers little oracular phrases and let fly at you with them. And if you ask for an explanation, you are transfixed with another garbled metaphor. You never get anywhere with them—nor do they get anywhere with one another, for that matter; for they take very good care to see that nothing gets settled, either in argument or in their own

> souls—thinking, I suppose, that this would constitute something stationary; and whatever is stationary they wage war on, and so far as they can banish it altogether from the universe!
>
> (*Theaetetus* 179 E)

Socrates conjectures that the Heracliteans may be in greater agreement when among themselves. Theodorus insists that each one of them is willful and committed to perpetual discord.

The Heracliteans did have a logical argument for the universality of change. If $x$ is identical to $y$ and $x$ has property $F$, then $y$ has property $F$. For instance, if the square root of sixteen is identical to four and four is even, then the square root of sixteen is even. Heraclitus's point is that this law implies that changing things do not endure through the change. If Socrates when ill is identical to the man who recovered, then every property possessed by the ill Socrates is possessed by the recovered Socrates. But then the healthy Socrates would still be ill. What appears to be a single individual, Socrates, enduring through time, is actually a succession of individuals. The Heracliteans conclude that our ordinary use of *identical* is loose talk founded on mere resemblance. Socrates before and after his illness are only identical in the way that distinct grains of salt are identical.

Philosophers who have been influenced by Einstein's physics respond to Heraclitus's paradox of change by portraying Socrates as a space-time worm. He is a sequence of individual stages. They concede to Heraclitus that Socrates does not *endure* through time. Instead, he *perdures* through time. Perdurance is a matter of having parts from different times. A momentary object does not perdure because all of its parts are from the same time. A number does not perdure because it has no temporal parts.

Other philosophers say that Socrates genuinely endures through time because the properties in question have a temporal aspect. The Socrates who had the property of being ill *in the morning* is identical to the Socrates who does not have the property of being ill *in the afternoon.*

## KNOWLEDGE AND IDENTITY

Heraclitus's paradox of change uses dynamic individuals as counterexamples to the substitutivity of identicals (the principle that if $x = y$ and $x$ has property $F$, then so does $y$). Euclides' riddle of the veiled figure uses static *subjective* properties as counterexamples to the same principle. At one and the same time, Euclides has the property of being known by Socrates and lacks the property of being known by Socrates. In addition to having objective properties such as being a man, Euclides has properties that at least partly depend on how people think of him. He can be popular only if many people *like* him. He can be famous only if many people *know* him.

The challenge posed by the veiled figure is to explain misidentifications. How can people fail to know true identity statements? Socrates knows Euclides. Euclides *is* the veiled figure. How could Socrates fail to know that Euclides is the veiled figure?

The paradox of the veiled figure involves an error of omission—failing to believe a true identity statement. Misidentifications can also be errors of commission in which one believes that a true identity statement is false. Before Socrates

learned of Euclides' disguise, he believed it false that the veiled figure was Euclides.

*Theaetetus* begins with the problem of explaining a more specific misidentification. How can people believe that a false identity statement is true? If someone knows both Socrates and Theaetetus, he will know that Socrates is not Theaetetus. If he does not know them both, then the issue of whether Socrates is Theaetetus will not arise. The thinker will not have the resources even to formulate the false statement. He can only refer to what he knows.

There is certainly some truth to this. Socrates could not have believed the false identity statement "Mencius is Mo Tzu." Although each of these Chinese philosophers overlapped in time with Socrates, they were too far away to be known by him. The word *Mencius* would have been meaningless in the mouth of Socrates. Therefore, he could not have had a thought that mixed knowns with unknowns such as "Theaetetus is Mencius."

## THE PARADOX OF ANALYSIS

The paradoxes of knowledge and identity can be used to challenge Socrates' assumption that definitions are informative. If the definiens (the terms used to do the defining) says something more than the definiendum (the term being defined), the definition is too broad (like the false definition "Human beings are bipeds"). If the definiens says something less than the definiendum, the definition is too narrow (like the false definition "Human beings are men"). If the definiens says neither more nor less than the definiendum, then the equivalence ensures that the definition is redundant

(like the true but trivial "Human beings are human beings"). Thus, all definitions are either false or circular.

The twentieth-century formulation of the paradox is due to C. H. Langford. He was raising a problem with G. E. Moore's principle that philosophy is mainly a matter of analyzing our concepts. An analysis breaks a concept down into components as in "A brother is a male sibling." Moore thought that knowledge could be broken down into justified true belief and that rightness could be analyzed as that which produces best consequences. Langford poses a dilemma:

> Let us call what is to be analyzed as the analysandum, and let us call that which does the analyzing the analysans. The analysis then states an appropriate relation of equivalence between the analysandum and the analysans. And the paradox of analysis is to the effect that, if the verbal expression representing the analysandum has the same meaning as the verbal expression representing the analysans, the analysis states a bare identity and is trivial; but if the two verbal expressions do not have the same meaning, the analysis is incorrect.
>
> (1968, 323).

The paradox of analysis resembles Meno's paradox of inquiry. Meno contends that if the inquirer knows enough to identify the correct answer to his question, then he already knows the answer. Langford alleges that an analysis that successfully identifies a concept with its meaning cannot give us knowledge because the identification is trivially correct. A definition can be illuminating only if one were earlier ignorant of an identity statement of the form $A = B$. If one understands

$A = B$, then one must grasp *A* and grasp *B*. But then one will know that *A* and *B* are one and the same!

Plato never formulates the paradox of analysis in his dialogues. However, there was a commentator on Plato's *Theaetetus* between 50 B.C. and 150 B.C. who displays a rudimentary awareness of the paradox. In the course of explaining a mistaken criticism of a definition, the commentator says

> This is a misunderstanding, they say: for the object and the definition are convertible, but the definition does not mean exactly the same as the name. For if one person asked "What is a man?" and the other replied "A rational mortal animal," just because a rational mortal animal is a man we won't say that when asked "What is a man?" he replied a "A man."
>
> (Quoted by Sedley 1993, 136)

The commentator is trying to prevent the principle of the substitutivity of identicals from undermining the informativeness of "Man is a rational mortal animal." The principle poses the same threat to the informativeness of "Euclides is the veiled figure." The paradox of analysis *is* the paradox of the veiled figure as applied to definitional identifications. When the definer says female fox is the meaning of *vixen*, he is identifying figures in a dark conceptual landscape. We know these identifications are helpful, but we face an unexpectedly good argument for the counteranswer that these identity statements are useless.

I have doubts about whether Euclides himself would have been alarmed by the paradox of analysis. As a Parmenidean, Euclides would solve the problem of the veiled figure by restricting knowledge to the *One*. Everything that exists is identical to one thing, so it is impossible for there to be distinct things that we could misidentify as being identical. The things in question encompass mental things. Ultimately, there are not many concepts and so there is no opportunity for misidentifications. Like Zeno, Euclides brandishes his paradox as a sword in defense of his master.

SEVEN

# Eubulides and the Politics of the Liar

The Greek paradoxes have reached us through a network of literature and oral tradition. Judging by how much nearly did not reach us and by the poor condition in which this material arrived, much must have been lost and much must molder in an unrecognized form on our library shelves. This chapter is about how paradoxes and our attitudes toward them have been shaped by their mode of transmission.

Paradoxes have not been handed down through the generations solely by virtue of their intrinsic interest. Often they hitch a ride on some weightier matter. For instance, the liar paradox owes some of its currency to the fact that Paul unwittingly packed it into the Bible.

And what appear to be mere accretions are sometimes the whole substance of the paradox. Many paradoxes of political philosophy and religion originated as incoherent compromises between vying factions.

The reverence or derision excited by a paradox is often an echo of the attitude first adopted toward those associated with the paradoxes. In Greece, dialectical struggle was generally a team effort. Philosophers had strong loyalty to their schools. Their competition for students and patronage was a matter of life and death—metaphorically for the group and literally for some members. Since the stakes were high, the tactics were more reminiscent of politics than of dispassionate inquiry. What could not be refuted was laughed down, stonewalled, or distorted.

## WAS ARISTOTLE A SPY?

The Megarian reputation for logic-chopping was consolidated by Euclides' student and successor Eubulides. Diogenes Laertius describes Eubulides as " . . . the author of many dialectical arguments in a question and answer form, namely, The Liar, The Disguised, The Electra, The Veiled Figure, The Sorites, The Horned One, and The Bald Head." (1925 11, 108) Eubulides' paradoxes are all discussed by Aristotle either directly or indirectly. But Aristotle's discussion is spare and stiffly dismissive.

The only report of Eubulides writing a book is by Eusebius, a fourth-century bishop of Caesarea. Eusebius says Eubulides accuses Aristotle of being a spy for Philip of Macedon and further charges Aristotle with being disloyal to Plato. There may be some truth to both charges.

Diogenes says that Aristotle was disappointed when he was not chosen to succeed Plato as the head of Plato's Academy. However, Aristotle was a foreigner from Macedonia and was forbidden to own land in Athens. Anti-Macedonian sentiment was growing because of Demosthenes' warnings about the growing power of Philip. Demosthenes was Aristotle's exact contemporary (both lived from 384–322 B.C.). Diogenes Laertius says that Demosthenes was probably a student of Eubulides. Perhaps Demosthenes was a channel of ill will between Eubulides and Aristotle. In any case, Aristotle left Athens and became the tutor of Philip's son Alexander. When Athens and Thebes were defeated by Alexander, Thebes was razed and its citizens sold off as captives. Alexander offered generous terms to Athens to secure the cooperation of her navy in his plans for the conquest of Persia. The Athenians agreed to pay for a Macedonian garrison in their city and to exile Demosthenes for his role in rallying the Athenians against the Macedonians. Once Macedonian hegemony was established, Aristotle returned to Athens and founded the Lyceum. His well-provisioned school functioned as an intellectual counterweight to the Academy.

Aristotle appears to have been an informal ambassador from Macedonia. Ambassadors are often suspected of orchestrating espionage. Many tales about Aristotle were told. Biographers such as Hans Kelsen and Anton-Hermann Chroust pool these stories into a portrait of Aristotle as a kind of James Bond or Mata Hari.

Aristotle's ambiguous status in Athenian society helps to resolve "Aristotle's paradox of monarchy." (Miller 1998) Aristotle says political justice and political community take place "among people naturally subject to law, . . . people who have an equal share in ruling and being ruled." (*Nichomachean Ethics*, 1134b15) He writes that "legislation has to do with those who are equal both in kind and capacity." (*Politics*, 1284b34–35) Yet there are also several passages in which Aristotle endorses kingship. A man of superlative virtue can surpass all others in his claim to rule. He is above the law and should rule permanently like the head of a household.

Scholars have tried to reconcile the conflict between Aristotle's assertions that monarchy is the best form of government and that citizens should function as equals using their own rationality to make decisions. The contradiction in Aristotle's writings arises from his need to appease the democrats in Athens and the need to appease Antipater, the regent of Macedon with whom he regularly corresponded. (Miller 1998) Aristotle also needed to appease Alexander himself. Although Alexander was thoughtful enough to send his teacher biological specimens, he also hanged Aristotle's nephew, the historian Callisthenes, for refusing to worship him as a god. There is a suggestive fragment from one of Aristotle's lost works that reads "Kings should not themselves be philosophers, but they should have philosophers as their advisors." (Aristotle, 1955, 62)

When news of Alexander's death reached the Athenians, they expelled the Macedonian garrison and recalled Demosthenes from exile. Aristotle, along with other Macedonian sympathizers, was charged by Demophilus and Eurymedon with impiety. Aristotle left for the city of Chalcis in Euboea where his mother's estate was still under Macedonian protection. Aristotle said he did not want to see Athens sin twice against philosophy.

Aristotle died the same year from a stomach ailment. Demosthenes also died that year. He was driven to suicide when Antipater crushed the Athenian revolt.

## ARISTOTLE'S CONTINUED INFLUENCE

After Macedon resumed its domination of Athens, Theophrastus, Aristotle's designated successor, revived the Lyceum. The core of the school was Aristotle's library. At about six hundred volumes, his library was one of the largest in the world. In addition to containing his own extensive works and notes, Aristotle's library contained a wide range of Greek literature. He pioneered the practice of prefacing his own treatment of a topic with a survey of what had been written before. Students at the Lyceum emulated Aristotle's methodology and his encyclopedic ambitions.

Theophrastus bequeathed the library to his pupil, Neleus of Skepsis. Theophrastus thought that Neleus would be his successor at the Lyceum and may have bequeathed the library to him to enhance the likelihood of his succession. However, the trustees of the school instead elected a younger man, Straton. Neleus, perhaps out of spite and perhaps in the hope of establishing his own school, carried the library of Aristotle and Theophrastus to the city of Skepsis. This contributed to the decline of the Lyceum. Neleus then bequeathed the library

> to his heirs, ordinary people, who kept the books locked up and not even carefully stored. But when they heard how zealously the Attalic kings to whom the city was subject were searching for books to build up the library in Pergamon, they hid their books underground in a kind of trench. But much later, when the books had been damaged by moisture and moths, their descendants sold them to Apellikon of Teos for a large sum of money, both the

> books of Aristotle and those of Theophrastus. But Apellikon was a bibliophile rather than a philosopher; and therefore, seeking a restoration of the parts that had been eaten through, he made new copies of the text, filling up the gaps incorrectly, and published the books full of errors.
> (Strabo 1929, 13.1.54)

Sulla seized Apellikon's library and shipped it to Rome. Plutarch, in his biography of Sulla, says that copies of Aristotle's writings were then made by the Greek philologist Tyrannion of Amisos (who had been in Rome since about 68 B.C.). Tyrannion gave them to Andronikos of Rhodes who edited them and compiled a comprehensive list of the works of Aristotle and Theophrastus. Although Andronikos's commentary and bibliography were eventually lost, they led to a tradition of scholarship that preserved Aristotle's work. What survives now is principally Aristotle's lecture notes for specialists. Aristotle had also written more accessible works. The Roman orator Cicero (106–43 B.C.) praised Aristotle's dialogues as composed in a "golden style" that he strove to emulate.

## CICERO'S TRADITION

As Aristotle's reputation reblossomed, the reputations of his adversaries withered. Cicero inaugurated a tradition of disparaging Eubulides. In *Academic Questions*, Cicero characterizes the Megarian paradoxes as "far-fetched and pointed sophisms." The sorites is dismissed as a "very vicious and captious style of arguing." Our principal source of information about Eubulides, Diogenes Laertius, quotes a comic poet:

"Eubulides the Eristic, who propounded his quibbles about horns and confounded the orators with falsely pretentious arguments, is gone with all the braggadocio of a Demosthenes." (1925, II, 108) The other commentators of antiquity also demonize Eubulides as a serpentine quibbler. Given this thin selection of uniformly negative "primary sources," future historians had no textual basis to veer from Cicero's verdict. Eubulides' ignominy became self-perpetuating. Each generation's dismissal expanded the basis for the next. As late as 1931, we find Eduard Zeller, in *Outlines of the History of Greek Philosophy*, characterizing Eubulides' paradoxes as "clever but worthless fallacies."

The emphasis on logic at the opening of the twentieth century elevated logical paradoxes to the status of instructive anomalies. Logicians lacked any historical grounds to challenge Cicero's tradition. Yet, they began to feel toward Eubulides what Mark Twain felt toward another figure of antiquity:

> I have no special regard for Satan; but, I can at least claim that I have no prejudice against him. It may even be that I lean a little his way, on account of his not having a fair show. All religions issue bibles against him, and say the most injurious things about him, but we never hear his side. We have none but the evidence for the prosecution, and yet we have rendered the verdict. To my mind, this is irregular. It is un-English; it is un-American; it is French.
>
> (from "Concerning the Jews")

In 1903, Gottlob Frege published his second volume of the *Grundlagen* which used a variation of the veiled figure to launch his theory of sense and reference. In 1905, Bertrand Russell published "On Denoting," which deploys the paradoxes of identity as tests for his theory of definite descriptions. In "Vagueness," Russell (1923) used the sorites to probe the applicability of classical logic to ordinary language. And Russell had previously used the liar paradox to model a refutation of naive set theory. In 1931, Kurt Godel was guided by the liar paradox in his construction of a proof of the incompleteness of arithmetic. And Alan Turing (1936) used the liar yet again in his derivation of the first uncomputable function (the halting problem). In 1950 Peter Strawson used the horned man paradox in "On Referring" to promote truth-value gaps. This led to a logic of truth-value gaps ("supervaluationism").

When William and Martha Kneale published *The Development of Logic* in 1962, they were cognizant of the heights that were reached on the backs of these riddles. They boggled at the traditional dismissive treatment of the Megarian paradoxes: "All are interesting, and it is incredible that Eubulides produced them in an entirely pointless way, as the tradition suggests. He must surely have been trying to illustrate some theses of Megarian philosophy, though it may be impossible for us to reconstruct the debates in which he introduced them." (1962, 114-15) Despite the meager historical record, the Kneales go on to make tentative suggestions as to how the paradoxes influenced Megarian logic and thereby Stoic logic through the efforts of Chrysippus.

There have been a spate of speculative reconstructions of Eubulides' paradoxes and ancient efforts to solve them. They follow William and Martha Kneale's suggestion that Eubulides should be understood in the same way as we understand Zeno (and Euclides): Eubulides' paradoxes were a defense of Parmenides.

## THE ETHICS OF PARADOX

Recall that Parmenides infers that there is only one thing from the premise that concepts which employ negations do not apply to anything. Parmenides and especially Zeno seem sensitive to the self-refuting nature of this singular conclusion and the process of arguing for it. There can be an argument for Parmenides' "All is one" only if there are premises that differ from the conclusion. But Parmenides' conclusion implies that there are no differences between premises and conclusions. If Parmenides is right, there are no arguments!

When faced with inescapable self-refutation, a buoyant philosopher will modestly portray his arguments as dispensable tools. Once you cross the river, you no longer need the raft. To help others reach the other side, you send the raft back to the opposite shore.

Does the end, enlightenment, justify the means? If you do not personally accept the arguments composing the raft, then it seems wrong to propound them. Those who insincerely propound arguments are lying. They assert what they do not believe with the intention that their hearers will believe.

There are broader definitions of lying that associate it with nearly any kind of deceit. These fail to respect the moral asymmetry between lying and misleading. All lies are *assertions*. When I assert *p*, I invite you to take my word for it. Lying is graver than merely misleading a person because lying betrays trust.

Actually, there are two forms of argument in which the premise is supposed rather than asserted. In a conditional proof, one assumes a proposition *p*, deduces *q*, and then concludes "If *p*, then *q*." In *reductio ad absurdum*, one assumes $p$, deduces a contradiction, and then concludes not $p$. *Reductio* is striking in that one assumes what one believes to be false. *Reductio* is frequently confused with *modus tollens* in which one argues: If $p$, then $q$; not $q$, therefore, not $p$. When $q$ seems patently false ("absurd"), then there is some temptation to call the argument a *reductio ad absurdum*. But in *modus tollens*, two premises are asserted and $q$ is merely some falsehood rather than a contradiction. Unlike the indirect forms of argument (conditional proof and *reductio*), *modus tollens* requires doctrinal commitments from the speaker.

Little can be proved without substantive premises. One loophole is to make one's adversary assert the premises. Riddlers do not assert anything. They just ask questions. Diogenes Laertius is particularly fond of question-answer pairs in which a philosophical attitude is expressed in the answer:

> [Thales] held there was no difference between life and death. "Why then," said one, "do you not die?" "Because," said he, "there is no difference." To the question which is older, day or night, he replied: "Night is the older by one day." Some one asked him whether a man could hide an evil deed from the gods: "No," he replied, "nor yet an evil thought." To the adulterer who inquired if he should deny the charge upon oath, he replied that perjury was no worse than adultery. Being asked what is difficult, he replied, "To know oneself." "What is the most pleasant?" "Success." "What is the divine?" "That which has neither beginning nor end."
>
> (1925 I, 34-36)

Some philosophical dialogues are just elaborations of this simple format. Others present the reasoning behind the answers.

Those who pose paradoxes are not asserting any of the propositions that comprise the paradox. They merely ask a question.

The Parmenidean master shies away from asserting "There are no negative truths" because that is itself a negative statement. But he can pose paradoxes that allow the student to attain the insight which is approximated by "There are no negative truths."

As we shall see, this basic maneuver runs throughout the whole course of Western philosophy. It is also a steady favorite in Eastern philosophy. Some sects of Buddhism revel in the enigmas raised by their tenets. How can I aim for freedom from desire without desiring that freedom and thereby ensuring the frustration of my goal? How can everybody be reincarnated if there are more people now than there have ever been in the past? As if these anomalies were not enough, Zen Buddhists heap on extra puzzles in an effort to trigger enlightenment. Master Shuzan takes a bamboo stick and poses a dilemma: "If you call this a stick, you fall into the trap of words, but if you do not call it a stick, you oppose the fact. So what will you people call it?"

## EPIMENIDES AND THE LIAR

Paul warned Titus, his bishop on the isle of Crete: "One of themselves, even a prophet of their own, said, The Cretans are always liars, evil beasts, slow bellies. This witness is true." (Epistles, 1:12-13)

The prophet was Epimenides. Various poems have been attributed to Epimenides but none of his philosophical writings have survived. He is reported to have been born about 659 B.C. in Phaestus or perhaps Knossus, the capital city of Crete. The two most common dates of death reckon him as the most long-lived of philosophers: 157 years by one account, about 230 years by the other. Diogenes says that when Epimenides' father sent him out to search for stray sheep, Epimenides lay down in a cave. He awoke fifty-seven years later. Epimenides returned to his fellow citizens with long hair and a flowing beard. He also had acquired superhuman knowledge of medicine and natural history. At his pleasure, his soul could leave his body and he could have intercourse with the gods—perhaps accounting for his gift of prophecy. His reputation as a seer led the Athenians to request his presence at rites of purification and propitiation to pave the way for Solon's legislative reforms. The Cretans paid him divine honors upon his death. In Crete, there is still an important street named after him.

Epimenides' remark "The Cretans always lie" was quoted for centuries because people realized that it is self-defeating for a *Cretan* to say "The Cretans always lie." There is irony in self-defeat. But irony is not inconsistency. After all, some Cretan has at some time asserted something that was not a lie. Epimenides' "The Cretans always lie" is just false. No paradox yet!

Eubulides may have poked through the ashes of Epimenides' remark and discovered a live ember; it would be odd if Epimenides' "The Cretans always lie" *entails* that some Cretan is not a liar. Sure, it is a historical fact that some Cretans sometimes tell the truth. But one should not be able to deduce this historical fact from logic alone. What if

Epimenides were the only Cretan? Then we could not make "The Cretans always lie" come out false by finding a truthful Cretan. We would have a statement that must be neither true nor false!

The element of historical contingency and the vagaries of lying are both stripped away in the classic reformulation of the liar paradox: *L: Statement L is false.* If statement L is true, then it would be a true statement that says that L is false. Therefore, L is false. But if statement L is false, then it is correctly reporting its truth-value. If a statement says only what corresponds to reality, then it is true. Therefore, L is true if false and false if true!

## THE HORNED MAN

A common first step toward a solution to the liar paradox is to maintain that "Statement L is false" is neither true nor false. One way to interpret this solution is as a repudiation of the law of bivalence. According to bivalence, every proposition has one of two truth-values: true or false. At this juncture, many philosophers claim a connection between the liar paradox and the paradox of the horned man: *What you have not lost, you still have. You have not lost your horns. Therefore, you still have your horns.* Deniers of bivalence go between the horns of the dilemma: "You have not lost your horns" *presupposes* that you had horns. A statement with a false presupposition is neither true nor false. A bachelor is not required to answer yes or no to "Are you still beating your wife?" Since none of the direct answers to this question are true, the bachelor must answer indirectly by correcting the false assumption that he is married. (Incidentally, "the horns of a dilemma" is derived from the name of the horned man paradox by means of the Latin *argumentum cornutum*.)

Samuel Wheeler (1983) conjectures that Eubulides solved the paradox by treating "your horns" as an empty name, like *Pegasus*. The second premise, *You have not lost your horns*, would then be meaningless rather than merely neither true nor false. Similarly, Wheeler suggests that Eubulides solved the liar paradox by denying that any statements are false. Falsehood concerns what is not, and what is not does not exist.

## THE SORITES PARADOX

The Parmenidean approach could also be applied to the sorites paradox. If you have a heap of sand and subtract one grain, then you still have a heap of sand. One grain cannot make a difference between whether a collection of sand is a heap or not a heap. Given this principle is true, you will have a heap of sand regardless of how many grains of sand we subtract. But this leads to the absurd conclusion that one grain of sand is a heap!

In a commentary on Aristotle's *Nichomachean Ethics*, Aspasius says that Eubulides used the sorites to criticize Aristotle's theory of virtue. (Moline 1969, 396) Aristotle believed that virtues are dispositions that lie between an excess and a deficiency. For instance, courage lies between foolhardiness and cowardice. Generosity lies between liberality and stinginess. Aristotle concedes that the mean is not the same for everyone. The mean for a soldier's courage is closer to foolhardiness than for a civilian. Perhaps the mean also shifts with one's stage of life or circumstances. But even with this flexibility, Aristotle's theory of virtue is vulnerable to a sorites argument. Suppose that in the case of Aristotle himself, a donation of one hundred drachmas to war widows would be generous. Donating ninety-nine drachmas would still be generous. A one drachma difference cannot make the crucial difference between a generous and nongenerous donation. Repeated applications of the principle leads to the conclusion that Aristotle would be generous if he donated a single drachma.

Aristotle frequently says that we should demand only as much precision as the subject matter allows. For instance, many factors of commerce depend on convention and fluctuating conditions. So a commentator on the economy must speak roughly and in outline rather than with the precision of mathematics or science. If Aristotle took these limitations about subject matter to be limits about the corresponding concepts, then he might have rejected Eubulides' challenge to draw the line between generous and nongenerous donations. That is, he might have insisted there is a certain looseness in the concept of generosity that makes it illegitimate to ask which amount is the minimum generous donation. He might even have denied that there is any fact to be discovered. Textual evidence suggests that Aristotle demands precision from ethical concepts:

> Similarly, too, we must state what quantity of money which he desires makes a man avaricious and what quality of pleasures which he desires makes a man incontinent . . . And similarly, in all cases of this kind; for the omission of any differentia whatever involves a failure to state the essence.
>
> (Aristotle's, *Topics* 146 b)

Aristotle's ethical theory does seem to imply that there is a minimum generous donation (Moline 1969). One of his themes is that the judgment of a generous man sets the standard of generosity. When the generous man stops judging the donation as generous, the donation stops being generous.

Eubulides would have doubted that the generous man's judgments are definite enough to support Aristotle's solution. There is often no way to tell whether a difference of one drachma would alter the generous man's opinion as to whether the donation was vague. Many generous men deny that there is such a thing as a minimum generous donation. If Aristotle lets the judgment of generous dissenters be the measure, his theory would be refuted. Their belief that there is no minimum would be enough to preclude a minimum.

The psychology of morality is as vague as morality itself. Sextus Empiricus liked to introduce the sorites paradox by first observing that it is not incest to touch your mother's big toe. This is a slippery slope for "incest." But it can also be pressed into service as a slippery slope for "judged to be incest by a virtuous man."

A sorites argument can be raised for nearly everything. Nearly all of our words have borderline cases. "Table" is vague because borderline cases can be created by shaving off slivers of the table. Nearly everything can be whittled down to a doubtful case. Why pick on Aristotle?

This is a fair criticism of Eubulides. But it plays into Eubulides' larger agenda. Parmenides reasoned that since nearly all of our concepts are concerned with differences between things, none of them applies to anything. Eubulides thought the sorites corroborated this sweeping nihilism. As followers of Parmenides, the Megarians would respond to all sorites arguments by denying the existence of the objects in question: there are no heaps or generous donations or incestuous acts. Ordinary things are illusions.

EIGHT

# A Footnote to "Plato"

> The safest general characterization of the European philosophical tradition is that it consists of a series of footnotes to Plato
>
> —Alfred North Whitehead

Most philosophers think that a paradox involves an argument that moves from acceptable premises to an unacceptable conclusion via acceptable reasoning. I have already objected that this definition is too narrow; it precludes the perceptual paradoxes of chapter one and the meaningless paradoxes of chapter three. I now want to criticize this reigning view as also being too broad. My counterexamples exploit the preface paradox and the "paradoxes of strict implication."

## THE TRUTH-TELLER

Plato's real name was Aristocles. "Plato" was a nickname. It means "the broad-shouldered one." The name was apt because of Plato's powerful build as a wrestler.

But was Plato's original name even more apt? Someone is well named if the predicate corresponding to his name describes him. Professor Sober is well named because he is sober. Professor Grim is ill named because he is not grim. Aristocles means *well-named.* So the issue is whether Well-Named is well named.

We would run into a dilemma if Plato had instead been named Ill-Named (Geach 1948). Either Ill-Named is well named or ill named. If Ill-Named is ill named, then the predicate corresponding to his name accurately describes him. So if he is ill named, then he is well named. But if Ill-Named is well named, then the predicate corresponding to his name does not apply to him.

The ill-named dilemma is a version of the liar paradox: *L: Statement L is false.* If L is true, then since it says that it is false, it must be false. But if statement L is false, then things are just as L says—in which case L is true after all. L is paradoxical because there is no consistent assignment of truth-values to it.

The opposite problem makes the truth-teller sentence paradoxical: *R: Statement R is true.* R is paradoxical because we can consistently assign either truth-value to R. Since there is no further basis for assigning a truth-value, R would be true or false without anything making it true or false.

Most logicians react by saying that R is neither true nor false. This is based on the feeling that the sentence is empty. But if R is neither true nor false, then R seems to *falsely* claim to be true.

"Well-Named is well named" is a version of the truth-teller paradox. We can consistently say that "Well-Named is well named" is true and we can consistently say that it is false. If we conclude that it lacks a truth-value, then "Well-Named is well named" seems false because *well named* fails to truthfully describe Well-Named. But if *well named* does accurately describe Well-Named, what is the property it so accurately describes? The very property of being well named?

Is Aristocles Aristocles? This philosophical question was missed by Plato. What a lost opportunity! Philosophy could have become a series of footnotes to Aristocles.

## THE PREFACE PARADOX

Was Plato aware of the liar paradox? The legend of Epimenides had been in circulation for hundreds of years before Plato's birth. Plato has Socrates raise an objection to Protagoras that tacks near the shores of the liar paradox. Protagoras's slogan "Man is the measure" is presented as implying that all beliefs are true: *What seems to a man, is to him.* To refute Protagoras, Socrates needs a criticism that will work within a single individual's belief system. He sees an opening in the fact that each person has beliefs about his beliefs:

> . . . there is no one in the world who doesn't believe that in some matters he is wiser than other men; while in other matters, they are wiser than he. In emergencies—if at no other time—you see this belief. When they are in distress, on the battlefield, or in sickness or in a storm at sea, all men turn to their leaders in each spheres as to God, and look to them for salvation because they are superior in precisely this one thing—knowledge. And wherever

> human life and work goes on you find everywhere men seeking teachers and masters, for themselves and for the other living creatures and for the direction of all human works.
>
> (*Theaetetus* 170 B–C)

Consider someone who believes that at least one of his own beliefs is false. Protagoras's principle that all beliefs are true implies that "At least one of my beliefs is not true" is true for this modest individual. Thus "All beliefs are true for the believer" when applied to the modest believer yields "Not all beliefs are true for the believer." Since Protagorean relativism implies its own falsity, Protagorean relativism is false.

Socrates' objection to Protagoras resembles D. C. Mackinson's (1965) preface paradox. In the preface of the book you are now reading, I apologize for the errors that are sure to be in the text. This acknowledgment of my fallibility is good common sense. Yet, it does make it impossible for all of my beliefs to be true. If the belief expressed in the preface is true, then one of the beliefs in the text is false. If all the beliefs in the text are true, then the belief in the preface is false. Either way, I have a false belief.

Although the preface paradox damages Protagoras's relativism, it also undermines Plato's assumption that rationality implies consistency. Since it is impossible for all of my beliefs about this book to be all true, they are jointly inconsistent. Yet, the belief I express in the preface is rational.

Indeed, this degree of intellectual humility is intellectually mandatory. Know thyself! If I failed to believe that some of the beliefs expressed in this text are false, then I would be a vain scholar.

## JUMBLE ARGUMENTS

In addition to being modest about whether my beliefs are true, I should be modest about whether all my beliefs are consistent. The more I say, the more opportunities I have to contradict myself. I say very much in this book and so believe that the assertions in this text (even apart from those in the preface) are jointly inconsistent.

Take the first 10,001 assertions I make in this book. I believe that any conjunction of 10,000 of them is inconsistent. Now consider any argument that takes 10,000 of my 10,001 assertions as the premises and takes the negation of the remaining assertion as the conclusion. This jumble argument would fit R. M. Sainsbury's definition of a paradox:

> This is what I understand by a paradox: an apparently unacceptable conclusion derived by apparently acceptable reasoning from apparently acceptable premises. Appearances have to deceive, since the acceptable cannot lead by acceptable steps to the unacceptable. So, generally, we have a choice: either the conclusion is not really unacceptable, or else the starting point, or the reasoning, has some non-obvious flaw.
>
> (Sainsbury 1995, 1).

The conclusion of the jumble argument is unacceptable to me because I sincerely assert its negation in my book. Each premise of the jumble is acceptable because I sincerely assert it in my book. The *reasoning* in the jumble argument is acceptable to me because I think the argument is deductively valid: Any argument with jointly inconsistent premises is automatically valid. This principle follows from the definition of *valid*: an argument is *valid* if there is no possibility that all its premises are true while its conclusion is false.

An argument is *sound* if it is both valid and has true premises. Since logicians do not have any special knowledge about the truth of premises, they focus on validity. They happily endorse silly arguments such as "All tortoises belong to the genus *Testudines*. Plato is a tortoise. Therefore, Plato belongs to the genus *Testudines*." *If* the premises were both true, then the conclusion *would be* true. Validity is merely a *conditional* guarantee of a true conclusion. If there is no way the premises could all be true, then the guarantee holds vacuously.

Euclides' disciples in Megara (most famously Philo) pioneered the logical doctrine that the indicative conditional "If $p$, then $q$" is false only when the antecedent, $p$, is true and the consequent, $q$, is false. This implies two "paradoxes of material implication." The negative version is that *any* indicative conditional with a false antecedent is true. For instance, "If Socrates visited the moon, then Plato visited the sun" comes out true. The positive version is that *any* indicative conditional with a true consequent is true. Thus, "If Socrates visited Atlantis, then Plato visited Megara" comes out true.

Some logicians softened the blow by emphasizing that *strict conditionals* have the form, "*Necessarily*, if $p$, then $q$." These conditionals are not made automatically true by the antecedent being false or the consequent being true. However, subsequent logicians discovered "the paradoxes of strict implication": a strict conditional is made automatically true by the *necessary* falsehood of its antecedent or the *necessary* truth of its consequent. Many minor paradoxes orbit the paradoxes of strict implication. My favorite is

Jaakko Hintikka's proof that it is immoral to do the impossible: One should never do anything that entails the destruction of the human race. One cannot do an impossible act without also destroying the human race. Therefore, one should not do the impossible.

An argument is valid if the conjunction of its premises strictly implies the conclusion. Thus, the paradoxes of strict implication affect some verdicts of validity. If the conclusion of an argument is a necessary truth, then the argument is automatically valid. If all the premises are true, then the argument will also be sound. This is the basis for some sophistical proofs of God's existence. Medieval logicians believed that "God exists" is a necessary truth and so bemusedly regarded "Plato philosophized, therefore, God exists" as a sound argument. The devout mathematical genius Leonhard Euler (1707–1783) sprang this logical trick on the French atheist Denis Diderot. Addressing Diderot before the court of Catherine the Great, Euler solemnly said, "Sir, $(a + b^n) / n = x$, hence God exists. Reply!." Since Diderot was not mathematically sophisticated, he did not know what to say. He was laughed out of St. Petersburg and hurried back to France.

A believer in classical logic can simultaneously perceive an argument as sound and as a positive instance of the paradox of strict implication. For instance, medieval logicians regarded "Plato philosophized, therefore, God exists" as a paradoxical argument even though they agreed that the proof was sound. The paradox can be in *how* you prove something rather than in what you prove. This point causes indigestion for those who say that all paradoxes feature unacceptable conclusions. Their accounts are too narrow.

Jumble arguments exploit a consequence of the negative paradox of strict implication: Any argument with premises that combine to form a necessary falsehood must be a valid argument. When a jumble argument is tailored to the belief system of a modest classical logician, he will accept the reasoning because he thinks that the conjunction of the premises is necessarily false. (Whether it is actually false does not matter for the purposes of the counterexample.)

If jumble arguments qualify as paradoxes, then any negation of one of my beliefs is a paradox. For it would be an unacceptable conclusion backed by an argument whose premises I (individually) accept and whose reasoning I accept.

Of course, I regard each jumble argument as unsound. But that is common for paradoxes. The conclusions of Zeno's arguments are plainly false and so Zeno's arguments must be unsound. But this obvious unsoundness does not stop me from classifying Zeno's conclusions as paradoxes.

We cannot exclude jumble arguments by requiring that paradoxes be *short* arguments. A sorites argument can have 10,000 premises. There are also paradoxical *truths*, such as Kurt Gödel's incompleteness theorem, that take a whole semester to prove. Gödel's proof is made lengthy by Gödel's caution rather than by any sophistry.

For many of us, there are *short* jumble arguments. Paradoxes have convinced many philosophers that they have *small* sets of beliefs that are individually plausible but jointly consistent. If those beliefs are used as the premises of an argument, and the negation of some other belief is used as the conclusion, then that conclusion will satisfy Sainsbury's definition of a paradox. Thus, from one genuine paradox we can grow as many short jumble arguments as we have beliefs.

I think the real difference between Zeno's paradoxes and jumble arguments is that jumble arguments can be diagnosed as unsound without violating a Socratic commandment: Thou shalt not rely on the implausibility of the conclusion when explaining what is wrong with an argument. I abide by this requirement when I infer that a jumble argument is unsound directly from the inconsistency of its premises.

The rationale for the Socratic commandment is that Socrates wants to use argument as a method of discovery. He disagreed with Myson who "used to say we should not investigate facts by the light of arguments, but arguments by the light of facts; for the facts were not put together to fit the arguments, but the arguments to fit the facts." (Diogenes 1925, I, 107–108) Socrates does not consider deduction as just an efficient way to unpack data that has been neatly stored in generalizations. Nor is deduction just a way to justify beliefs that you already hold. Socrates thinks of deduction in the same way that we think of an experiment: as a neutral method that can overturn our strongest convictions.

As we saw in his description of lawyers, Socrates despised "special pleading" in which one first has a conclusion and then comes up with reasons for holding that conclusion. The rationalizing of a propagandist is merely aimed at making a conclusion *look* reasonable. Socrates blinds himself to the outcome of his reasoning to ensure that he is being solely guided by the premises and the rules of inference. Admittedly, Socrates' self-blinding throws away information. But this trade-off is familiar to us in the form of double-blind experiments, in which scientists prevent wishful thinking by keeping their subjects and themselves in the dark as to who receives the active treatment and who receives the placebo.

When we say Zeno's bisection argument "looks sound," we only mean it looks sound from a certain perspective—a perspective that does not include knowledge of the conclusion's absurdity. The columns of the Parthenon look straight when viewed from the ground but do not look straight from the roof. From up high you can see that the columns slant inward to make them look straight to the people below. When Socrates follows an argument wherever it leads, he refuses to take a perspective that uses information about the conclusion's plausibility. Socrates always reasons forward from the premises, never backward from the conclusion. (The only exception is when he reasons by *reductio ad absurdum.*) Even nowadays, many feel that a philosopher relying on outside evidence about the conclusion is like a student peeking at the answer book.

Many illusions require special viewing conditions. I have an "impossible crate" suspended from my office ceiling by an invisible thread. When an inquisitive visitor asks about this irregularly shaped mobile, I station him at a predetermined distance, have him close one eye, and then tell him to align his line of sight along the near and far corners of the "crate." Under those special conditions, the crate looks like a three-dimensional counterpart of figure 8.1. Many paradoxical arguments require the same disciplined contemplation. Instead of evaluating them normally, you must start from premises that you only pretend to accept, proceed with inference rules that you regard as questionable transport, and then suppress the urge to backpedal from your destination.

Fig. 8.1

No one believes that the crate is as it appears. Nor do they expect to. They make the effort partly for the sheer spectacle and partly in the hope of being edified. Cognitive paradoxes have the same mixture of aesthetic and theoretical allure. A scientist who goes through the observational contortions needed to witness a double rainbow will concede that rainbows are illusions. Yet, he will value the experience as much as an observation of a real phenomenon such as a solar eclipse.

## THE ELENCHUS PROBLEM

The eminent Plato scholar Gregory Vlastos (1983) used to interpret Socrates as refuting his interlocutors by deriving a contradiction. This was the standard view as reflected in the *Encyclopedia of Philosophy* entry for "Dialectic":

> The Socratic elenchus was perhaps a refined form of the Zenoian paradoxes, a prolonged cross-examination which

> refutes the opponent's original thesis by getting him to draw from it, by means of a series of questions and answers, a consequence that contradicts it. This is a logically valid procedure, for it corresponds to the logical law "if *p* implies not-*p*, then not-*p* is true."
>
> (Hall 1967, 386)

But Vlastos eventually noticed that Socrates usually achieves only the weaker result of showing that the interlocutor's beliefs are jointly inconsistent. Vlastos finds this alarming because Socrates is under the impression that he has refuted a particular member of the inconsistent set. From a logical point of view, consistency can be regained by rejecting *any* member of the set. Therefore, Socrates has not refuted anything. All he has done is shown that his interlocutor needs to revise some of his beliefs.

Maybe not even that! News that a set of beliefs is inconsistent only justifies a hunt when there is some prospect of success. When a few false beliefs are concealed in a mass of true beliefs, then the cost of correction is high. Each belief enjoys a high probability. Under these poor hunting conditions, we resign ourselves to inconsistency.

Actually, Socrates does tend to ensure that good hunting conditions prevail. The inconsistencies exposed by Socrates consist of a *small* set of beliefs. They also tend to be *minimally* inconsistent: eliminating even just one member of the set would be enough to gain consistency. In other words, the beliefs in that small search space are nearly consistent. Just a little tinkering might solve the problem!

Socrates did not *plan* to create a *minimally* inconsistent set. His goal is to detect an inconsistency. He stops eliciting commitments when he thinks the job is done. A by-product of this dialectical efficiency is that you leave the inconsistent individual with the hope of becoming consistent by changing a single belief.

## IS THE ELENCHUS NEUTRAL?

Socrates acts as if the elenchus is a universal method that allows him to take on all comers no matter what they believe. But the method does have some presuppositions. First, the elenchus presupposes that there are inconsistencies. Antisthenes of Athens argued that no statement can contradict another statement. The idea is inspired by Parmenides: A statement can be about Socrates only if it applies to Socrates. If it applies to Socrates, it is a true statement. Therefore, no false statement can be about Socrates. A statement about Socrates can be contradicted only if a false statement can be about Socrates. Consequently, no statement about Socrates can be contradicted. What goes for Socrates, goes for all things. Therefore, there are no contradictions.

Plato appears to target Antisthenes in the *Euthydemus*. Antisthenes is portrayed as a sophistical wrangler busy in the practice Protagoras advertised as "making the weaker argument appear the stronger." Antisthenes in turn wrote a polemic against Plato under the naughty title *Sathon* or *Little Willy*. The Greek expression for "Little Willy" is a near pun of "Plato." Antisthenes used *Sathon* as a name for Plato.

The elenchus assumes contradictions cannot be true. Since Antisthenes thinks there are no contradictions, he agrees that there are no true contradictions. However, there have been philosophers who have affirmed both the existence of contradictions and their truth. A contemporary example is

Graham Priest (1987). He thinks a minority of contradictions are both true and false. According to Priest, paradoxes figure prominently in this provocative minority.

Priest realizes that his position is untenable in contemporary classical logic. As we saw with the negative paradox of strict implication, anything follows from an impossibility. When the impossibility is a strict logical contradiction, we can even formally derive the arbitrary consequence: From the premise *p* and *not-p*, we can infer *p*. From *p* we can infer *p or q* (where *q* is any proposition). Now we can go back to *p* and *not-p* and infer *not-p*. When *not-p* is combined with the earlier result of *p or q*, we can deduce *q*.

Classical logic is "explosive"; one contradiction implies every proposition. Is there any way for Priest to avoid an indiscriminate acceptance of everything?

Ludwig Wittgenstein (1889-1951) poked fun at the logicians who trumpeted contradictions as intellectual disasters. In real life, when people discover they have fallen into contradiction, they unceremoniously patch up the problem—if they do anything at all. Wittgenstein looked forward to the day when logicians would adapt to this anthropological reality: "Indeed, even at this stage, I predict a time when there will be mathematical investigations of calculi containing contradictions, and people will actually be proud of having emancipated themselves from consistency." (1964, 332)

And indeed there soon arose "dialethic logicians." They take their name from Wittgenstein's remark that the liar sentence is a Janus-headed figure facing both truth and falsity (1978, IV.59). A dialetheia is a two(-way) truth. As a dialetheist, Graham Priest values consistency but only in the comparative way he values simplicity, generality, and empirical fruitfulness. Consistency is just one desirable feature among many. In the case of the liar paradox, Priest thinks we should trade a little consistency to get much simplicity. In particular, we should concede that "This sentence is not true" is *both* true and false and then use "paraconsistent logics" to stop the contradiction from spreading.

Paraconsistent logics are designed to safely confine the explosion. For instance, they reject the inference rule "*p*, therefore, *p* or *q*" on the grounds that a valid argument must have premises that are relevant to the conclusion. They extend this relevance requirement to conditionals in an effort to head off the paradoxes of implication.

Dialetheists portray themselves as friends of contradiction. They remind me of ranchers who present themselves as friends of the horses they castrate. A gelding is not just a tamer sort of stallion; it is not a stallion at all. The dialetheist's "contradictions" may look like contradictions and sound like contradictions, but they cannot perform a role essential to being a contradiction; they cannot serve as the decisive endpoint of a *reductio ad absurdum*. At best they can be the *q* in a *modus tollens* argument: If *p* then *q*; not *q*, therefore, not *p*. So in the end, I think Priest falls into Antisthenes' skepticism about contradictions.

Whether or not Priest agrees with me about his skeptical kinship with Antisthenes, he should agree that jumble arguments create a problem for Sainsbury's definition of *paradox*. For I have been careful to subjectivize my examples. The reasoning in jumble arguments will be acceptable to those who *believe* in classical logic. Even if the reasoning in my jumble argument is unacceptable to Graham Priest, he will correctly calculate that the reasoning is acceptable to me—and to the majority of logicians. So according to Sainsbury's definition, the jumble argument should count as a paradox to me. But since jumble arguments are not really paradoxes, they show that Sainsbury's definition is too broad.

NINE

# Aristotle on Fatalism

The Irish writer Lord Dunsany was fond of chess. He devised chess problems that convey insight without presupposing anything more than competence at the game. In my favorite problem, White is to play and checkmate in four moves (fig. 9.1). Since Black has all his pawns, he looks far more powerful than White. But something is awry; the black queen is not on a black square as required for the start of a legal chess game. The black king and queen must have moved. That means some of the pawns must have moved. Since pawns can only move forward, the black pawns must have reached their present positions by advancing to the seventh rank. So the only black pieces that can move are the knights. Black has far less liberty than it seems! The white knight can checkmate by first jumping in front of the king, then in front of the queen and finally to either side of the black king for checkmate. Black can only delay the inevitable by one move: he can move his knight to the bishop file.

This inevitability is conditional on White playing rationally. If White dallies, then Black can quickly promote a

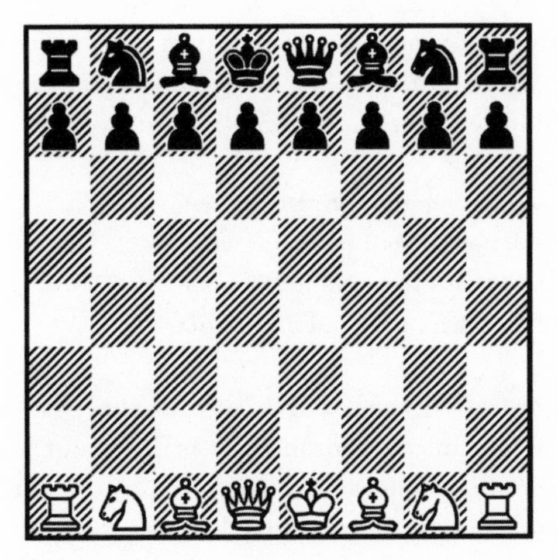

Fig. 9.1

pawn to queen and finish off White. But in solving chess problems, we are supposed to assume the players are rational and pursuing the aim of the game. The actions of other players are just further instruments of fate.

## THE INALTERABILITY OF THE PAST

Time is like chess. Moments proceed by rules. The rules have instructive implications. Consider the Greek mothers who offered sacrifices when they heard that a ship had been lost in battle. They prayed that their sons were not on the sunken ship. For Aristotle, retrospective prayers are futile. In the course of emphasizing that we only deliberate about the future, Aristotle cites the poet Agathon: "Of this power alone is even a god deprived, To make undone whatever has been done." Either your son was on the ship or not. It is too late for anyone to do anything about it. As Omar Khayyam wrote fourteen hundred years into Aristotle's future:

> The moving finger writes, and having writ,
> Moves on; nor all your piety nor wit
> shall lure it back to cancel half a line,
> Nor all your tears wash out a word of it.

Aristotle contrasted the fixed nature of the past with the openness of the future. No one can bring about a past sea battle, but some people can bring about a future sea battle.

Fatalists deny this asymmetry between the past and the future: Right now, it is either true that there will be a sea battle tomorrow or not. If it is now true that there will be a sea battle tomorrow, then there is nothing that can be done to prevent it. What will be, will be. If it is now false that there will be a sea battle tomorrow, then nothing can be done which will bring about the sea battle. What won't be, won't be. For instance, if the admirals order the battle to commence, something will prevent the orders from being executed.

Contemporary commentators on time travel respect the fixity of the past when solving the grandfather paradox. In H. G. Wells's *The Time Machine*, an inventor travels into the past and alters history by stepping on a butterfly. Characters in other time travel stories worry constantly about this peril of changing history. They tiptoe through the plot to preserve the established course of events. But if history were so fragile, then a less conservative time traveler could bring about a contradiction. Suppose this revisionist travels back to the days when his grandfather was a boy. He kills his grandfather with a rifle. Since the grandfather never produces a grandson, the shooting undermines a necessary condition of its own occurrence. Since the scenario is contradictory, one may be tempted to conclude that time travel is incompatible with the laws of logic. Defenders of time travel concede that the shooter cannot kill his grandfather. He might pull the trigger, but the bullet will go wide of the mark. Or maybe the bullet hits its mark but the grandfather recovers. Time travelers cannot alter the past because they are already part of the past. Contrary to the novelists, there is no need to tiptoe through the plot to avoid altering the past.

## THE MASTER ARGUMENT OF DIODORUS CRONUS

Aristotle's adversary in this debate is one of his younger contemporaries from Megara, the logician Diodorus Cronus. There is a legend from the Athenian colleges that Diodorus Cronus committed suicide when unable to solve a logic problem set for him by Stilpo in the presence of Ptolemy Soter. Historians mostly value the tale because it helps to date the activities of Diodorus (since Ptolemy conquered Megara in 307 B.C.). It also conveys the stereotype of the Megarians as obsessed with dialectical one-upmanship.

Diodorus was renowned for arguments about the nature of motion. He propounded these in the same spirit as Zeno. However, he is most famous for an argument that Epictetus recounts:

> Here, it seems to me, are the points upon which the Master Argument was posed: there is, for these three propositions, a conflict between any two of them taken together and the third; "Every true proposition about the past is neces-

> sary. The impossible does not logically follow from the possible. What neither is presently true nor will be so is possible." Having noticed this conflict, Diodorus used the plausibility of the first two to prove the following: "Nothing is possible which is not presently true and is not to be so in the future."
>
> (Epictetus 1916, II, 19, 1-4)

Epictetus goes on to describe how some philosophers reject other members of the triad. His presentation is the fully modern one of presenting a paradox as a small set of propositions that are individually plausible but jointly inconsistent. This style of presentation is more economical than characterizing a paradox as an argument. If we count paradoxes in terms of distinct arguments, Diodorus's three propositions would constitute three paradoxes instead of one.

Although we know the premises and conclusion of Diodorus's master argument, we do not know the steps that he used in his proof. His contemporaries appear to have conceded that the conclusion follows from the premises. For they try to resist Diodorus by rejecting his premises only. This has stimulated many scholarly attempts to reconstruct the master argument of Diodorus Cronus. Frederick Copleston (1962, 138) suggests the argument went like this:

1. What is possible cannot become impossible.
2. If there are two contradictory alternatives and one has come to pass, then the other is impossible.
3. If the nonoccurring alternative had been possible before, then the impossible would have come out of the possible.

4. Therefore, the nonoccurring alternative was not possible before.
5. Thus, only what is actual is possible.

This interpretation has the advantage of making the argument valid; if the premises are true, the conclusion must be true. But commentators complain that Copleston has left the first premise too easy to deny. Last winter I had it in my power to walk across Walden Pond. Now it is summer and the walk across Walden Pond has become impossible. The change in seasons affects what I have the power to do.

The traditional interpretation of Aristotle's solution is along these lines: Right now, it is neither true nor false that there will be a sea battle tomorrow. If a sea battle occurs, then the statement will *become* true. The future is open because statements about upcoming contingencies have no truth-values. In the traditional interpretation, Aristotle concedes that some statements about the future have truth-values. It is true now that "Either there will be a sea battle tomorrow or not" because that exhausts all the possibilities. Aristotle also thought that statements about natural necessities have a truth-value. "There will be a total solar eclipse on August 23, 2044, visible for two minutes in northern Asia" is true because the laws of astronomy dictate it to be true.

The traditional interpretation readily explains why Aristotle never discusses time travel. If the future does not yet exist, one cannot travel from the present to the future. Nor can someone from the future travel to the past. No one discusses time travel until nineteenth-century physicists speculate about time being a fourth dimension.

In 1956, Elizabeth Anscombe challenged the traditional interpretation of Aristotle's solution. Truth-value gaps for future contingent statements conflict with the principle of bivalence: every proposition is either true or false. Anyone who takes the momentous step of postulating truth-value gaps should be tempted to use these gaps to solve many problems. For instance, the most popular contemporary solution to the sorites paradox is to say that applying a predicate to one of its borderline cases yields a statement that lacks a truth-value. Yet we saw that Aristotle did not make this move when the issue arose as to what specific amount of money marks the transition to avarice. Lastly, Aristotle pioneered the very distinctions and principles that contemporary philosophers use to defuse logical fatalism. They note that, necessarily, either a farmer is a bachelor or is not. But this does not imply that it is either a necessary truth that he is a bachelor or a necessary truth that he is not a bachelor. Similarly, it is a necessary truth that the farmer will reap his corn or that he will not. It does not follow that it is either a necessary truth that the farmer will reap his corn or a necessary truth that he will not.

Many philosophers think that distinctions such as these, codified in Aristotle's freshly invented modal logic, are enough to disarm the fatalist. We followers of Anscombe think it more likely that Aristotle applied these logical tools rather than momentously breaking with the principle of bivalence.

## VACUOUS FATALISM

Diodorus is generally assumed to be a substantive fatalist, that is, a fatalist who believed that time is real. Inspired by Anscombe's iconoclasm, I challenge this interpretation. Belief in time would grate against Diodorus's allegiance to the Megarian school of philosophy. As a Parmenidean, Diodorus should believe that time is an illusion. He should not be the kind of fatalist who thinks that the past and future exist and are surprisingly symmetrical aspects of the universe. Diodorus should be a *vacuous* fatalist who merely thinks that *if* there is a past and future, then the future is no more open than the past. The point of collapsing all possibilities into what is actually the case is to show the untenability of time and to prove that the existence of the One is a necessary truth. The universe did not just happen to contain exactly one thing. The One is a necessary being that could not have failed to have existed. The appearance of there being many things is necessarily false.

Recall that Parmenides constructed an "as if" theory of physics that could be used to account for appearances. Diodorus was free to construct an "as if" theory of time. Just as Parmenides tidied up his instrumental physics theory by eliminating reference to voids, Diodorus might have tidied up his theory of time by eliminating reference to genuine future alternatives. But Diodorus's underlying account of time would be that it is an illusion. Unlike a fatalist who believes that time is real, Diodorus need not have counseled people to resign themselves to fate. Diodorus is merely exposing another absurdity in the common belief that there are many things changing through time and the belief that our world is one of many possible worlds. Or so say I.

## ARISTOTLE'S COMMON SENSE

Aristotle was methodologically and temperamentally receptive to common opinions and the beliefs of experts. He made advances in logic to disarm arguments for paradoxical conclusions. Aristotle was not the sort of man who would follow a syllogism to the death. He feels free to use the conclusion of an argument to judge its soundness. He usually trusts the testimony of the senses. After reviewing the arguments of the followers of Parmenides, Aristotle writes

> Reasoning in this way, therefore, they were led to transcend sense-perception, and to disregard it on the ground that "one ought to follow the argument": and so they assert that the universe is *one* and immovable. Some of them add that it is *infinite*, since the limit (if it had one) would be a limit against the void.
>
> There were, then, certain thinkers who, for the reasons we have stated, enunciated views of this kind as their theory of *The Truth* . . . Moreover, although these opinions appear to follow logically in a dialectical discussion, yet to believe them seems next door to madness when one considers the facts. For indeed no lunatic seems to be so far out of his senses as to suppose that fire and ice are one: it is only between what *is* right and what *seems* right from habit, that some people are mad enough to see no difference.
>
> (Aristotle's *Generation and Corruption* I, 8, 325a4–23.)

Aristotle thinks you should have the same attitude toward arguments as you do toward clocks. If a clock gives a reading within the bounds of your expectation, then you accept the result. But if the clock gives a reading that seems too high or too low, then you doubt that the clock is functioning properly. In some situations, the clock *might* be nonetheless right. But you at least have reason to check.

Socrates would reject the analogy between arguments and clocks. Our faculty for reason uses measurements but it is not itself some kind of gauge. Reason is what we use to make sense of gauges. There is nothing further to fall back on. Reason must have the last word.

Since reason compels us to seek what is good and shun what is bad, we have no choice about whether to follow reason. Socrates realized that this ethical determinism makes us sound like slaves to reason. But he presents freedom as determination by what is good. When ignorant, we are determined by our false beliefs about what is good. As we gain knowledge, the objective good determines our will. Knowledge makes us free.

Aristotle thought that Socrates' ethical determinism flies in the face of the fact that many people are weak willed—and even wittingly wicked. Consider the case of Nathan Leopold. A brilliant son of a millionaire, he was given every educational advantage. He skipped several grades, learned several languages, became an expert on birds, and earned a bachelor of philosophy degree by age eighteen. Leopold was a fatalist who preferred the writings of Friedrich Nietzsche over Socrates. In books such as *Beyond Good and Evil* Nietzsche extolled supermen who would throw off the chains of "slave morality": "A great man, a man that nature has built up and invented in a grand style, is colder, harder, less cautious and more free from the fear of public opinion. He does not possess the virtues which are compatible with respectability, and with being respected, nor any of those things which are counted among the virtues of the hard." Along with his submissive friend Richard Loeb (age eighteen), Leopold (then nineteen) decided to commit the perfect crime. They meticulously planned a murder-kidnap plot. On May 21, 1924, Leopold and Loeb lured fourteen-year-old Bobby Franks into a car and killed him with a chisel. Leopold and Loeb were arrested ten days after the murder. After they confessed, their prospects for avoiding the death penalty seemed remote. They were poor candidates for the insanity defense. Leopold and Loeb were from wealthy, supportive families. Leopold was actively studying law at the University of Chicago! Although Loeb was of only average intelligence, he was a popular, handsome student studying history at the same institution as Leopold. At the trial, these defiant college boys smirked and giggled. Their lawyer, Clarence Darrow, resorted to one of his pet philosophical themes:

> Nature is strong and she is pitiless. She works in her own mysterious way, and we are her victims. We have not much to do with it ourselves. Nature takes this job in hand, and we play our parts . . . What had this boy to do with it? He was not his own father; he was not his own mother; he was not his own grandparents. All of this was handed to him. He did not surround himself with governesses and wealth. He did not make himself. And yet he is to be compelled to pay.
>
> (1957, 64–65)

Judge Caverly sentenced Leopold and Loeb to life imprisonment for the murder plus ninety-nine years for kidnapping. Many suspected that Judge Caverly's sentence was an incoherent compromise between free will and determinism.

If Darrow's fatalism were correct, Leopold and Loeb were not guilty (even though Darrow had shrewdly counseled them to plead guilty). We are not guilty for acts that we could not have refrained from performing. Consequently, Leopold and Loeb would have no basis to feel remorse for killing Bobby Franks. Clarence Darrow could not consistently maintain that Judge Caverly *ought* to spare Leopold and Loeb. Judge Caverly was determined to sentence the killers to death or determined not to.

In ancient Greece, there was a popular story about the founder of Stoicism, Zeno of Citium (not to be confused with Zeno of Elea). He beat his slave for stealing. The slave, something of a philosopher himself, protested: "But it was fated that I should steal." "And that I should beat you," retorted Zeno.

## THE MANY BASES OF FATALISM

Darrow had also used science to support his fatalism. The whole methodology of psychology seemed to demand the kind of deterministic outlook later articulated by the behaviorist B. F. Skinner: "If we are to use the methods of science in the field of human affairs, we must assume that behavior is lawful and determined. We must expect to discover that what a man does is the result of specifiable conditions and that once these conditions have been discovered, we can anticipate and to some extent determine his actions." (1953, 6) The psychologists were preceded by the historians in their demand for determinism. Oswald Spengler presented his *Decline of the West* as a "venture of predetermining history."

According to Karl Marx's historical materialism, the outcome of history is fixed by unalterable economic forces. But if resistance is futile, then isn't compliance superfluous?

Marxism as a political philosophy involved a call to struggle. Why bother? Since Marxism is both a historical theory and a moral theory, the conflict between freewill and determinism is internalized within it.

Christianity incorporates the same conflict. As author of all creation, God foresees everything that will happen from the beginning of time. Yet people must be assigned enough freewill to make them accountable. People must be the appropriate recipients of the rewards of heaven and the punishments of hell.

If there is a genuine conflict between determinism and freewill, then it is not clear that determinism can win. Whenever we deliberate, we presuppose that we are free to choose between genuine alternatives. If you are persuaded that only one outcome is possible, then you cannot try to decide which outcome to bring about. Since we cannot stop deliberating, we cannot shake the belief that we are free. There is no choice about whether to believe in free choice.

Proof that we are compelled to believe that we are free is not proof that we are free. However, it does limit the feasible resolutions of the paradox of determinism. We do not have the same practical compulsion to believe determinism. Indeed, we are receptive to evidence against causal determinism. Thanks to quantum mechanics, many physicists (rightly or wrongly) believe that there is objective chance in the universe. Since these austere physicists think they can get along on a lean diet of statistics, psychologists and historians come off as gluttons when demanding determinism as a transcendental precondition for their own fields.

## THE MORAL OBJECTION TO FATALISM

Aristotle worried that fatalistic belief would induce lethargy. In *De Fato*, Cicero (106–43 B.C.) formulated this concern as the "idle argument":

> If the statement "You will recover from that illness" has been true from all eternity, you will recover whether you call in a doctor or do not; and similarly if the statement "You will recover from that illness" has been false from all eternity, you will not recover whether you call a doctor or not . . . therefore, there is no point in calling a doctor.
> (1960, 225)

The Stoic Chrysippus argued that you are just as fated to call the doctor as you are fated to recover. "Condestinate" facts depend on one another. If you had not called the doctor, you would not have recovered. But there is no possibility of your not calling the doctor. The fatalist should concede that your actions and decisions are causes. Chrysippus's point is that the choices are not between real alternatives. What actually happens is the only ways things could possibly happen.

As a Stoic, Chrysippus defended moral responsibility from metaphysical attacks. In the next chapter, we shall see Chrysippus marshal a second resourceful defense of morality against a very different metaphysical paradox.

TEN

# Chrysippus on People Parts

This chapter is devoted to the paradoxes of material constitution. They form an emerging field of puzzles about objects and people. The character of this development is conveyed by Fig. 10.1. Fortunately, these riddles have been recently organized with a paradox template. We shall use the template to connect past confrontations with the paradoxes with contemporary solutions.

## THE GROWING ARGUMENT

In the opening decades of the fifth century B.C., Epicharmus wrote a play with a philosophically precocious plot. A man is approached for payment of his portion of a fee for a forthcoming banquet. Lacking money, he resorts to a riddle: If you have a number of pebbles and add a pebble or subtract a pebble, do you have the same number of pebbles? No, replies the creditor.

Fig. 10.1

Or again, if you have a length of one cubit and add or subtract a bit, then would that length still exist? No, replies the creditor. The debtor then invites the creditor to think of men the same way. Men are always changing, some growing, some diminishing. Since this applies to both the creditor and the debtor, neither of them is the same as they were yesterday or the same as they will be in the future. The creditor acquiesces to this philosophical point. The debtor then triumphantly concludes that he owes nothing. After all, he is not the one who contracted to pay the fee. That man is gone. Nor will he be the one enjoying the banquet. That man is yet to be.

The creditor does not know what to say. Finally, he strikes the debtor. Reeling from the blow, the debtor angrily protests the assault. The creditor expresses sympathy but explains that he is not the man who struck him.

Which premise should the creditor deny? If he denies that the debtor is identical to the collection of parts that constitutes him, then the creditor would be saying that there are two things in the same place at the same time: the creditor and the collection of particles. This seems like double vision. What stops the collection of particles from being a person in its own right? The "mere collection" looks like a man, walks like a man, and talks like a man.

According to mereological essentialism, each part of an object is essential to it. The number of objects may grow but not the objects themselves. What appears to be a single individual is a rapid succession of individuals.

Epicharmus's "growing argument" generalizes to a case in which the number of parts stays the same. Recall Heraclitus's assertion that when one steps into a river twice, one steps into different bodies of water. The river stays the same even though all of its parts change. Can an artifact survive complete replacement of its parts?

> The ship wherein Theseus and the youth of Athens returned had thirty oars, and was preserved by the Athenians down even to the time of Demetrus Phalereus, for they took away the old planks as they decayed, putting in new and stronger timber in their place, insomuch that this ship became a standing example among the philosophers, for the logical question as to things that grow; one side holding that the ship remained the same, and the other contending it was not the same.
>
> (Plutarch 1880, 7–8)

In the seventeenth century, Thomas Hobbes improved the riddle of the Ship of Theseus. He supposes that someone hoards the old planks and finally reassembles them into a ship. Is the hoarder's ship the Ship of Theseus?

The hoarder compares the Ship of Theseus to an object that is dismantled and reassembled. Consider London Bridge, which was built in 1831. In 1962, the British government auctioned off the obsolete bridge to a land developer, Robert McCulloch, for $2,460,000. He reassembled the blocks in Lake Havasu City, Arizona. The process was completed on October 10, 1971, and the bridge was dedicated by the lord mayor of London. The local radio station KBBC continues to invite tourists to visit London Bridge in its new location.

Those who deny that the hoarder's ship is the Ship of Theseus insist that the Ship of Theseus was in continuous existence while its old parts were being replaced. It did not pop out of existence when the hoarder reassembled all the old planks.

Suppose McCulloch used the blocks of London Bridge to make a castle in California, and preservationists subsequently complain that he destroyed London Bridge by reconfiguring its blocks into his California castle. McCulloch could not plausibly defend himself by claiming that London Bridge continues to exist; that it now just happens to share the exact location of his California castle. Further, suppose that a repentant McCulloch dismantles the California castle and assembles the blocks into a bridge at Lake Havasu City. Is this bridge identical to the old London Bridge? If so, is it also identical to his California castle?

## STOIC ORGANICISM

The growing argument is mentioned by Plato and Aristotle. Neither gives it much attention. Paradoxes about parts and wholes only became intensively discussed after the skeptic Arcesilaus took over Plato's Academy. Having undermined

Platonism from within, Arcesilaus commenced a campaign against the Aristotelians and the Stoics across town.

Arcesilaus thought the Stoics were especially dogmatic. Instead of lowering expectations about what philosophy can achieve, the Stoics offered just what one naively hopes to secure from philosophical reflection: overall knowledge of the universe integrated with moral wisdom.

The Stoics believed that the universe was an organic whole. Their analogies have been inadvertently updated by the twentieth century's James Lovelock. This biochemist defends the "Gaia hypothesis" that the earth is a living organism. (In Greek mythology, Gaia is the goddess who drew the living world forth from Chaos.) In the 1960s, the National Aeronautics and Space Administration (NASA) Jet Propulsion Laboratory asked Lovelock to design experiments to detect life on Mars. They wanted to send the Viking lander to Mars to check whether life existed there. Lovelock disappointed the rocketeers by claiming that atmospheric analysis already showed there is no life on Mars. Astronomers knew that the Martian atmosphere is static. In contrast, Earth's atmosphere is dynamic. This indicates an underlying regulative process. Extra-terrestrials would not need to visit Earth to learn whether it has life. Lovelock further speculated that the hypothetical astronomers would be in a position to know that Earth itself is now alive: about one billion years after its formation, a nonliving Earth was occupied by a metalife form that transformed this planet into its own substance. Just as cell colonies develop into organs and bodies, organisms coevolve to promote the growth of the whole, Gaia.

The Stoics went further than Lovelock. They believed the whole universe is a rational animal. God is just the most creative aspect of nature. Rocks and other inanimate things have the least creative tension, plants more, animals yet more. At the top of this chain of being are rational animals. Since their rationality makes human beings mirror the universe as a whole, they are microcosms—miniature counterparts of nature. People are healthy and happy to the extent that their inner order corresponds to the outer order of nature. To learn how to live, learn about *life*.

In Stoic cosmology, growth is the most fundamental process of all living things. Arcesilaus used the growing argument to challenge the coherence of this organic theme. If the only change is a succession of momentary objects, then no individual can develop better harmony with the universe. From the conquered stronghold of Plato's Academy, Arcesilaus was picking off students from the dwindling ranks of the Stoics.

This decay was reversed when Chrysippus became third head of the Stoa. He saved Stoicism by writing over 705 books in its defense. None of them survives as a whole. The fragments that subsist in quotation and paraphrase are often obscure. Given the fragmentary nature of the record, the historian is often in the position of knowing Chrysippus's answer but not knowing the question. For instance, commentators have been puzzled by Chrysippus's taxonomy of four levels of existence: substrate, qualified, disposed, and relatively disposed. What theory lies behind this jargon? David Sedley says these distinctions were drawn in response to Epicharmus's growing argument:

> There has been much recent debate about the nature and purpose of this theory, but I think that some of the mystery is dispelled once one sees that it originated at least

> partly in response to the Growing Argument. It is founded on the recognition that an ostensibly unitary object may under different descriptions have different and even incompatible things truly said of it. The insight was not in itself a new one, but Chrysippus' scheme is the first attempt to derive from it a formal classification of the levels of description available.
>
> (Sedley 1982, 259-60)

Sedley interprets Chrysippus as a relativist about identity: the debtor is identical to both a lump of matter and a man. As a specific lump of matter, the debtor does not persist through growth. But as a man, the debtor does persist. The relativist about identity believes that "Is $x$ the same as $y$?" is meaningless; we can only ask "Is $x$ the same $F$ as $y$?" Under this view, many things can simultaneously exist in the same spot.

The relativist's strategy presupposes that we can reidentify individuals in terms of their qualities. The debtor's quality of being a man is not specific enough to do the job. We need a quality peculiar to the debtor. Yet the quality must be general enough to cover him for an entire lifetime. The debtor's hair color, shape, and size change over time, so these cannot be the peculiar quality. One might try a psychological quality like having the same memories. But even if this solution worked for the debtor, it would not extend to inanimate things.

The debtor might be unique in being the only man to have four uncles who fought in Ionia. But this distinction cannot be the basis of the debtor's identity. He would still exist if someone else had four uncles who had fought in Ionia. The property of having four uncles who fought in Ionia belongs to Chrysippus's fourth level of existence, of being "relatively disposed."

Chrysippus's search for peculiar qualities is further complicated by a doctrine introduced by the founder of Stoicism. Zeno of Citium responded to skepticism by insisting that some truths are infallibly known. If your mother approaches you in broad daylight, you know she is your mother. Chrysippus took this to mean that your mother has an unchanging peculiar property that allows you to *re*-cognize her.

The skeptics denied that you can know that your mother is present simply by virtue of looking at her in good light. You cannot rule out the possibility that your mother has a duplicate. Perseus once refuted the Stoic Ariston by inducing one of a pair of twins to deposit money with Ariston and afterward having the other twin reclaim it.

One may doubt that any quality is necessarily peculiar to an individual. If one individual has a quality, what prevents another individual from having the same quality? Consider two planks that are exactly alike except one is painted green. The principle that distinct things must have distinct properties will not stop us from painting the other plank green!

## DION AND THEON

Chrysippus's reaction to the growing argument was not limited to the defensive task of finding a solution. He realized that if he could formulate a variation of the paradox that did not involve growth, then the skeptics would have no grounds to blame the paradox on growth. The growing argument would no longer be a special embarrassment for Stoicism. Here is how Philo of Alexandria reports Chrysippus's paradox:

> Chrysippus, the most distinguished member of their school, in his work *On the Growing (Argument)*, creates a freak of the following kind. Having first established that it is impossible for two peculiarly qualified individuals to occupy the same substance jointly, he says: "For the sake of argument, let one man be thought of as whole-limbed, the other as minus one foot. Let the whole-limbed one be called Dion, the defective one Theon. Then let one of Dion's feet be amputated." The question arises which one of them has perished, and his claim is that Theon is the stronger candidate. These are the words of a paradox-monger rather than of a speaker of truth. For how can it be that Theon, who has had no part chopped off, has been snatched away, while Dion, whose foot has been amputated, has not perished? "Necessarily," says Chrysippus. "For Dion, the one whose foot has been cut off, has collapsed into the defective substance of Theon, and two peculiarly qualified individuals cannot occupy the same substrate. Therefore it is necessary that Dion remains while Theon has perished."
>
> (Long and Sedley 1987, 171–72)

Philo makes it seem as if Chrysippus conceded that there were two men already in the pre-amputated body and that the amputation crowds one of them out. The question given this interpretation is "Who goes and who stays?" But Chrysippus could not accept this interpretation because of his allegiance to the principle that two *men* cannot occupy the same body at the same time. Relativists about identity generally require that the colocated objects be of distinct sorts.

Michael Burke (1994) has recently advanced an argument for Chrysippus's surprising conclusion. He does not claim to be using the same reasoning as Chrysippus. Burke's reasoning is certainly different from the relativism about identity that Sedley attributes to Chrysippus. Burke thinks it is absurd that two things could be in the same place at the same time. Burke is not placated by the qualification that the sorts must be distinct. If $x$ and $y$ share all the same parts, then how could they fail to be of the same sort? Any property of $x$ would be shared by $y$.

Following Aristotle, Burke thinks there is a hierarchy of substances. Once a mere collection of bricks is arranged into a patio, the mere collection no longer exists. The bricks that now compose the patio can no longer fall under the lower sort "mere collection of bricks" because it would be qualitatively identical with a patio. Since nothing would stop the collection of bricks from being a patio, it would be a patio rather than anything less than a patio. Higher substances dominate lower substances in the sense that their "persistence conditions" prevail. (Persistence conditions are rules for deciding whether an object survives a given change. A patio survives replacement of a brick but a *set* of bricks does not.) Burke thinks Theon is a lower substance than Dion because Theon has been defined as Dion's body minus exactly one foot. Given the stipulated meaning, Theon would perish if another foot were removed.

The practice of applying the personal name Theon to a body part exacerbates our puzzlement; we tend to assume Theon names a *man*. But "Theon" only labels a large body part. Before the amputation, Theon can exist because it is the dominant substance in that region of space. But after the amputation, Theon would be colocated with Dion. Since Dion is a higher substance than Theon, the persistence conditions of the object are those of Dion rather than of Theon. Theon therefore collapses out of existence under the weight of Dion's higher status.

As Burke sees it, the puzzles all turn on the premise that the same parts can constitute different sorts of things at the same time. These sorts have conflicting persistence conditions. Burke preempts this conflict by saying that there will always be a highest sort that dominates the others. Since an object is an instance of a sort only if it has the persistence conditions of that sort, the dominant sort forces the subordinate sort to pass out of existence when they would otherwise be exactly colocated.

Burke's strategy also applies to a recent variation of the paradox that makes the rival substances exactly coincide spatially and historically. Allan Gibbard (1975) has us imagine that Goliath is a statue and Lumpl is a piece of clay that constitutes Goliath. A sculptor first fashions the top half of Goliath, then the bottom half. When he joins them, Goliath comes into existence and Lumpl comes into existence. After the clay dries, the sculptor becomes dissatisfied and smashes the sculpture—thereby simultaneously destroying Lumpl and Goliath. Burke's solution is that only Goliath existed. The sort statue dominates the sort *lump of clay*.

Many philosophers regard Burke's talk of dominant substances as a lapse back into Aristotelian metaphysics. They are egalitarian about sorts. This leaves them with a conflict when one thing falls under two sorts that have conflicting persistence conditions.

## PARADOXES AND PARADOX TYPES

Michael Rea (1995) characterizes the growing argument, the Ship of Theseus, Dion and Theon, and Lumpl and Goliath as instances of a more general problem of material constitution. The problem is a conflict between five individually plausible but jointly inconsistent principles:

1. *Existence Assumption.* There is a whole $F$, and there are parts that compose it.
2. *Essentialist Assumption.* If the parts compose $F$, then the parts must have composed that $F$. Those parts are necessary and sufficient for that $F$ to exist.
3. *Principle of Alternative Compositional Possibilities.* If the parts compose $F$, then $F$ could have been composed of some different parts.
4. *Identity Assumption.* If $x$ and $y$ share all the same parts at the same time, then $x = y$.
5. *The Necessity Assumption.* If $x = y$, then it is a necessary truth that $x = y$.

Since the problem is composed of fill-in-the-blank sentences rather than complete propositions, the set of sentence schemas is a template for paradoxes rather than a paradox. If we substitute "man" for $F$ and let $x$ be Dion and $y$ be Theon, then we get a paradox very similar to Chrysippus's paradox. The propositions that conform to the schema are individually plausible but jointly inconsistent. Rea believes that the resulting paradoxes tend to be stronger than natural specimens: any solution to the paradoxes conforming to Rea's scheme is a solution to the historical paradoxes but not vice versa.

Just as there is a common form to the paradoxes, there is a common form to their solution. To solve the paradox, one must refute at least one member of the set.

The nihilist rejects the existence assumption. Peter van Inwagen (1981) denies that Theon exists prior to the amputation on the grounds that arbitrary undetached body parts do not exist.

Actually van Inwagen goes much further. He denies that there are any nonliving complex things. He believes that there are only organisms and simple, indivisible things. There are babies but there are no baby carriages. Carriages are nonliving complex things. If they existed, we would fall into absurdities. Suppose Plato and Socrates each have a carriage and systematically swap each component. Does Socrates wind up with Plato's carriage and Plato with Socrates'? Van Inwagen regards our tendency to give conflicting answers as evidence that complex material things are incoherent.

Van Inwagen does not go around correcting mothers who say that there are carriages. Just as astronomers see little harm in talking of sunrise (even though they believe the sun does not rise), van Inwagen sees little harm in talking of carriages (even though he thinks they are impossible).

Nihilists make no exception for organisms. Peter Unger (1980) argues that there are no men; there are only particles arranged in a manly way. Unger enforces this point with the "problem of the many." From microphysics, we know that each object is a cloud of particles. Each cloud lacks a determinate boundary between the particles that are part of the cloud and the particles that are part of the cloud's environment. Since there are many equally good candidates for being "the cloud," either they are all clouds or none are clouds. Unger thinks it is more absurd that there are many clouds (as opposed to one cloud) and so concludes that there are no clouds.

Parmenides and Zeno are even more severe than Unger. They deny the possibility that there could be a plurality of simple things. According to Parmenides, there is exactly one simple thing.

The second assumption, essentialism, says that if a bunch of things manage to compose something, then they do it on their own. The feat of composition does not depend on anything external. Thus, one can figure out whether the parts constitute the *F* just by concentrating on them and ignoring everything else. Burke denies this principle. He says that the parts that constituted Theon stop making Theon when the amputation occurs. For although the subtraction of the foot leaves all of Theon's parts intact, it does force Dion to occupy that exact region. Since *man* trumps *body part*, Theon is pushed out of existence.

The third assumption, the principle of alternative compositional possibilities, says that the same thing can be composed of different parts. We have already seen the debtor reject the third member of the set. This denial is known as mereological essentialism and has been espoused by Roderick Chisholm (1979, ch. 3). He thinks only Theon survives. Each part is essential, so Dion ceases to exist when he loses his foot. Practical interests are served by ignoring minor changes and talking *as if* Dion survives. But strictly speaking, the loss of even a molecule would end Dion. Notice that this theory does not help with cases of complete coincidence such as Lumpl and Goliath.

The fourth assumption, the identity principle, says that whatever has the same parts is the same thing. This principle is acceptable to four-dimensionalists only if temporal parts are included. According to four-dimensionalism, Theon-plus (Dion's intact body) and Theon are space-time worms that completely overlap until the amputation. Theon-plus ceases at the amputation while Theon continues (since he does not require a foot). Dion himself is a larger space-time worm who converges with Theon after the amputation.

Four-dimensionalists do not have a complete solution to the problem of material constitution. They cannot find any difference between Lumpl and Goliath because they perfectly coincide. Sort-relativists are more comprehensive. They say Lumpl and Goliath peacefully coexist. They differ in whether they would continue to exist *if* they lost a little matter (Goliath would, Lumpl would not) and *if* their matter were drastically rearranged (Lumpl would, Goliath would not).

Even those who have no theoretical position on personal identity can have doubts about the identity principle. The slogan "Same parts, same object" will be rejected by anyone who thinks that an object can be permanently destroyed by being temporarily disassembled.

There are religious implications. Catholics believe that they will be resurrected on Judgment Day. Although our bodies will have disintergrated, God will gather up our scattered remains and reassemble us. Doubters have asked why a man who is assembled from Lazarus's parts is Lazarus rather than a duplicate of Lazarus.

Incidentally, Thomas Aquinas showed that Catholics need to take the further step of not requiring God to use the very same parts in the reassembly process. If a cannibal baby grows up on a pure diet of human remains, then how is God to resurrect the pure cannibal on Judgment Day? There are not enough parts to go around. Aquinas's solution permits the resurrector to use different particles than those originally composing the individual—just as long as the same *kind* of matter is employed.

Aquinas's liberalism is also required by *Star Trek* fans who want character continuity. Most of the crew contentedly use the transporter. It disassembles you and almost instantly reassembles you at another location. Or does it just kill you and make a duplicate? Suppose the teletransporter malfunctions: you learn that the machine successfully created an exact copy of you at the destination but failed to disassemble the original. You are asked to push the override button to remedy the omission. Should you push?

Some readers may comfort themselves with the thought that these paradoxes only arise for science fiction scenarios and in the fever of religious speculation. We are not surprised when common sense falters in strange circumstances.

However, this view of common sense needs to be qualified. For common sense is sometimes confounded by familiar situations that are of practical significance. The Ship of Theseus shows that common sense is sometimes embarrassed by completely ordinary transitions.

And let's be fair: common sense also performs well in some strange circumstances (holding still for dental surgery, flying in a plane, etc.). The nature of common sense is not itself common sense. We should be braced for surprises about how well it performs.

Common sense has undesigned strengths for the same reason our eyes do. Although our eyes evolved for terrestrial viewing, they work well on the moon and for seeing distant stars. This is because simple solutions tend to be general solutions. Our eyes can see far more than they were designed to see and our common sense can accurately judge far more than it was designed to judge.

The fifth and final assumption of the puzzle of material constitution, the necessity of identity (if $x = y$, then necessarily $x = y$), is rejected by those who believe that identity can be contingent or even temporary. Gibbard solves his Lumpl and Goliath problem by saying that Lumpl and Goliath happen to be identical. This answer seems refuted by the fact that Lumpl and Goliath have different hypothetical properties. Goliath could survive the loss of a finger and Lumpl could survive flattening. By the principle that identical things have identical properties, Goliath and Lumpl are distinct. Gibbard retorts that Lumpl and Goliath are *contingently* identical. He thinks necessity is by linguistic convention and that makes it a matter of psychological perspective. Goliath and Lumpl are the same thing that can be looked at in different ways. When viewing it as a statue, we allow that it could survive the loss of a finger but not flattening. When viewing it as a specific piece of clay, we allow that it could survive flattening but not the loss of a finger. Goliath would have been distinct from Lumpl if it had been formed from different clay.

For many years, philosophers believed that the contingency of some identity statements followed from the fact that scientists have *empirically discovered* "Water is $H_2O$" and "Lightning is an electrical discharge in the atmosphere." If it is merely a matter of an empirical fact that these identity statements are true, then couldn't they have been false?

The contingency of identity was important for philosophers who believed that the mind is identical to the brain. They were familiar with an old argument against contingent identity: If $a = b$, then $b$ has all the properties that $a$ has. Individual $a$ has the property of being necessarily identical to $a$. Therefore, if $a = b$, then it is a necessary truth that $a = b$. They dismissed the argument as a sophism. After all, were there not empirical demonstrations of contingent identities such as "Water is $H_2O$"?

In *Naming and Necessity*, Saul Kripke defended the little sophism as a decisive demonstration. He does not attempt to shore up the proof with extra premises. Kripke merely disinhibits our inferential mechanism by removing confusions and distractions. Nowadays, most philosophers agree with Kripke. Despite the enormous popularity of contingent identity in the 1950s, few philosophers would now accept Gibbard's solution to the paradoxes of material constitution. His solution is too late!

Whether or not Chrysippus's solution to the growing argument is correct, he did effectively thwart the attack on Stoicism launched by the Academy's Skeptics. However, as we shall see in the next chapter, a leaner skeptical threat matured after Chrysippus's death.

ELEVEN

# Sextus Empiricus and the Infinite Regress of Justification

We know almost nothing—about Sextus Empiricus. We do not know when this codifier of Greek skepticism was born or when he died. We do not know where he was born or taught or even if he was Greek rather than a barbarian. He appears to have been a physician and the head of some school of philosophy. Most scholars place him in the second century. But they are guessing.

What we do know is that Sextus Empiricus authored *Outlines of Pyrrhonism* and *Against the Logicians*. These books, along with several others that are commonly attributed to him, compile two hundred years of skeptical arguments. Since Sextus wanted to counter the dogmatists of his day, he patiently describes the doctrines of Aristotle, Diodorus Cronus, the Stoics, and many others. Sextus only records philosophical positions with a view to undermining them.

Ironically, Sextus's survey of sites slated for demolition is much responsible for their preservation. Like the other accidental historian of ancient philosophy, Diogenes Laertius, Sextus's works were widely and persistently circulated because he had a flair for paradoxes.

Sextus leaves us uncertain as to his specific brand of skepticism. Sextus has long been construed as advocating suspending judgment on all matters. The ancients knew that the Pyrrhonists were inspired by Pyrrho of Elis. Diogenes Laertius reports that Pyrrho learned his philosophy in India. Pyrrho could have visited India by tagging along with Alexander the Great's expedition. Scholars have pointed out several features of Pyrrho's philosophy that seem alien to Greek philosophy and that were indigenous to Indian philosophy. Diogenes also reports that since Pyrrho trusted no belief more than any other, he went "out of his way for nothing, taking no precaution, but facing all risks as they came, whether carts, precipices, dogs or what not." (1925 II, 61-62) Nevertheless, Pyrrho managed to reach age ninety because of the many students and friends who "used to follow close after him."

## THERAPEUTIC PYRRHONISM

Sextus treats philosophy as a kind of mental disorder that can be quieted by dialogue. As physicians are wont to do, Sextus presents his cure as a serendipitous discovery. Like other seekers of the truth, the skeptic began as a dogmatist frustrated by his failure to solve the paradoxes. Weary, he lapsed into a state of suspended judgment. Ironically, this doubt relieved him of the anxiety that he had hoped to dispel by finding the truth. Sextus recalls the story of Apelles, who was trying to paint the mouth foam of a horse. This famous painter used a sponge to clean the paint from failed efforts. Apelles became so frustrated that he threw the sponge at the picture. To his surprise, the mark left by the sponge produced the effect of the horse's foam. Similarly, the skeptic unintentionally happened upon a resolution of problems that vexed him. Pyrrhonism consolidates this dumb luck.

Sextus's basic strategy is to treat inconsistency as a tranquilizing ally rather than as an adversary. When you find yourself becoming opinionated on a topic, try to think of opposing arguments. As the pros and cons cancel out, peace of mind dawns.

This method of equipollence must be understood psychologically. It would be dogmatic to rate one argument as being equally cogent as another. Sextus's aim is to balance the persuasive force of the arguments, not their real merits. The persuasive force is gauged passively, by noting how the argument affects the subject in question. In one's own case, it is difficult to separate one's opinion of the argument's cogency from its objective logical force. Self-therapy gives you no psychic distance. But when Sextus is curing others, he can freely tailor his talking therapy to the patient in question. The skeptic

> . . . desires to cure by speech, as best as he can the self conceit and rashness of the dogmatists. So just as the physicians who cure bodily ailments have remedies which differ in strength, and apply the severe one to others whose ailments are severe and the milder to those mildly affected—so too the skeptic propounds arguments which differ in strength and employs those which are weighty and capable by their stringency of disposing of the Dog-

> matist's ailment, self conceit, in cases where the mischief is due to severe attack of rashness, while he employs the milder arguments in the case of those whose ailment of conceit is too superficial and easy to cure, and whom it is possible to restore to health by milder methods of persuasion.
>
> (1933a, III, 289-91)

Sextus is interested in what *is* the effect of an argument rather than what *ought* to be the effect. He calmly narrates the experience of deduction just as Albert Hoffman relates the phenomenology of lysergic acid diethylamide (LSD) in his 1943 "Laboratory Notes."

Sextus's method of titrating arguments with counterarguments must be exercised on a laborious case-by-case basis. Conveniently, Sextus also prepares all-purpose argument patterns that help the patient argue other positions to a draw. As the patient becomes a well-rounded dialectician, he absorbs the lesson that "reason is a such a trickster" and stops taking philosophical arguments seriously.

Sextus cannot *assert* the therapeutic philosophy outlined above. Anyone who asserts a proposition implies that he knows it is true. Accordingly, Sextus severely hedges his philosophical remarks. To cover occasional lapses, he peppers his writings with blanket disclaimers:

> For, in regard to all the Skeptic expressions, we must grasp first the fact that we make no positive assertion respecting their absolute truth, since we say that they may possibly be confuted by themselves, seeing that they themselves are included in the things to which their doubt applies, just as aperient drugs do not merely eliminate the

> humours from the body, but also expel themselves along with the humours.
>
> (1933a, 1, 206–7)

Sextus advertises Pyrrhonism as a way of life rather than a doctrine.

Pyrrhonism differs from the Academic Skepticism that flourished after Arcesilaus took over Plato's Academy. The greatest representative of the new academy, Carneades contended that knowledge is impossible. The Stoics had objected that doubt is paralyzing. One does not know what to do next. The skeptics of the new academy replied that decisions can be made on the basis of probabilities (of a qualitative character, not the numeric sort introduced by Pascal and Fermat in the seventeenth century).

Some propositions are more justified than others. Many contemporary scientists are mitigated skeptics of this cautious sort. They are fallibilists who think we can be mistaken about anything. By a testable mixture of observation and theory, scientists instead assign probabilities to hypotheses. As new evidence comes in, the probabilities are revised. Science is a raft that is constantly being repaired. No part is essential. The raft is kept afloat by the *process* of revision.

Sextus denies that the Academic Skeptics are entitled to assert the sweeping generalization "Knowledge is impossible." A proof that "There is no proof whether *p* is true" tends to be more demanding than proof of a typical theorem. To prove a conclusion, one need only find a single cogent argument for it. To prove that *p* can be neither proved nor disproved, one must prove the universal proposition that there are no such arguments for *p* and no such arguments for not *p*. Universal propositions impose a heavier burden of proof than singular propositions. Consequently, the assertion that "Knowledge is impossible" merely substitutes negative dogmatism for positive dogmatism.

More radically, Sextus thinks it is dogmatic to affirm that probability is the guide of life. To change your mind on the basis of probabilities, you need to assign some probabilities prior to any inquiry. These prior probabilities are assigned without any reason. But then one is assigning some propositions higher status than others without any basis. This favoritism is dogmatic. Sextus casts himself as the open-minded inquirer who refuses to acknowledge that any belief is more probable than any other. Since he does not want to commit himself to any proposition, he does not want to assert that we lack knowledge. For all we know, we know as much as we seem to know.

Since Sextus is unwilling to assert premises, he can only mount indirect arguments. In *reductio ad absurdum* and conditional proof, one merely *supposes* a premise. Sextus lets the premises be the dogmatist's beliefs and then confines himself to internal criticisms in which he exposes contradictions or shows that his adversary's position has implausible consequences. Sextus does not seek decisive arguments that will convert his adversary from being a believer to being a disbeliever. After all, disbelief is just belief in the negation of a proposition. Sextus encourages neutrality rather than disbelief. He does not want to win or lose; he only wants to play long enough to show the futility of the game.

Sextus opposes *philosophical* beliefs, not the ordinary beliefs one has in everyday life. Sextus encourages us to follow appearances, to abide by local customs and laws. This conservatism includes religious observances—as long as this piety does not froth over into religious metaphysics and fanaticism. To get along, go along.

Sextus is free to claim knowledge in his ordinary dealings with people. If he is challenged by a philosopher, the conversation becomes philosophical and Sextus will retreat to the claim that it *appeared* to him that he had knowledge.

## THE PROBLEM OF THE CRITERION

Many of Sextus's arguments are specific objections directed against the live options of his day: Stoicism, Atomism, Aristotelianism. He called one of his most effective general arguments "the wheel." If you want to sort good apples from bad apples, then you need a criterion. But how do you know that the criterion correctly classes the good apples as good and the bad apples as bad? It seems you could only know the criterion is accurate if you already know which apples are good and which are bad. But if you know that, you do not need the criterion!

Now consider the problem of sorting good beliefs (justified beliefs or knowledge) from bad beliefs. To know whether the criterion is accurate, one must be able to independently sort good beliefs from bad beliefs. But if one could sort them without the criterion, then the criterion is redundant.

The problem of the criterion locks into a classic infinite regress. The following four propositions about justification seem plausible but are jointly inconsistent:

1. Some beliefs are justified.
2. A belief can only be justified by another justified belief.

3. There are no circular chains of justification.
4. All justificatory chains have a finite length.

Much of epistemology can be seen as an attempt to extinguish this paradox about the regress of justification.

Epistemological anarchists reject 1, the assumption that some beliefs are justified. This position is self-defeating because it implies that "No beliefs are justified" is itself unjustified. Notice that anarchism is incompatible with Carneades' probabilism. Although Sextus cannot assert that no beliefs are justified, he nudges his reader toward arguments that imply that conclusion.

Foundationalists reject 2, the requirement that every justified belief be grounded by another justified belief. The Stoics contended that some perceptual judgments are self-evident truths. This made them the butts of practical jokes. After hearing Sphaerus the Stoic deny that a wise man assents to mere opinion, King Ptolemy Philopator secretly placed waxen pomegranates on the dinner table. When Sphaerus reached for one, the king invited all to conclude that even a wise man might assent to a false presentation.

Sextus embarrasses foundationalists by exhibiting their disagreements as to which truths are self-evident. The foundationalists look dogmatic because of their refusal to defend their self-evident propositions with argument.

Coherentists reject 3, the prohibition against circular reasoning. They agree that one cannot justify a proposition by arguing in a small circle, such as "Sextus was a contemporary of Galen, therefore Sextus was a contemporary of Galen." But they think that some large circles justify a belief. Nelson Goodman (1954) has characterized the method of reflective equilibrium as *virtuously* circular: We formulate a general principle and see whether it conforms to our judgments about particular instances. When we discover a conflict, we must decide whether to retain the principle or our opinion about the particular case. If we amend the principle, we go on to consider other cases. We work back and forth between principles and particular cases trying to get a better and better fit. This process justifies the beliefs we have reflected upon even though we have been reasoning in an expanding ring.

Infinitudists reject 4, the requirement that all justificatory chains be finite. The first and almost only philosopher to espouse this position was Charles Pierce (1839-1914). Most philosophers think finitely long chains of justification provide no practical escape from anarchism: Finite thinkers do not have enough time to form infinite chains. Therefore, the theory implies that finite beings lack any justified beliefs.

## THE CIRCULARITY OF DIRECT ARGUMENTS

A direct argument infers a conclusion from an asserted premise. Sextus questions whether direct arguments can rationally persuade anyone. In *Against the Logicians*, he contends that all direct arguments must either encourage a hasty inference or be superfluous:

> By what means, then, can we establish that the apparent thing is really such as it appears? Either, certainly, by means of a non-evident fact or by means of an apparent one. But to do so by means of a non-evident fact is absurd; for the non-evidence is so far from being able to reveal anything that, on the contrary, it is itself in need of

> something to establish it. And to do so by means of an apparent fact is much more absurd; for it is itself the thing in question, and nothing that is in question is capable of confirming itself.
>
> (1933b, II, 357)

Socrates exhorts us to follow the argument wherever it leads. But if "follow" implies belief, this is bad advice. To ignore the plausibility of the conclusion is to waste a clue about the reliability of the argument. Such profligacy is irrational because it violates the requirement that belief be based on the total available evidence. The implausibility of Socrates' conclusions provides ample reason to doubt the cogency of his arguments. Sextus makes a sensible comparison: "For just as we refuse our assent to the truth of the tricks performed by jugglers and know that they are deluding us, even if we do not know how they do it, so likewise we refuse to believe arguments which, though seemingly plausible, are false, even when we do not know how they are fallacious." (1933a, II, 250)

We associate such circumspection with promoters of common sense! For instance, G. E. Moore (1873-1958) appeals to the principle of weighted certainties. Moore was impressed by subtlety of skeptical arguments and frequently found it difficult to pinpoint a fallacy. Nevertheless, he was sure there had to be a flaw somewhere because the conclusion was obviously false. For example, many skeptical conclusions implied that he could not know that a particular object was a finger.

> It seems to me a sufficient refutation of such views as these, simply to point to cases in which we do know such things. This, after all, you know, really is a finger: there

> is no doubt about it: I know it and you all know it. And I think we may safely challenge any philosopher to bring forward any argument in favor either of the proposition that we do not know it, or of the proposition that it is not true, which does not at some point, rest upon some premise which is, beyond comparison, less certain than is the proposition which it is designed to attack.
>
> (1922, 228)

Moore seems to assume that proof yields a fresh belief only when unopposed by an entrenched belief. In other words, a proof can only be persuasive when it pushes into a blank area, not when it must displace preexisting belief or disbelief. But why should belief always spread into neutrality but never vice versa? Neutrality is not a void that lacks any positive causal power. When a traveler on a tight schedule comes to neither believe nor disbelieve that he is on the right road, that neutrality topples his belief that he will arrive on time.

However, we must concede to Moore that there is nothing irrational or illogical in distrusting arguments that lead to strange conclusions. Indeed, the textbook technique of refutation by logical analogy rests on the legitimacy of harnessing our knowledge of conclusions as a test of the cogency of arguments. The technique is a sign of our logical modesty; our past troubles with fallacies and sophisms and the many logical errors of peers provide ample inductive grounds for caution. Logical analogy can also be viewed as an application of the widely accepted methodology of reflective equilibrium. Rules are to be checked against the intuitive acceptability of the particular inferences they allow or disallow. If the rule leads us from intuitive truths to intuitive falsehoods, the rule is ripe for rejection. Thus, orthodox logical methodology endorses peeking at the conclusion.

The Socratic commandment forbids us from appealing to the implausibility of the conclusion when explaining what is wrong with an argument. This strategy is compatible with acknowledging the relevance of the conclusion's plausibility. When an editor keeps the identity of an author secret from a referee, the editor can admit that the knowledge of the author's identity is relevant in appraising the manuscript. The author's reputation is a fast and fairly accurate indicator of the quality of the manuscript. The editor is free to use this information at a later stage of her deliberations. However, she does not want her referee to use the author's identity as a mental crutch and she does not want him to be biased. The editor wants the referee to focus on the manuscript itself.

Similarly, philosophers want us to wear blinders when trying to pinpoint the flaw in a paradoxical argument. If there really is something wrong with the premises or the reasoning, we should be able to locate the problem without relying on knowledge of the conclusion. Like any diagnostician, the philosopher wants the failure to be *predictable* from features of the original situation.

## THE PARADOX OF DOGMATISM

A little logical humility is a good thing. But how are we to prevent Sextus from expanding our caution into logical paralysis? The question has been deepened by a puzzle that Gilbert Harman (1973, 148) attributes to Saul Kripke. Suppose I believe that my friend Ted drinks and you try to dissuade me: "Ted has an allergy to alcohol, so since no one with such an allergy drinks, Ted does not drink." I am unmoved. I reveal my reasoning:

1. Ted drinks.
2. If Ted drinks, then if you present a valid counterargument that implies Ted does not drink, then that counterargument has a false premise.
3. Therefore, if you present a valid counterargument to "Ted drinks" that implies Ted does not drink, then it has a false premise.
4. You have presented such a valid counterargument to "Ted drinks."
5. Therefore, your counterargument has a false premise.

By hypothesis, I believed the first premise prior to your counterargument. I also fully believed the second premise because it is analytically true. Since the third statement follows by *modus ponens*, I took this warning to heart. By advancing your counterargument, you make the fourth premise obvious to me. Conjoining it with the third yields the final conclusion by another *modus ponens* inference. This metaargument can be generalized to yield Sextus's conclusion that no one can be rationally persuaded by a direct argument.

Sextus was aware that it seems too self-defeating to *argue* that nothing can be justified by argument. However, "Nothing can be justified by argument" is not a contradiction; nor is there any contradiction in "Sextus argued that nothing can be justified by argument." Since both these sentences are consistent, Sextus does not feel pressure to disavow them.

Anyone who hopes to score off of this paradox is merely engaged in rhetoric.

Of course, Sextus is not one to draw a sharp distinction between rhetoric and logic. The next chapter is devoted to a rhetorician who blurs this line with pragmatic paradoxes.

TWELVE

# Augustine's Pragmatic Paradoxes

*I cannot start this chapter.* This opening sentence is undermined by my very act of writing it. Yet my opening sentence describes a possible state of affairs. Pragmatic paradoxes are contingent sentences that behave like contradictions or tautologies. In Aristophanes's *The Clouds*, the debt-ridden Strepsiades swears that after Sokrates teaches him enough sophistry to evade creditors, Strepsiades will pay him a huge fee. Strepsiades' promise to pay for knowledge of how to break his promises *resembles* a contradiction, but it is not a logical falsehood like "Someone promised something and no one promised anything." After all, Strepsiades could keep his promise if Sokrates is trusting enough to accept a self-undermining assurance. Pragmatic paradoxes were common in Greek comedies. Greek orators used them as rhetorical devices. But Greek philosophers did not take pragmatic paradoxes seriously.

Augustine is the first on record to use them dialectically. Unlike traditional paradoxes that are normally cited in attacks against established beliefs, pragmatic paradoxes are normally cited *in defense of* established beliefs.

## A CRITIQUE OF REASON

Until Erasmus's *In Praise of Folly* in 1509, the last treatment of the skeptical paradoxes was Augustine's *Contra Academicos*. As a brilliant student of rhetoric, Augustine (354-430) admired Cicero's presentation of Academic Skepticism. However, at the age eighteen, feeling that he was overcoming a fear of inquiry, Augustine became a follower of the Persian prophet Mani. The Manichees considered themselves Christians. Like Yoda in *Star Wars*, Mani taught that the world is a moral arena in which two cosmic forces contend. The force of good, which is identified with light, is equally matched against the force of evil, which is identified with darkness. God, who is also identified with the force of good, tries his best to combat evil but his opponent is too formidable to extinguish. Mani easily explained the presence of evil. God is not in total control. Events need to be ultimately explained in terms of two conflicting superagents, not a single all-powerful creator of the universe. The Manichees did not require a division between material reality and spiritual reality. Everything is corporeal. Nor did the Manichees ask for a leap of faith. The Manichees claimed all of their tenets were demonstrable by reason alone.

Around 383, Augustine concluded that the Manichees had overstated their logical credentials. He returned briefly to the skepticism of the Academy. However, a stream of probabilities could not quench Augustine's thirst for certainty. He waded into the Neoplatonism of Plotinus. During that period, he worked on a response to skepticism. Eventually, Augustine had a religious experience and converted to the Christianity of his mother. Much of Plato's influence persisted.

Augustine felt that the skeptic can only be answered with God's assistance. Citing Scripture, Augustine averred that the power of human reason was degraded by the original sin of Adam and Eve. From his own experience, Augustine believed that human beings often refuse to accept the consequences of their beliefs. When he understood that he ought not to fornicate, Augustine prayed "Give me chastity and continence, but not yet!" As a boy, he joined his friends in stealing pears from an orchid. He did not steal because he was hungry. He stole for the joy of trespass and theft. Augustine disagreed with Socrates about the relationship between knowledge and virtue. Augustine believed people wittingly and even intentionally pursue evil. Augustine presented his pear-thieving as living testimony. From his own case, Augustine also concludes that people form many beliefs because of the benefits that accrue from those beliefs rather than on the basis of evidence. In the case of philosophers, arrogant pride in their powers of reason lead them to irrationally insist upon beginning all inquiry with reason.

Augustine regularly cites Isaiah 7.9, which he reads as "Unless you believe, you will not understand." Sometimes this prefaces a defense of knowledge based on authority. To learn about the world, children must believe in their parents and take their testimony on trust. They cannot first study whether their parents are reliable informants. As children mature, they form further bonds of trust with friends and teachers and spouses. These attachments give them basic beliefs necessary for understanding more subtle propositions.

Some assertions must be accepted without reason as a precondition for understanding other assertions.

"Unless you believe, you will not understand" is also invoked by Augustine to underscore the emotional dimension of understanding. Augustine insists that when he first read the Scriptures, he knew what they meant but did not understand them. To understand "Jesus died for your sins," you must be motivated to act upon it. This motivation requires a combination of gratitude, awe, shame, and love. These emotions rest on beliefs. An atheist cannot be grateful to God for surviving a lightning strike. He cannot feel shame for his sins. The atheist can hold nothing sacred.

Augustine thinks reason plays a role in sorting out reliable authorities from unreliable authorities. He objects to astrology by recounting how a slave woman and a rich woman simultaneously gave birth. The slave child and the rich child had very different futures. If their futures were determined solely by celestial conditions at the time of their births, then their futures would have been the same.

Reason plays a role in distinguishing authentic religious texts from spurious ones. Church fathers relied on intricate deductions to prevent the New Testament from being polluted with apocryphal stories about Jesus. Even inadvertent *omissions* can corrupt Scripture. In 1631 a royally authorized edition of the Bible overlooked just one word. The omission rendered the seventh commandment as "Thou shalt commit adultery." When the bishop of London reported the mistake to the king, the errant Bibles were rounded up and the printers were fined 3,000 pounds.

Even if the sacred text is uncorrupted, Augustine concedes, reason is needed for its interpretation. Augustine regards "Jesus is a rock" as a metaphor and "Jesus is light" as the literal truth.

Augustine's concession that reason is needed for sorting out authorities is poignant. Augustine's Latin Bible fumbles the verse that serves as Augustine's springboard for discussing the relationship between reason and faith (Kretzmann 1990). The modern Revised Standard Version renders Isaiah 7.9 less paradoxically: "If you will not believe, surely you shall not be established."

Despite a few paragraphs in which Augustine disparages reason, he regularly engages in long chains of inferences. He meets his reservations about reason by wrapping each deduction in a prayer. Sometimes he prays to avoid fallacies. Sometimes he prays for positive guidance.

Can praying improve your reasoning? I once questioned a student about his suspicious behavior during a logic examination. He confessed that he was praying for the correct answer. I felt this was cheating. Even if God did not give him the answer, the student was soliciting the answer from Someone Else.

If you think there is a knowledgeable deity that is responsive to your pleas, then it is perfectly logical to ask for help. From earliest antiquity, the ancient Greeks believed prayer improves memory. Like the bards who prayed that they might remember the poems they were about to recite, Socrates prayed to recall a complicated sophistical argument from the previous day. He prayed for success in discovering the nature of justice and for general aid in an argument. Plato has the Athenian precede his proof of the existence of the gods with a prayer for their help in making their own existence evident to reason:

> To the work, then, and if we are ever to beseech a god's help, let it be done now. Let us take it as understood that the gods have, of course, been invoked in all earnest to

> assist our proof of their own being, and plunge into the waters of the argument before us with the prayer as a sure guiding rope for our support.
>
> (*Laws*, 893 b1–4)

Since the prayer presupposes that the gods exist, the point is only to supplement faith with reason. But even someone who was uncertain whether the gods exist might be inclined to pray; he might reason that a call for assistance could not hurt and it might help!

Augustine begins his *Confessions* with a prayer. The prayer concerns an epistemological paradox about prayer. How can one know God through prayer? To address God rather than someone else, Augustine needs to know something about God. But if God can only be known through prayer, then Augustine would have no way of making first contact. In a culture swamped with false gods, how does a pious man commune with the true instructor?

Protestantism correlates with less worry about misaddressed supplications. When the antiwar agitator Bertrand Russell reported to Brixton prison to serve his sentence in 1918, the warder at the gate took his particulars. When asked "Religion?" Russell replied "Agnostic." The warder heaved a weary sigh, entered the answer into his log, and took solace in the fact that "Although there are many religions, they all worship the same god." Prisoner 2917 said this kept him happy in his cell for a week.

Catholic intellectuals deny that idol worshippers, heathens, and Buddhists worship the same God. One's beliefs about God need to be roughly on target to count as praying to God. Although Augustine does not develop his epistemological paradox about prayer, contemporary Catholics are careful to grant reason independent access to the Almighty.

Following Augustine's example, medieval philosophers commonly inject paradoxes into prayers. Saint Anselm (1033-1109) has an almost irreverently wide range of them. Devout philosophers used paradoxes as foci in their meditations just as philosophy teachers use paradoxes to stimulate class discussion. Augustine's feeling of being dizzy with sin makes it natural for him to punctuate speculative ascents with the pure oxygen of prayer. With divine inspiration, Augustine's fallen faculties can be resuscitated to meet superhuman tests of faith.

For the next thousand years, Christian philosophers prayed on the job. They prayed even to learn what can be known without praying: John Duns Scotus (ca. 1266-1308) begins "A Treatise on God as First Principle" with "Help me then, O Lord, as I investigate how much our natural reason can learn about that true being which you are . . . "

## AUGUSTINE'S *COGITO*

Augustine believed that reason alone is enough to secure some knowledge against the skeptic. With an originality that is commonly overlooked, Augustine credits us with knowledge of appearances. Even if an apple is not yellow, the sufferer of jaundice knows that it *looks* yellow to him. Unlike Sextus Empiricus, Augustine treats statements about appearances as assertions that are true or false. Sextus assumes that a speaker always tries to fit an appearance to an external reality. When Sextus uttered sentences of the form "It appears to me that *p*," he took himself to be merely expressing a feeling. "Ouch!" can be uttered sincerely or insincerely, but it is neither true nor false. Augustine innovates by construing appearance statements as reports of an interior reality.

Augustine also believes that we can know tautologies such as "If Cicero executed the Catliniarian conspirators, then Cicero executed the Catliniarian conspirators." Sextus never bothers to attack tautologies because he does not consider them to be assertions. They do not try to match appearance to reality. When people talk about the weather, they do not predict "Either it will rain or not." Tautologies are empty remarks akin to the schema "Either_____or not____." If you cannot get it wrong, you cannot get it right!

But Augustine is right. People do mistakenly reject tautologies and mistakenly accept contradictions. In a *reductio ad absurdum*, you demonstrate that the supposition implies a contradiction and, on that basis, you *assert* the negation of the supposition. Sextus often seems to assume that he can block proofs merely by refusing to grant premises. But many philosophical arguments do not employ premises; they just use inference rules. Indeed, Sextus's own internal criticisms are indirect arguments of this sort. When he uses conditional proof, he concludes by asserting a conditional proposition even though he never asserted a *premise*.

Augustine's third class of certainties (in addition to reports of appearances and tautologies) involve pragmatic paradoxes. If Augustine were to say "I am dead," then his assertion would be a pragmatic contradiction. But it cannot be a semantic contradiction because when I say "Augustine is dead," I utter a truth.

The opposite of a pragmatic contradiction is a pragmatic tautology. My utterance of "I am awake" is vindicated by my very act of asserting it. Augustine believed that pragmatic tautologies could be turned into a reply to the skeptic. Academic Skeptics argued that every judgment about what exists is fallible because it is always the case that one might be merely dreaming that the thing exists. In the *City of God* Augustine is heartened by an exception:

> I am not at all afraid of the arguments of the Academicians, who say, What if you are deceived? For if I am deceived I am. For he who is not, cannot be deceived; and if I am deceived, by this same token I am. And since I am if I am deceived, how am I deceived in believing that I am? For it is certain that I am if I am deceived. Since, therefore, I, the person deceived, should be, even if I were deceived, certainly I am not deceived in this knowledge that I am. And, consequently, neither am I deceived in knowing that I know. For, as I know that I am, so I know this also, that I know.
>
> (1872, xi, 26)

This is an anticipation of Rene Descartes's *cogito ergo sum* ("I think, therefore, I exist"). When this passage was pointed out to Descartes, he replied in a letter of November 14, 1640, to Colvius, that Augustine fails to use the argument to show that "this *I* which thinks is *an immaterial substance* with no bodily element." However, in *The Trinity* (10.10.16), Augustine does seem to gravitate toward this conclusion from the premise that he can doubt that he has a body but not that he has a mind.

Descartes claimed that he had never heard of Augustine's *cogito*. Descartes's Catholic education at La Flèche makes this unlikely. Augustine's writings were popular among Descartes's Jesuit instructors. Augustine presents his *cogito* seven times in such intensively studied works such as *The Trinity* and *City of God*.

Augustine's loosely strung anticipations of Descartes's *Meditations* do not constitute an attempt to systematically found a philosophy inside out à *la* Descartes. Descartes is far and away the more precise and organized thinker. Yet Augustine clearly had more than a lucky premonition of the Cartesian mind-set.

Sextus Empiricus was aware of an argument that you cannot deny the existence of your soul because you must have a soul to make the denial. Sextus underestimated the significance of the argument because he lacked Augustine's preoccupation with the distinction between the interior realm of the mind and the outer material world.

Augustine is unprecedently introspective—even for a Christian anticipating the apocalypse. Augustine is the first to propound the argument from analogy to other minds. (*The Trinity* 8.6.9) By introspection, he can see that his actions are correlated with feelings and thoughts. Since others engage in the same types of actions, Augustine infers that there are similar feelings and thoughts underlying their actions.

The argument from analogy supports the method of empathy. A historian understands the decisions of Alexander the Great by hypothetically adopting Alexander's beliefs and desires. The historian tries to survey the battlefield through the eyes of Alexander and then replicate his thinking.

Mental simulation is effective only to the degree that the parties truly resemble each other. After Alexander conquered Egypt, the Persian king offered Alexander fabulous terms for peace. Alexander sought advice from his general Parmenion, who answered, "If I were Alexander, I would accept these offers." "So would I," retorted Alexander, "if I were Parmenion."

Augustine displays no anxiety about the inference to other minds being based on a single case (one's own). If I discover a flea in my hat, I gain evidence that someone else has a flea in his hat. But this sample is too small to support the hypothesis that everybody with a hat has a flea in it. Augustine knows that, in his own case, his moans are caused by pains. But what entitles him to infer that the same holds for all other human beings? Augustine needs a larger sample. Alas, he can only introspect his own mind.

From a logical point of view, solipsism ("Only I exist") is a straightforward alternative. But the hypothesis that only you have a mind is nearly unthinkable for normal people. Solipsism is such an unneighborly thought that no one took it seriously until John Stuart Mill (1806-1873) started to codify practices of inductive reasoning. Mill was an extreme empiricist, a phenomenalist, who struggled to explain how we know that other people have experiences. Mill maintained that the self is just a bundle of actual and possible experiences. Thomas Reid (1710-1796) had earlier objected that if the self is not a substance, then no one would be able to tell whether other bodies have experiences. Mill's reply was that phenomenalism did not introduce any extra difficulty in ascertaining whether there are other minds. He suggests that people reason by analogy to the existence of minds other than their own. Mill concedes that if the evidence was simply a correlation that holds for one's own case, "the inference would be but an hypothesis; reaching only to the inferior degree of inductive evidence called Analogy. The evidence, however, does not stop here." (Mill 1979, 205) Mill goes on to maintain that the real proof of other minds springs from our knowledge that mental events and bodily events are connected by laws. Isaac Newton does not need to drop a great variety of objects to prove that each object is attracted to every other object. People do not need direct access to other people's experiences to grasp the laws binding experience and behavior. The problem of other minds became more alarming as philosophers became increasingly persuaded by the negative remarks of both Reid and Mill and less persuaded by their positive remarks: Yes, phenomenalism did not give one basis to believe that there are other minds. Yes, this is not a problem peculiar to phenomenalism. But no, phenomenalism lacks the resources to justify the inference. Common sense is equally impotent. Gosh, belief in other minds seems like a leap of faith! It is a dogma no sane person can forbear—but it is dogma all the same.

"Do I know that others have minds?" is an example of a paradox that was posed and carefully answered for fifteen hundred years prior to being revealed as a paradox. Only in the nineteenth century did philosophers discover surprisingly good arguments for a negative answer.

## AUGUSTINE'S SUBJECTIVE THEORY OF TIME

Augustine deployed Christian dogmas to drown the skeptical paradoxes. However, Christianity itself generates paradoxes—at least for Christians. (The phenomenon is general; introducing almost any apparatus to resolve paradoxes makes that tool the subject of other paradoxes.)

To oppose the Manichees, Augustine had to portray God as all-powerful. This generates the problem of evil. If God knows that there is evil and is able to stop it, then how could he be all-good if he refrains?

Augustine offers two inharmonious answers. His Neoplatonic answer is that, strictly speaking, evil does not exist. What is real is good. What we call evil (blindness, poverty, hopelessness) is the *absence* of certain things. There are degrees of reality; evil is a tear in being.

Augustine's more classically Christian solution is that human beings are responsible for evil because of their own freewill. God cedes people control that they frequently abuse. This freedom does not mean that God is surprised by our misbehavior. Since God is all-knowing, there was never a time at which he failed to know that Eve would tempt Adam to eat an apple from the forbidden Tree of Knowledge. There was never a time when God did not know the whole course of human depravity. So why did God make creatures he knew would disappoint him?

Shipwrights made boats they knew to be vulnerable to fire. Timber has this engineering limit. Could God be resigned to limits imposed by raw matter itself?

Not according to Augustine. Deferring to Genesis, he denies that God made anything from material that predated his activities as creator. God created the whole world from nothing. In *The Timaeus*, Plato allowed that the demiurge began the universe in the sense of organizing a preexisting state of chaos. But everyone in antiquity agreed that the universe could not have had a beginning.

The Manichees teased Christians by asking what God was doing before he created the universe. If God waited, then he was an idler. And an arbitrary idler at that; there would be no justification for starting the creation at one point of time rather than another.

Augustine answers that God created time when he created everything else. By this, he does not mean that time depends on the existence of periodic public phenomena such as the movement of planets. We can make sense of there being no *physical* events occurring. For instance, we can perceive a long silence. What is inconceivable is for time to pass in the absence of *mental* change.

Augustine warns that if we think of time as a mind-independent phenomenon, we fall into a paradox of measurement. The objective present is a boundary between the past and the future. If that boundary has duration, we can divide the present's earlier stage into the past and its later stage into the future. But what *was* the case cannot be what is *now* the case. And what *will* be the case cannot *now* be the case. Thus, the objective present must be a durationless instant. Since the past no longer exists and the future is yet to exist, things are available only for an instant—according to the objective mode. But wait! To measure the length of a spoken sentence, one must hear the beginning of the sentence and its end. All utterances take longer than an instant. Therefore, it is impossible to measure the length of an utterance—or of anything else!

Augustine dismisses this result as absurd. He traces our false step to the attempt to model measurement in terms of the objective present. Measurement requires a *subjective* present—what early-twentieth-century psychologists called "the specious present." Some measured its duration as six seconds, others measured it as twelve seconds. When a doorbell goes ding-dong you hear the ding and the dong as a single pattern. Similarly, short melodies and sentences can be taken in as a single chunk. When the sounds become too long, you must rely on memory rather than perception. According to the subjective account of time pioneered by Augustine, the past corresponds to what we remember, the present to what we perceive, and the future to what we anticipate. We can measure intervals in the specious present because it does have a duration.

Since observers vary in their span of perception, the meaning of "present" is relative to an observer. Since the human perceptual span is less than a minute, the present is less than a minute. Much is in the past. Much is in the future.

God has an unlimited perceptual span. Everything is in the present for him. He grasps the entire history of the universe in one panoramic glimpse. If we relativize "past" to God, there is no past. Hence, God cannot literally have waited to create the world. If we relativize "future" to God, then there is no future. Hence, God cannot literally have *fore-*knowledge of Adam and Eve's wicked decisions. God is omniscient in virtue of what he perceives, not in virtue of what he predicts.

We naturally tend to relativize our temporal vocabulary to a human perspective. This is fine for understanding ordinary affairs. But if we hope to solve theological paradoxes, we must scale up to the mind-boggling terrain of eternity. Augustine agrees this stretch may be too far for a human being to achieve on his own. But if you put your hand out, the Lord might take hold and guide you to a vision of eternity.

THIRTEEN

# Aquinas: Can God Have a Biography?

In *God: A Biography*, Jack Miles, a former Jesuit, cautiously situates his subject in literature: "I write here about the life of the Lord God as—and only as—the protagonist of a classic of world literature; namely, the Hebrew Bible or Old Testament. I do not write about (though I certainly do not write against) the Lord God as the object of religious belief." (1995, 10) Miles does not want to offend or to be perceived as a blasphemer. He resolves to discuss the character God rather than God.

Whereas Augustine worried that he would fail to refer to God, Miles worries that he will refer to God. Augustine tries to secure reference with theology. Miles tries to avoid reference with literary theory.

## IMMUTABILITY

The Old Testament seems to provide Miles with ample material for an action-packed biography. But if God is immutable, as maintained by Augustine and the medieval tradition which culminated with Thomas Aquinas, then God's life is not composed of a succession of events. Everything is in the present for God—an instantaneous whole. As Boethius (480–524) wrote in his prison cell:

> Eternity, then, is the total and perfect possession of life without end, a state which becomes clearer if compared with the world of time, for whatever lives in time lives in the here and now, and advances from past to future. Nothing situated in time can at the one moment grasp the entire duration of its life. It does not as yet apprehend the morrow, and it has already relinquished its yesterday; and even in your life of today, you humans live for no more than that fleeting and transient moment. So anything subject to a status within time, even if it has no beginning and never ceases to exist, and even if its life extends without limit in time, as Aristotle argued is the case with the world, is not yet right accounted eternal; for it does not grasp and embrace at the one moment the whole extent of its life, even if that life is without end. It does not yet possess the future, and it no longer owns time past.
>
> (2000, 110–11)

An immutable subject makes for a boring life story. Miles points out that the bulk of the Bible presents God as acting in time: creating, destroying, cursing, and rejoicing. He dismisses the doctrine of immutability as an artificial import from Aristotle.

However, Aristotle's metaphysics only became available to the medieval schoolmen in the second half of the twelfth century. Augustine's doctrine of an eternal God had already been entrenched for eight hundred years. Although Augustine was influenced by Plato through Plotinus, Augustine's account of God's relationship with time is a Christian innovation.

Aquinas (ca. 1225–1274) was responsible for integrating Aristotle's philosophy into Christianity. He mainly used Aristotle's distinctions and principles to consolidate extant Catholic dogmas. Aquinas was a moderate. He looked for the truth that lies between extreme opinions. He was not interested in importing Greek novelties. Aquinas's aim was to achieve an overall synthesis that would stand up to learned challenges from the Moslems, Jews, and heretics. He faces paradoxes with equanimity: "Since faith rests on infallible truth, and since the contrary of a truth can never be demonstrated, it is clear that the arguments brought against faith cannot be demonstrations, but are difficulties which can be answered." (1929, Ia.I.8) Aquinas's conservativeness outraged Bertrand Russell:

> There is little of the true philosophic spirit in Aquinas. He does not, like the Platonic Socrates, set out to follow wherever the argument may lead. He is not engaged in an inquiry, the result of which it is impossible to know in advance. Before he begins to philosophize, he already knows the truth; it is declared in the Catholic faith. If he can find apparently rational arguments for some parts of the faith, so much the better; if he cannot, he need only fall back on revelation. The finding of arguments for a conclusion given in advance is not philosophy, but special pleading. I cannot, therefore, feel that he deserves to be put on a level with the best philosophers either of Greece or of modern times.
>
> (1945, 463)

Regardless of how Aquinas should be ranked, he had astounding success with his theoretical unification. After a period of resistance, Aquinas's teachings became orthodoxy. He is the only individual mentioned in the 1917 Code of Canon Law. Echoing the Second Vatican Council, the 1983 Code says priests in training should take Aquinas "in particular as their teacher."

Aquinas acknowledges that the doctrine of immutability requires that one treat biblical descriptions of God as metaphorical. Augustine had already discussed passages in which God appears to change his mind: "Then the word of the Lord came to Samuel: 'I repent of having made Saul king.'" (1 Sam. 15.10–11) Augustine handled such passages by making a distinction between God changing his will and God willing a change. A father who schedules different children to sit at his right during the week's dinners is not changing his mind each day. Similarly, God's will that Saul take a turn as king does not mean he has changed his mind when Saul's time was up.

According to Aquinas, the will of an immutable being changes from now to then only in the way that an obelisk changes from being thick at the base to being thin at the tip. God is impassible; nothing can cause God to do anything. This is guaranteed by God being fully realized; whichever property he can possibly have, he actually has.

Although God cannot have most emotions, he does have knowledge. God's omniscience reinforces the point that God makes no decisions; he already knows what will happen.

### IS GOD ALIVE?

If life requires change and God is immutable, then God cannot be alive. He could be a force, like gravity. But gravity is not a fit subject for a biography.

Thomas Aquinas boldly argues that God is supremely alive. Organisms are alive by virtue of a principle of movement lying in themselves. They are "automobiles." Since God is the cause of everything, he has life in the highest degree.

One may suspect that Aquinas is committing the genetic fallacy of inferring that the origin has the same properties as the outcome. Astronomers and biologists agree that the sun is the origin and sustainer of all life on the earth. The sun controls the movements of the earth and all the other planets of the solar system. But none of this confers any degree of life upon the sun.

Aquinas pictures God as a knowing maker of the *whole* universe. Aquinas's proofs of God's existence treat the universe as a big object. He asks simple questions: Where did it come from? What keeps the universe going? According to Aquinas, God wittingly organizes his creation and attracts everything toward himself.

Aquinas's thesis that God is supremely alive also grates against his sympathy with negative theology. This principle only permits negative descriptions of God. "God is wise" only means that God is *not* stupid, *not* foolish, *not* ignorant. We can only apply positive properties to the material things of which we have experience. "Alive" designates a positive property.

The difficulty of saying God is alive is not restricted to theologians. When Jack Miles says God is alive, he wishes to be construed as saying "According to the Old Testament, God is alive." That is why Miles feels free to ignore history when writing *God: A Biography*. Miles's book is a fictionalized biography. If the Old Testament turns out to be accurate, then this make-believe chronicle of the life of God would be a helpful guide to God's actual life. Would it be about God? A pretend biography that *coincidentally* matches the life of

Aquinas would not be about Aquinas. Similarity is not enough. But if the Old Testament's accuracy was due to the source it claims for itself, then there would be an appropriate causal connection between Jack Miles's use of "God" and God. Miles would have inadvertently written a real biography of God.

Aquinas thinks that we can know "God is alive" as a literal truth. The hitch is that we cannot comprehend the state of affairs that makes the statement true. Consider a girl who is informed by her father that she has two brothers who are not brothers of each other. Although she is not in doubt about the revelation, she is puzzled as to what "it means." She futilely tries to draw a family tree that could generate this outcome. She accurately interprets the problem as a weakness of her imagination, not a reason to doubt the revelation that she has two brothers who are unrelated to each other.

## TIMELESSNESS AND ETERNITY

In *A History of π*, Peter Beckman chronicles how π was first assumed by mathematicians to be a rational number and then came to be known as an irrational number. But π did not undergo any real change. Each intrinsic property of π is essential to π. Since π cannot have a property at one time and not at another, π is immutable.

Believers in a timeless God think he is much like a number. God possesses all his properties essentially. God cannot change his mind or stop doing anything. As a perfect being, he cannot change for the better or change for the worse. He is absolutely simple and so cannot gain or lose parts. Facts about God can change—but only in virtue of changes in things other than God. For instance, God is no longer honored by animal sacrifices made by the Jews. But this is a change in the Jews rather than a change in God. God can only acquire new properties in the attenuated sense that numbers acquire new properties.

The timelessness of God has grammatical reverberations. The "is" in "$\pi$ is a transcendental number" is tenseless. To criticize a mathematical thesis as "out of date" is a grammatical joke. The "is" of mathematics is never given a tense. Similarly, the debate about the nature of God gets played out at the level of syntax. When Friedrich Nietzsche puts "God is dead" in the present tense, he is taking a swipe at *ahistorical* theology.

Perhaps Beckman will next write *The Geography of* $\pi$. After all, the wheels and buildings that are designed with $\pi$ occupy space. Once again, remarks about the location of $\pi$ must be interpreted as indirect comments about the material things that have been affected by $\pi$. If God is like a number, then "Where is God?" is a defective question. Augustine's *City of God* could not be about God's residence.

But Aquinas thinks "Where is God?" has an answer; namely, "Everywhere." Since God is in all locations, God cannot travel. Instead of thinking of God as timeless, Aquinas pictures God as in a big Now unflanked by a past or future. God cannot move through time as we can. In some circumstances, Aquinas uses this static quality of divine time to solve problems in much the same way as believers in a timeless God. For instance, when trying to show that foreknowledge is compatible with freewill, Aquinas will talk as if dynamic time does not apply to God.

Yet when Aquinas approaches other issues, such as potentiality, he assumes God's knowledge and power gets altered by the passage of time. Time narrows the field of possibilities.

God can help a woman retain her virginity but cannot restore her virginity. Thus, God's power is conditioned by time.

Thomists work hard to find consistent interpretations of Aquinas's remarks. But I suspect that he is caught by an underlying schizophrenia in the language of time. This double nature has been exposed bit by bit since the middle ages. It was first fully exhibited by a British philosopher writing seven hundred years after Aquinas.

## FLOWING TIME VERSUS STATIC TIME

Generally, children abandon philosophical questions after failing to make any progress in answering them. There are a few exceptions. Like Aquinas, John McTaggart (1866-1925) was a precociously abstruse boy, shambling about in a cloud of ruminations about the Almighty. Unlike Aquinas, McTaggart became a boy atheist. This caused consternation until McTaggart's schoolmates decided he was deranged.

Surprisingly, McTaggart combined his atheism with a belief in immortality. This conviction was based on mystical experiences. McTaggart devoted his philosophical career to devising arguments that would yield the conclusions he took to have been independently revealed to him.

In 1908, he published "The Unreality of Time." McTaggart points out that our words for time divide into two series. What he calls the A series is comprised of *past*, *present*, and *future*. McTaggart's B series is comprised of *earlier*, *simultaneous*, *later*. He notes that the A series suggests a flow of time whereas the B series is static. What is in the future becomes present and then becomes past. The A series guides our emotions. After giving birth, a new mother exclaims "Thank goodness that is over!" She is pleased that her labor is in the past, not that her labor precedes a particular date. The A series also guides our actions. Knowing that the baby is scheduled to be fed at noon leads to action only when coupled with the belief that it is *now* noon.

McTaggart believes that the A series (*past*, *present*, *future*) is more fundamental than the B series (*earlier*, *simultaneous*, *later*). He defines "$x$ is earlier than $y$" as "Either $x$ is past when $y$ is present, or $x$ is present when $y$ is future." He then argues that the A series (and therefore the B series) is subjective. McTaggart agrees with Augustine that the paradox of measurement refutes the objectivity of time. But he thinks Augustine's equation of *past-present-future* with the psychological series *memory-perception-anticipation* makes time *viciously* subjective. Time cannot vary from mind to mind. If your perceptual span increases from childhood, there is no corresponding change in the duration of the present. If there is time, there must be a single perspective from which all temporal statements can be harmonized. Since there is no such perspective, time is an illusion.

McTaggart offers a battery of intriguing arguments for the unreality of time. What binds them together is their exploitation of tensions between the A series and B series. Metaphysicians credit McTaggart for specifying the conceptual origin of a whole family of temporal paradoxes. In retrospect many earlier metaphysicians can be seen as responding to the disharmonies between the A and B series.

Aquinas generally writes in a way that makes the B series more fundamental than the A series. Most twentieth-century thinkers share Aquinas's preference for the B series. They define the A series in terms of the B series—with the help of the demonstrative term "this." Under one scheme "now" means simultaneous with this utterance, "past" means earlier than this utterance, and "future" means later than this utterance. Given facts about the speed of light and sound, it is natural for human beings to organize time in a past-present-future series. Think of how navigational concerns led us to develop the longitude-latitude system. This imaginary grid organizes complicated geographical facts. The relationships between the equator and the prime meridian can be studied in a precise mathematical way, just like the "logic of time" implicit in the A series. But the system is a useful fiction rather than an x-ray of reality.

The Pythagoreans took amenability to mathematical analysis to be the mark of truth. McTaggart takes the precision of calendars and stop watches to be a sign of a fabricated order. The order we "discover" is the order of a notational scheme that we project onto the world.

This conventionalism already had deep roots in Aquinas's era. The medieval nominalists rejected Plato's realm of universals and analyzed words as having no more behind them than custom. They believed we frequently misconstrue the hand of man as the hand of God. As we shall see in the next chapter, accusations of this kind of mistake easily escalate into charges of blasphemy and heresy.

FOURTEEN

# Ockham and the Insolubilia

Socrates thought that paradoxes are best approached through free inquiry. This is not an option if you adhere to a sacred text. These creeds channel inquiry. As a rule, the effect is stifling. This chapter reviews an exception to the rule.

## THE DOCTRINAL STORM OF 1277

Nine years before William of Ockham (ca. 1285–1349) was born, a logician was elected pope. Peter of Spain, who became Pope John XXI, is the author of three logical treatises. A few scholars are not sure the *logician* Peter was the pope. But then it would be a miracle that Peter's *Summulae Logicales* became the most popular logic text with 166 editions printed over the next three hundred years.

Peter of Spain drew a highly influential distinction between two ways of parsing sentences that use the word "infinite." Under the mild interpretation, "The number of dead men is infinite" means that for every natural number *n*, there is a stage of history at which the number of dead men is greater than *n*. Under the more problematic reading, "The number of dead men is infinite" means that there is a stage of history such that for every natural number *n*, the number of dead men is greater than *n*. Peter suggests that the paradoxes of infinity can be conjugated away by choosing the milder reading. Peter's proposal is a linguistic replacement of Aristotle's metaphysical distinction between potential and actual infinity. By keeping the distinction at the level of grammar, Peter avoids Aristotle's problem of explaining why the potentially infinite cannot become actual.

Like twentieth-century linguistic philosophers, Peter preferred to cast issues in terms of words rather than things. He was especially suspicious of pagan cosmology. Peter preferred Augustine over Aristotle. To continue his research, the pope had a private chamber added to the papal palace at Viterbo. But while he was using his new room, the ceiling collapsed. The pope died of his injuries less than a week later.

Five months before the ceiling fell in, Pope John XXI commissioned the bishop of Paris, Etienne Tempier, to investigate whether the radical Aristotelians at the University of Paris were heretics. In addition to the Thomists, there were characters such as Siger of Brabant. Whereas Aquinas thought that the Christians had argued the Greeks to a draw (at least) on all key issues, Siger thought that the Islamic commentators on Aristotle had shown that reason favors a universe with an infinite past. Siger therefore maintained that faith must sometimes run *contrary* to reason (not merely *beyond* reason). After Bishop Tempier issued his unexpectedly detailed condemnation of 219 propositions of "Latin Averroism," Siger had to flee Paris. He was rumored to have been murdered. Aristotelians worried that Rome would sin twice against philosophy.

The bishop of Paris had exceeded his commission but Pope John XXI went along with the downgrading of Aristotle. Negatively, the condemnation of 1277 created a tradition of Aristotle-bashing that continued long after the Aristotelians reasserted themselves. In 1536, the French logician Peter Ramus presented a master of arts thesis reputedly entitled "Whatever Aristotle Has Said Is False." Peter Ramus continued to peck away at Aristotle for thirty years. When this French logician was murdered on the third day of the Massacre of St. Bartholomew, there was a report that the assassins had been hired by an academic opponent.

The condemnation of 1277 strongly reaffirms the all-powerful nature of God: anything that is logically possible can be done by God. Aristotle's natural necessities do not circumscribe the divine sphere of action. Aristotle says nature abhors a vacuum, but since God can create empty space, Christian physicists were obliged to take vacuums seriously.

The Christian elite viewed purges much as a forest ranger views controlled burns. Yes, there is the immediate horror of destruction. But clearing the old, dead wood makes way for fresh, safer growth. The condemnation of 1277 relieved many Christian scholars from the stifling obligation to respond to Aristotle. There was a wave of fresh thought experiments in physics: What would happen if a feather and a stone were dropped in a glass cylinder free of air? Would they reach the bottom simultaneously? Could one see into the vacuum or does one need a medium to see? How would heavenly bodies look if the speed of light were infinite?

At the same time, logic entered a golden age. As an unexpected bonus, a scientific revolution was conceived—only to be tragically aborted by the Black Death.

Researchers on motion and perception were free to question the common sense that Aristotle so ably fortified. Instead of having to take on this intellectual giant with infant theories, the post-1277 scholar was entitled to ignore him.

These liberated theorists could also ignore most theology. In times of intellectual persecution, prudent thinkers seek safety in specialization. They become newly appreciative of the intrinsic interest of their esoteric subject matter. They claim that their research is irrelevant to the controversies of religion and politics. For extra protection, these professionalized Christians claimed their research was irrelevant to neighboring fields of research. Like-minded researchers clustered together, achieving critical mass within and uncritical mass without. Each group operated with the understanding that they would not interfere with those outside their specialty. Good fences make good neighbors.

Purges also create academic vacancies. Inoffensive specialists can hope to swiftly climb institutional ladders that were recently thick with senior faculty. Technically oriented logicians were in an especially good position to move up. Since logic is only concerned with what follows from what, it is topic neutral. By being about no doctrine in particular, logic is heresy-proof (at least with respect to consistent dogma). Yet this topic neutrality also makes it applicable to all arguments whatsoever.

## WHAT OCKHAM RAZED

The condemnation of 1277 served as a garden trellis for Ockham's reasoning. He had *faith* in the absolute power of God. He adopted Augustine's interior perspective. Ockham emphasizes that what matters morally is the intention behind the act, not the act or its consequences. A man who attempts adultery and fails is just as guilty as a man caught in the act. A man who throws himself off a cliff in suicidal despair is forgiven if he manages to repent halfway down.

Each agent has intuitive knowledge that his will is free. No proof of freewill is possible. Indeed, very little is provable. Ockham felt that reverence for Greek philosophy led Aristotelian Christians to overintellectualize Christianity. Little of positive theology can withstand careful logical scrutiny. Since theology is not the queen of the sciences, it should step aside and let other areas of study develop on their own.

Part of wisdom is recognizing one's limits. In the case of paradoxes, this means a willingness to concede that one is unable to reconcile some apparent inconsistencies. For instance, in his *Commentary on the Sentences,* William of Ockham declared, "It is impossible for any [created] intellect, in this life, to explain or evidently know how God knows all future contingent events." (d. 38, *q.*1) Yet he denies that this irresolvable appearance of inconsistency compels him to weaken his belief in God's foreknowledge or to hedge his belief in human freedom. Ockham is not merely asking for patience. He thinks we will *never* figure out the solution because we *cannot* figure it out.

This impotence is embarrassing. To avoid the *appearance* of irrationality, most theologians fell into the reality of irrationality by worshiping in houses of cards. Their systems are rationalizations for propositions that must stand on faith. The light of logic exposes cracks in the foundations and reveals how much of Christianity rests on the grace of God.

Intellectual pride prejudices theologians into accepting flawed formulations of the problems they "solve." For instance, Ockham thought Aquinas merely exploited formulations of the problem of foreknowledge that make time important. The real challenge lies in the fact that God's absolute power is determining our actions to the same degree that it determines any other event.

God's omnipotence is not entirely bad news on the problem-solving front. Ockham thinks God's absolute power explains why God is not to blame for the evil in the world (since God knowingly and voluntarily created the world). Ockham accepts the divine command theory of ethics: An action owes its rightness solely to the fact that God approves of it. An act owes its wrongness solely to the fact that God disapproves of it. Since God does exactly what he wills, he cannot do anything blameworthy. If God made a world worse than the actual world, that gratuitous inferiority could not be the basis for reproaching him.

Although the divine command theory is so popular with laymen that it tends to be presupposed rather than asserted, theologians are impressed with an objection Socrates musters in the *Euthyphro*. Is an act pious because it pleases the gods or are the gods pleased because it is pious? If the gods approved of cruelty would that make cruelty right? The divine command theorist cannot answer by saying that God would never approve of cruelty because cruelty is wrong. For under their theory, God's approval of something *makes* it right.

Instead of rushing to answer the *Euthyphro* dilemma, Ockham calmly pushes the dilemma to a logical extreme.

Suppose God commands a man to disobey him. The man is obliged to disobey God (because anything commanded by God is obligatory). Yet the man is also obliged not to disobey God. "The man disobeys God" is a consistent proposition. If God is free to will any consistent state of affairs, then he is free to will that.

## OCKHAM'S POLITICS

Ockham rode the condemnation of 1277 into a protoscientific dawn. By restraining theology, he encouraged a rigorous, piecemeal approach to theoretical issues. Little improvements could accumulate without external meddling. He was making the academic world safer and more productive.

Ironically, the autonomy he promoted for puzzle specialists came at the price of high-level disruption of his own career. Ockham's influential attacks on the theological establishment alarmed John Lutterell, the chancellor of Oxford University. He prevented Ockham from obtaining a masters of arts degree at Oxford, thereby denying him a license to teach. Lutterell also denounced Ockham to church authorities. With no more official status than an undergraduate philosophy major, Ockham was summoned to papal court in Avignon to meet charges of being a heretic. During the four-year process, the general of the Franciscan order (to which Ockham belonged) maintained Pope John XXII was mistakenly opposed to the doctrine of apostolic poverty. This is the issue Umberto Eco dramatizes in the "Fifth Day" chapter of *The Name of the Rose.* Eco's monks raucously debate the vexed issue whether Jesus owned the clothes he wore. If the clergy should imitate Christ and Jesus failed to own even his loin cloth, they should own nothing as individuals. If the religious *groups* should imitate Christ, then even collective ownership is forbidden. Ockham was asked to investigate the history and doctrinal aspects of apostolic poverty.

Ockham concluded that the pope was a heretic. In 1327 it became evident that Pope John XXII was going to enforce his rejection of apostolic poverty. Ockham and his companions fled from Avignon and sought the protection of Emperor Louis of Bavaria. They were immediately excommunicated. For the next twenty years, Ockham devoted himself to writing treatises on issues of papal authority and civil sovereignty. His polemics angered the pope so much that he threatened to burn down the city of Tournai if the citizens did not capture Ockham and turn him over. After the death of his protector Louis, Ockham realized his antipapal crusade was a lost cause and may have attempted a reconciliation. He died in 1347, probably from the Black Death.

## THE INSOLUBLES

The medievals called the liar paradox an "insoluble." Just as sailors do not imply absolute invisibility when they describe sandbars as invisible, Ockham does not imply that the liar paradox is absolutely recalcitrant. Ockham thinks the liar paradox is merely difficult for us to solve.

The insolubles encompass what current philosophers call the "paradoxes of self-reference." Twentieth-century philosophers rediscovered most of them independently, but some have been directly mined from medieval literature. For instance, Stephen Read (1979) blew the dust off of a paradox discussed by Pseudo-Scotus (so named because he was long confused with Duns Scotus). Under the traditional definition, an argument is valid if and only if it is impossible for the premises to be true and the conclusion false. In a commentary on Aristotle's *Prior Analytics*, Pseudo-Scotus presents an apparent counterexample: "God exists, therefore, this argument is invalid." Pseudo-Scotus is presupposing that "God exists" is a necessary truth. Less-devout readers are free to substitute any necessary truth, say, "All equilateral triangles are equiangular." If the argument is valid, then since the premise is true, the conclusion must be true. But then the argument is both valid and invalid. Contradiction. Therefore, the argument is not valid. But wait! If the argument is invalid, then it is possible for the premise to be true and conclusion false. Since the premise is a necessary truth, the argument is invalid only if the conclusion is false. But then the argument is valid! Contradiction again!

Pseudo-Scotus suggests that the counterexample can be avoided by adding an extra requirement for validity: the conclusion must not deny its own validity. Here he is applying Ockham's proposal that the insolubility be stopped by banning self-reference.

Ockham realized that a ban on all self-reference would mean the loss of innocent sentences such as "This sentence is in English." He was willing to accept such casualties as collateral damage. When a gardener poisons aphids, he foresees that he will poison innocent insects along with the pests. There might be more specialized poisons but the gardener does not feel under an obligation to avoid all side-destruction. The medievals are interested in eliminating the glitch but are not expecting the solution to be deeply illuminating. They just want to de-bug their logical systems.

This engineering attitude toward the liar paradox contrasts with the pure theoretical concerns of the ancient Greeks. Diogenes lists Chrysippus as devoting at least six works to the subject. Athenaeus reports that the poet and grammarian Philetas lost much sleep over the liar paradox. He also lost his appetite. Philetas became so thin that friends had to attach lead weights to his feet. They feared the emaciated insomniac would be blown over by the strong winds of Cos (the beautiful Aegean island where Philetus lived). His epitaph: O Stranger: Philetas of Cos am I. 'Twas the Liar who made me die, And the bad nights caused thereby. Most medievals only lost sleep over the liar paradox in the way a bookkeeper loses sleep over ledgers that will not tally. The bookkeeper does not think the inconsistency has dark implications for the foundations of arithmetic.

I have suggested that the technical attitude toward paradox was sharpened by the condemnation of 1277. However, this merely amplified a preexisting tendency of late-medieval thinking. The full story only emerges when we examine the strange saga of the Christian liar paradox.

## THE ORIGIN OF THE INSOLUBLES

Ockham's insights emerged from an educational system (much still intact) that was guilded together after the European economy began to revive around 1100. Prior to this period, schools clustered around ecclesiastical centers. Scholars were not required to take higher orders. But most did, partly out of religious devotion and partly because of practical advantages: clerical status offered scholars independence and protection against the brutality of the locals.

With the decline of the Roman empire, paradoxes that seemed irrelevant to religious issues lapsed into desuetude. They were either forgotten or demoted to the status of intellectual diversions. The liar paradox is a particularly striking example (Spade 1973). One might expect it to be kept steadily before the Christian eye because it is repeated in the Bible: "One of themselves, even a prophet of their own, said, The Cretans are always liars, evil beasts, slow bellies. This witness is true." (Epistles 1: 12–13). But Christians had the same attitude toward the liar paradox as they did toward a mosquito that is preserved in a reliquary; they were curious as to how the pest became ensconced but were not curious about the creature itself. Augustine cites the verse only to raise the issue of why sacred Scripture should quote pagan sources. Many Christian scholars had access to Cicero's remarks about the liar paradox in his *Academica*. It is also explained in Aristotle's *Sophistic Elenchi* (25, 180a27-b7) which appeared in the Latin West around 1130. But this led to no competent commentary.

Is the liar paradox so hard to understand? In the twentieth century, the liar paradox became part of popular culture. In the 1967 *Star Trek* episode "I, Mudd," the android leader Norman short-circuits when he hears the following exchange:

> *Captain Kirk*: Everything Harry tells you is a lie. Remember that—everything Harry tells you is a lie.
> *Harry Mudd*: I am lying.

The scriptwriters could safely presuppose that most of their audience could follow Norman's oscillations: If Mudd is lying, then Mudd is telling the truth—and if Mudd is telling the truth, then he is lying.

One might suggest that the liar is only easy in hindsight. Medieval pictures of construction sites depict wheels and hand barrows but never depict wheelbarrows. The wheelbarrow is an obvious combination once you see it, but it requires insight to discover.

This analogy is marred by the fact that the medievals had access to the specimen liar paradoxes—plus intelligent commentary about them. The real problem was that the medievals were at a false summit. They had enough sophistication to escape sloppy formulations of the liar paradox but not enough sophistication to strengthen the paradox in a way that exposes pseudosolutions.

The first hundred years of commentators on *Sophistic Elenchi* simply accept Aristotle's cursory "solution." Aristotle says the liar paradox commits the fallacy of *secundum quid et simpliciter*: treating a statement that is true in one respect as if it were true absolutely: for instance, "Ethiopians are white with respect to their teeth, therefore, Ethiopians are white." Consider a man who swears he will break his oath to go to Athens. If he breaks his oath to go to Athens, has he sworn truthfully? On the one hand, he has done what he swore he would do (break the oath to go Athens). On the other hand, he has not done what he swore to do (go to Athens). If we forget to relativize "true" and "false" to the distinct oaths indicated in parentheses, then "The perjurer kept his oath" seems both true and false. Similarly, says Aristotle, we will appear to fall into contradiction if we do not relativize for the liar paradox. Aristotle leaves it to the reader to fill in the details.

The medievals do not express dissatisfaction with the sketchiness of Aristotle's answers. For centuries, most scholastics mention the liar paradox only as an example of a fallacious argument. They actually show more interest in Aristotle's case of the perjurer who swears to break his oath. For instance, Giles of Rome became interested in the moral implications of the perjurer. If you swear to break an oath to go to Athens, should you break your oath to go to Athens? Giles concludes that you ought not. Although it is bad to swear to break an oath, it is worse to fulfill the tainted oath.

As time passed, commentators gravitated toward leaner formulations of the liar paradox. In *De fallaciis* Thomas Aquinas writes: "Likewise here, 'The Liar speaks the truth in saying that he speaks falsely. Therefore, he speaks the truth.' It does not follow. For to speak the truth is opposed to what it is to speak falsely, and conversely." Perhaps inadvertently, Aquinas undermines the analogy with the perjurer's statement by putting the liar paradox in the present tense. This frees the liar paradox from an association with the thorny issue of future contingent propositions. Albert the Great tends to formulate the perjurer example in the present tense to preserve the analogy.

Sadly, the analogy with the perjurer's oath became a way of defeating non-Aristotelian solutions to the liar paradox. For instance, those who suggested that the liar statement "says nothing" were ridiculed because the perjurer's oath is obviously meaningful.

The historical puzzle about the liar paradox has three parts. The first subproblem is to explain a thousand years of Christian incomprehension of the liar paradox. The second task is to explain how these "dunces" could go on to rapidly reach a new pinnacle of understanding. The third stage of the historical puzzle is to explain why understanding of the liar paradox then declines again into a four-hundred-year plateau of facile complacency. In the next chapter I will focus on these three tasks.

FIFTEEN

# Buridan's Sophisms

Jean Buridan (1295-1356) practiced what William of Ockham preached. He abstained from theology and concentrated on semantics, optics, and mechanics. In the case of insolubles, his secular focus on details led to an understanding of the "paradoxes of self-reference" that was only matched in the twentieth century.

Buridan's career follows the pattern encouraged by Ockham. He enrolled in the University of Paris, which was then the most prestigious school in Europe. He was later hired as an instructor and rose through the ranks. Buridan did not pursue the usual master of arts degree and so was not licensed to teach theology. He was a "secular cleric," a priest who did not affiliate with an order. Consequently, his work was not promoted in the way Dominicans perpetuate Thomas Aquinas and Franciscans advance Duns Scotus. Buridan's fame and influence came from research and administrative service. Buridan served as university rector in 1328 and again in 1340. In 1345 he was chosen to defend the interests of the University of Paris before Philip of Valois at Rome. To quell strife, the pragmatic

Buridan banned some of Ockham's nominalist writings (which, logically enough, eventually led to some of Buridan's own writings being posthumously banned).

## THE EDUCATIONAL SYSTEM

As a side effect of the medieval educational system, sophisms had become standard classroom tools. A sophism is a sentence that poses an instructive analytical difficulty. Usually the problem is an embarrassment of riches: there is an argument in favor of the sentence's truth *and* an argument against it. Albert of Saxony's eleventh sophism in his *Sophismata* is:

> A. All men are donkeys or men and donkeys are donkeys.

Here is the argument that A is true: A conjunction is an "and" statement and so is true when all of its conjuncts are true. "All men are donkeys or men" is true and "Donkeys are donkeys" is true. Therefore, A is a true conjunction. Here is the argument that A is false: A disjunction is an "or" statement and so false when all of its disjuncts are false. "All men are donkeys" is false and "Men and donkeys are donkeys" is false. Therefore A is a false disjunction. The quandary is that A is both true and false. This completes Albert's *exposition* of the sophism.

Now comes Albert's *solution*. Statement A is ambiguous:

> A1. (All men are donkeys or men) and (donkeys are donkeys).
>
> A2. (All men are donkeys) or (men and donkeys are donkeys).

The sophism prompts students to distinguish between the main connective of a sentence and subordinate connectives. If "and" is the main connective, then A means A1. If "or" is the main connective, A means A2.

In addition to logical sophisms, there are grammatical sophisms. Linguistics began with puzzle sentences such as "Love is a verb." Twentieth-century linguists continued the practice with counterexamples to increasingly sophisticated grammatical generalizations. For instance, one natural theory of how pronouns work is that they borrow the reference of an earlier referring phrase (unless the meaning is supplied from outside the sentence, as when we point). Thus, "Francis touched the beggar and cured him" is solved as "Francis touched the beggar and cured the beggar." In 1967, Emmon Bach and Stanley Peters pointed out that this theory leads to an infinite regress when applied to cross-referential sentences such as "The pilot that shot at it hit the Mig that chased him." In the Mig sentence "it" means "the Mig that chased him" and "him" means "the pilot that shot at it." Substituting one phrase for the pronoun always leaves the other pronoun. Since we are finite beings, we cannot go round and round substituting forever. Do we understand the sentence by leaving some pronoun ungrounded? Or is the Mig sentence meaningless? Buridan would have loved the Bach-Peters paradox.

As sophisms became more challenging, their solutions became controversial. Writers of logic manuals would then review past solutions, present their own, and finally show the advantages of their proposal. The insolubles lie at the extreme end of this continuum of difficulty.

But how did the medievals come by the insolubles? In the previous chapter, I argued that they were unable to recover them from the fossil liars embedded in the Bible, Cicero, Aristotle, and sources now unknown to us. The insolubles were not simply imported to medieval Europe from the Greeks. Nor do the Islamic commentators play a role. The medievals reconstructed the insolubles from a pedagogical practice of their own design—the obligational dispute.

## FORCED ERRORS IN A DEBATING GAME

At the University of Paris, virtually all students were in the Arts Faculty. All of these students were required to spend the first two years studying logic. As is still true, logic is taught by frequent assignments and tests. But since the costs of writing were much greater, far more of the course work was oral. Beginning students were obliged to engage in formal debating games. More advanced students participated in the contentful debates recounted by Peter Abelard and Thomas Aquinas. But I trace the recovery of the insolubles to the introductory-level debates.

The scholastic obligational dispute is a skeletalized descendant of the debating game Aristotle sets out to codify. He states this purpose in the opening of the *Topics*: "Our treatise proposes to find a line of inquiry whereby we shall be able to reason from reputable opinions about any subject presented to us, and also shall ourselves, when putting forward an argument, avoid saying anything contrary to it." The topics indicated by Aristotle are similar to the ones still debated in high school and college debating competitions. Whereas modern debaters are judged principally on rhetorical criteria, the measure for Aristotle's debaters was logical consistency. Since the point of the debate is to check for contradictions, Aristotle shapes the debate to make internal conflicts easier to spot and prove:

> With regard to the giving of answers, we must first define what is the business of a good answerer, and of a good questioner. The business of the questioner is to develop the argument as to make the answerer utter the most implausible of the necessary consequences of his thesis; while that of the answerer is to make it appear that it is not he who is responsible for the impossibility or paradox, but only his thesis; for one may, no doubt, distinguish between the mistake of taking up a wrong thesis to start with, and that of not maintaining it properly, when once taken up.
>
> (*Topics* VIII 4)

Aristotle is picturing a cooperative exchange between knowledgeable, mature individuals. The point of the dispute is to create a specimen for postgame analysis.

Medieval obligational disputes were an adaptation for a rowdy, naive crowd. The format does not presuppose any knowledge. Obligational disputes appeal to the male appetite for mock combat (which is intensified in isolated, male-only institutions such as medieval universities). Yet obligational disputes have a surprisingly pure logical structure. An obligational dispute resembles the children's game king of the hill, in which the defender on the hill wins unless he is dislodged. But here the king's *opponent* chooses the hill. Specifically, the opponent in an obligational disputation posits a proposition. If the proposition is consistent, then the respondent is obliged to *consistently* defend the proposition against the opponent's cross-examination. The respondent has a limited range of answers. In the early history of the game, the only responses are "I grant it" and "I deny it." Ockham describes a later version in which the defensive repertoire is enriched with "I doubt it" and even "I distinguish it." If the opponent extracts contradictory answers from the respondent, then the respondent loses. After all, a pair of conflicting answers is a sure sign that the respondent committed a logical error: a consistent proposition cannot have inconsistent consequences.

Opponents usually saddled the respondent with a patently false posit. This strategy is shrewd. Since the respondent does not believe what he must defend, his background beliefs conflict with the thesis in the foreground. If the respondent fails to censor his real beliefs, a later answer will be inconsistent with earlier answers. This mental leakage explains why prevaricators have trouble sustaining consistency.

The length and pace of the debate needs to be regulated because the players have opposite strategic preferences about how much is said by the respondent. The opponent's chance of detecting a contradiction increases with the number of replies made by the respondent. Thus, the opponent wants to maximize the number of answers while the respondent wants to minimize this exposure.

The opponent has the exciting role. He is motivated to keep the pace fast. He has a far wider range of possible moves than the respondent's meager stock of "I grant it" and "I deny it." When not diverted by compassion, people prefer to identify with those who have the more pleasant perspective.

Since human beings also prefer offense to defense, audiences have a tendency to root for the *opponent* in an obligational dispute. And the rooting was sometimes boisterous. There were university statutes excluding students who demonstrated by "clamoring, hissing, making noise, stone-throwing by themselves or by their servants and accomplices, or in any other way." (Thorndike 1944, 237)

Devious opponents eventually noticed that respondents can be disarmed with pragmatic paradoxes. These posits make false comments about the respondent. If you posit "You do not exist," then I must defend this proposition because it is consistent. If you follow up with "You are a handsome fellow," then what am I to reply? If I say "I grant it," my answer implies that I exist and so I have contradicted my earlier position that I do not exist. If I say "I deny it," my answer also implies that I exist and so I have still contradicted my earlier position that I do not exist. You never gave me a chance!

Instructors tried to rescue respondents by outlawing "You do not exist" as a posit. But clever students deployed variations such as "You are asleep" (which was not always false; courses ran from 4 A.M. to 7 P.M. with hardly a break). Here the problem is that an obvious truth about the *act* of disputing conflicts with the content of what is said in the dispute.

Some instructors reacted by rescinding the opponent's freedom to choose the starting position themselves. However, as Jean Buridan points out, at any stage of a yes-no obligational dispute, the respondent can be trapped with "Your reply will be negative." If a respondent replies yes, he is affirming that he is not affirming. If he replies no, then he is denying that he is denying.

## BURIDAN'S BRIDGE

Buridan repackages "Your reply will be negative" as a stepping stone to a more famous sophism: Suppose Plato is a bridge keeper. Plato is enraged and tells Socrates, "If what you say is true, then I will let you cross the bridge; and if what you say is false, then I will throw you into the water." Socrates replies, "You will throw me into the water." What Socrates said is true if and only if it is false.

Although Buridan is sometimes credited with being the inventor of the bridge paradox (Jacquette 1991), the puzzle probably goes back to Chrysippus. In "The Auction of Philosophers," Lucian (ca. 115–ca. 200) depicts a slave market with Zeus in charge and Hermes as auctioneer. The offerings include Pythagoras, Diogenes, Aristippus, Democritus, Heraclitus, Socrates, Epicurus, Chrysippus, Aristotle, and Pyrrhon. The philosophers are put through their paces. As a fatalist, Chrysippus is resigned to being sold as a slave. He illustrates his value as a logician with an exhibition of paradoxes: the Reaper, the Electra, and the Sorites. Finally, he rescues a customer's child from a hypothetical dilemma:

*Chrysippus*: Now, suppose a crocodile, finding the child roaming about the river's side, should perchance seize it and then promise to restore it to you, provided you state correctly what he has made up his mind to do about giving up the brat—what would you say was his intention in the matter?

*Customer*: Your question is a poser. For I'm at a loss what to say first, so as insure the recovery of the child. But, for Heaven's sake, do you make answer

> and rescue me the little fellow, lest the monster
> be too quick for me, and eat him up.
> (Lucian 1901, 413)

Chrysippus does not answer but the grammarian Aphthonius is on the record recommending that the crocodile be told "You do not intend to restore it."

In the second century A.D., the Roman Pausanias (1971) pioneered the literary genre that we call the travelogue. To convey local history, he recounts legends associated with particular sites and artworks. Pausanias's section on Eleia contains a story about how Anaximenes pleaded with Alexander the Great. The king had just conquered Anaximenes' native city of Lampsacus. Since the citizens had sided with the Persian king, they feared that the enraged Alexander would enslave them and destroy their city. They sent the respected philosopher Anaximenes to petition for mercy. Before Anaximenes could speak, Alexander interrupted and

> swore by the gods of Greece, whom he named, that he would verily do the opposite of what Anaximenes asked. Thereupon Anaximenes said, "Grant me, O king, this favour. Enslave the women and children of the people of Lampsacus, raze the whole city even to the ground, and burn the sanctuaries of their gods." Such were his words; and Alexander, finding no way to counter the trick, and bound by the compulsion of his oath, unwillingly pardoned the people of Lampsacus.
> (1971 6.18.2–4)

Since Anaximenes lived two centuries before Alexander, this anecdote is chronologically impossible. Even so, the tale shows that the topsy-turvy aspect of countersuggestibility was already well known in the second century.

Storytellers continue the Greek tradition of incorporating paradoxes. Miguel de Cervantes used Buridan's bridge in *Don Quixote*. This made the bridge an element of the western literary canon.

Buridan may have adapted the bridge from the story related by Pausanias. Although Pausanias received almost no attention for hundreds of years (his papyrus rolls were impractically bulky for travelers), lovers of antiquities eventually realized that Pausanias's travelogue had aged into an atlas of treasure maps. This kept the ancient legends in circulation.

## THE MEDIEVAL THEORY OF PROPOSITIONS

To salvage the obligational disputes, the logic teachers needed to formulate a *general* rule about how the game should start. One reform was to prohibit personal posits that described the respondent. But students would side-step this rule with impersonal posits such as "No one exists." If reference to any individual was prohibited, Buridan suggested that opponents choose "No proposition is negative." The medievals regarded "No proposition is negative" as a contingent proposition because they took propositions to be actual assertions. This magnified the importance of pragmatic paradoxes.

William of Ockham proposed that the respondent's commitments not include facts about the game itself. This requires a distinction between the content of what is said and what follows from the fact that it was said. If I assert "The

Black Death was caused by fleas," I invite the inference that I believe the Black Death was caused by fleas. This goes some way in explaining why it is difficult to assert "The Black Death was caused by fleas but I do not believe it." The sentence is consistent but I cannot consistently believe it. This limit to consistent belief is interesting because we tend to assume that any consistent proposition can be consistently believed.

## BURIDAN ON THE INSOLUBLES

Buridan's sophisms can be traced to loopholes in obligational disputes. They are dialectical variants of pragmatic paradoxes and the liar paradox.

Buridan's first sophism in his chapter on the insolubles is "Every proposition is affirmative, so none is negative." Is the argument valid? *Pro*: the premise implies the conclusion because it is an instance of the valid argument from "All *F*s are *G*s, therefore, no *F*s are non-*G*s." *Con*: a contingent proposition cannot imply a necessarily false conclusion. "No proposition is negative" is false whenever it is uttered.

Buridan's solution is to insist that a proposition can be possible even if it cannot be a true utterance. It is good enough if the facts could be as the proposition says. For instance, "No sentence on this page is nine words long" expresses a possibility because there could be an absence of nine-word sentences on this page. But the sentence cannot be both true and inscribed on this page because it is itself nine words long. Under this conception of possibility, the argument is valid.

Buridan's second sophism is "No proposition is negative, therefore some proposition is negative." The argument seems invalid because the conclusion contradicts its contingent premise. Yet the argument also seems valid because the conclusion is made true by the premise. The premise is a negative proposition and so the conclusion is confirmed by the premise. However, Buridan thinks this is the wrong kind of support. Given the conception of possibility and validity he promotes in his first sophism, Buridan must reject this second sophism as an invalid argument. For what counts is whether the conjunction of the premises and the negation of the conclusion could be made true by a fact. If such a fact is possible, the argument is invalid. If no propositions were uttered, then the premise of the second sophism would be true and the conclusion false.

Buridan's discussion accumulates insights and constraints that guide the development of subsequent sophisms. As a prelude to the direct liar paradox ("What I am saying is false"), he reviews indirect liar paradoxes. The simplest specimen, sophism nine, consists of Plato saying "What Socrates says is true" and Socrates replying "What Plato says is false." If Plato's statement is true, then it is false. If Plato's statement is false, then Socrates' statement is also false—which means that Plato's statement is true after all.

This looped liar shows that no direct self-reference is needed for the liar paradox. It also shows that the paradoxical nature of an utterance need not be an intrinsic property of the sentence itself. The paradoxical aspect of Plato's "What Socrates says is true" depends on another utterance. If Socrates had instead said "My father was Sophroniscus," then Plato's remark would have been unparadoxical.

Although there is no direct evidence that the Greeks were aware of looped liars, some of their humor shows they understood that the paradoxical nature of a statement can rest on other statements. In his essay "On False Modesty," Plutarch relates an incident involving Menedemus, a student of the Megarian Stilpo, who had a reputation for teasing others with paradoxes: "When he heard that Alexinus often praised him, he said 'And I'm always chiding Alexinus; so Alexinus must be a bad man, since he either praises a bad man, or is chided by a good one.'" Alexinus's otherwise innocent remark has been dragooned into a paradox.

These contingent paradoxes refute subjective definitions of "paradox" that require any paradoxical statement to seem absurd to someone. Plato could have drawn a random statement from an urn, declared it true without reading it, and then cast the unread message into the sea. If that unread statement was "What Plato says is false," then Plato's original remark was paradoxical even if it never seemed absurd to anyone.

Paradoxes are as objective as diseases. My subjective sense of disorder is evidence of a disorder but is not itself a disorder. I can be sick without feeling sick and without the possibility of a physician being able to detect any illness. Just as there are diseases that will never be discovered, there are paradoxes that will be forever unknown.

## THE DECLINE OF SCHOLASTICISM

Many of these paradoxes will never be known because of a real disease: the Black Death. In addition to killing Buridan, Ockham, and a third of Europe, this plague lowered the prestige of the Church and its satellite institutions. Insights into the liar paradox were packaged in an esoteric terminology and format that received blanket condemnation by disaffected survivors. As intellectual life reconstituted, thinkers turned toward accessible writers such as Cicero and Augustine. Contempt for the liar paradox enjoyed a renaissance.

Obviously, the Church was still an important institution. Scholastic philosophy lingered for centuries. However, the intellectual superstructure of Christianity was increasingly marginalized by humanists. The future belonged to skeptics and scoffers such as Erasmus (1466–1536) and Montaigne (1533–1592). These men were fideists who denied that complicated reasoning could improve on simple faith. They lampooned the scholastics' efforts to draw positive morals from philosophical paradoxes. Paradoxes were either dismissed as piffles or deployed negatively to humble the pretensions of reason.

People were more receptive to the "new" paradoxes emerging from empirical discoveries. In 1522, all of Europe was astounded by the circumnavigator's paradox. When Ferdinand Magellan's ship sailed around the world, a whole day apparently was lost. One of the eighteen survivors of the original 270-odd crew relates the incident:

> On Wednesday, the ninth of July, we arrived at one these islands named Santiago, where we immediately sent the boat ashore to obtain provisions. . . . And we charged our men in the boat that, when they were ashore, they should ask what day it was. They were answered that to the Portuguese it was Thursday, at which they were much amazed, for to us it was Wednesday, and we knew not how we had fallen into error. For every day I, being always in health, had written down each day without any intermission. But, as we were told since, there had been no mistake, for we had always made our voyage westward and had

> returned to the same place of departure as the sun, wherefore the long voyage had brought the gain of twenty-four hours, as is clearly seen.
>
> (Pigafetta 1969, I, 147–48)

It turns out that one of Buridan's young colleagues, Nicole Oresme, wrote extensively on this paradox. (Lutz 1975, 70) (Oresme may have picked up the paradox from Syrian geographers.) In "Traitié de l'espére," Oresme describes two imaginary travelers Jehan and Pierre who go around the equator in opposite directions and rendezvous simultaneously at their point of departure. Each covers 30 degrees of longitude per 24-hour day. Jehan, who goes west, reports that his journey took eleven days and nights. Pierre, who goes east, says that it lasted thirteen days and nights. As a control, there is a third man, Robert, who remains at the starting point. Robert says that only twelve days and nights had elapsed since both travelers had set out. Oresme realized if you travel in the same direction that the sun appears to move, you will lengthen the interval to the next sunset or sunrise. After a complete circuit, the increases will add up to a whole day.

Lewis Carroll (1850, 31-33) embellishes the circumnavigator's paradox by imagining a strip of land circling the earth in which everyone speaks English. You embark Tuesday from London at 9 A.M. and travel quickly enough to keep the sun in the same position in the sky. As you go along, you check the time by asking the locals, "What time is it?" They always answer, "9 A.M." Indeed, that is the answer when, 24 hours later, you return to London. But the Londoners also report the day as Wednesday rather than Tuesday. So where did Wednesday begin?

The circumnavigator's paradox was rendered obsolete in 1878 when the International Date Line was declared at 180 degrees east from Greenwich, England. It is a credit to scholasticism that the need for such a convention was noted five hundred years earlier by Nicole Oresme. He thought through these issues in an entirely hypothetical manner. In deference to the condemnation of 1277, Oresme denied that strict demonstrative proofs were possible in the physical sciences. First, he would argue that the earth goes round the sun. Then, he would turn around and argue that the sun goes round the earth. Oresme invites us to conclude that neither reason nor experience can settle the issue. He adopts the traditional view, that the earth does not move, on faith.

Was the circumnavigator's paradox a theoretical paradox when debated in the sixteenth century? On the one hand, a widely acknowledged expert, Nicole Oresme, had definitively solved the problem in the fourteenth century. So it was no longer a paradox to those attending Oresme's lectures; there was no longer any conflict between observation and calendar theory. However, in the sixteenth century, Renaissance men were opting out of the old system of intellectual division of labor. Their experts did not include fourteenth-century philosophy professors. The medieval syllogisms of Buridan and Oresme was likened to spiders' webs; hard for any man to precisely imitate but only strong enough to ensnare the feeble. By disavowing the past, Renaissance men created a new environment for the circumnavigator's paradox.

SIXTEEN

# Pascal's Improbable Calculations

Inventors put paradoxes into practice. *Horseless carriage* and *wireless telephone* were oxymorons before they became terms for commonplace artifacts. These wonders *subtract* some essential feature. At nineteen, Blaise Pascal (1623-1662) subtracted thought from subtraction.

## MINDLESS COMPUTATION AND DESCARTES

In 1651 Pascal built an arithmetic machine to ease his father's work as tax commissioner. This was a historic feat of engineering. For years, Pascal labored closely with carpenters and experts at gear assembly.

An arithmetic machine seemed especially absurd in the aftermath of René Descartes. He refined the common-sense distinction between mind and matter into a formidable metaphysical dualism.

Your body takes up space, has weight and other properties studied by physicists. Descartes recommended that bodies be studied as machines.

Your mind has no size or weight or other physical properties. Little wonder that your mind is private; only you have direct access to your thoughts. We outsiders only have indirect access to your mind—principally through what you say. Your words betoken thoughts and your thoughts manifest your essential nature as a thinking being. You can conceive of yourself existing without a body but it is self-defeating to conceive of yourself as a nonconceiver. Therefore, you are identical to your mind and only contingently occupy your body.

Descartes went to the morgue to find the point at which mind interacts with the body. He found that brains were symmetrical except for the pineal gland. Descartes deduced that this is the point of interaction. He hoped his discovery would help solve a paradox raised by Johannes Kepler's advances in optics. Kepler had shown that the retinal image must be inverted relative to the physical world. Descartes directly confirmed Kepler's discovery by looking through the eyeball of a dead ox. Why does the world look right side up when the retinal image is upside down? Descartes answered that the representation of the optical image is *reinverted* before it reaches the pineal gland. But dissections never revealed a reinversion mechanism.

George Berkeley eventually persuaded everybody that there was no need for reinversion. Descartes had mistakenly pictured himself as observing the world through his own eyes (in the way he looked through the ox's eye). There is no internal observer inspecting the optical image. (If there were a little man inside your head, then how would *he* see?) Once we refrain from relativizing up/down to this homunculus, the paradox fails to get off the ground. The riddle of the inverted image is an example of a paradox that was raised by experiments and resolved by conceptual analysis.

According to Descartes, your body is determined by the laws of nature. But your mind is free. Indeed, Descartes blamed all errors on human willfulness. We jump to conclusions out of laziness and desire. We should be ashamed because God's goodness ensures that he has given us enough resources to ascertain the true nature of reality. If God had rigged up the world in the way feared by the skeptics, then God would be a deceiver—which is incompatible with God's beneficence and power. God must have given us a fair opportunity to learn about the nature of the external world beyond our minds. Descartes's *Discourse on Method* shows philosophers and scientists how to exploit this opportunity.

In the *Meditations* Descartes endeavors to prove all this from an indubitable basis. The possibility of dreams and illusions drives him to a purely internal perspective. If he can prove that God exists, Descartes will prove that we can know the external world. But until God is proved, Descartes can only use the data available to his immediate consciousness. Thus Descartes is confined to a priori proofs of God's existence. Descartes's first proof portrays his idea of God as an infallible trace of God himself. All other sources for the idea are methodically excluded: Descartes could not have obtained that idea from himself because he is finite. Nor can an idea of God result from adding two finite ideas (in the way Descartes gets the idea of a unicorn by combining the idea of a horn and the idea of a horse). Adding finite things together only produces finite things. Nor can the idea of God come from subtracting one idea from another. Infinity is not a subtraction from finitude. So the idea of God must have come from God himself. Descartes also uses Saint Anselm's ontological proof: God is the greatest conceivable being. It is better to exist than not exist. Therefore, we must conceive of God as existing.

We may think that Descartes's philosophy overworks God. But after Descartes visited Pascal in 1647, Pascal complained to his sister Gilberte, "I cannot forgive Descartes: in his entire philosophy he would like to do without God; but he could not help allowing him a flick of the fingers to set the world in motion; after that Descartes had no more use for God." (Coleman 1985, 19)

Descartes is impressed that we have access to abstract truths such as 10,000 - 2,000 = 8,000. This truth is not a summary of past experiences in which you have removed 2,000 objects from 10,000 objects and found the remainder to be 8,000 objects. You have never actually counted so many objects. And if you did, you would not accept any "counterexample" to 10,000 - 2,000 = 8,000. The equation transcends experience. From this lofty perspective, it is hard to see how gears could perform the fundamental operations of arithmetic. Yet, there sat Pascal's calculator grinding out differences on the tax commissioner's desk.

When descendants of Pascal's adding machine acquired the versatility of the 1950s "electronic brains," these mechanical marvels were increasingly regarded as near counterexamples to Descartes's dualism. We now feel an awkward kinship with computers—especially the robots in science fiction.

Disciples of Alan Turing (1912-1954) welcome our inclination to attribute minds to machines. They see automata as an opportunity to demystify consciousness. What matters to functionalists is what the thing *does*, not what it is made of. This is the thrust of Turing's test for thought: if a computer can converse in a way that is indistinguishable from a human

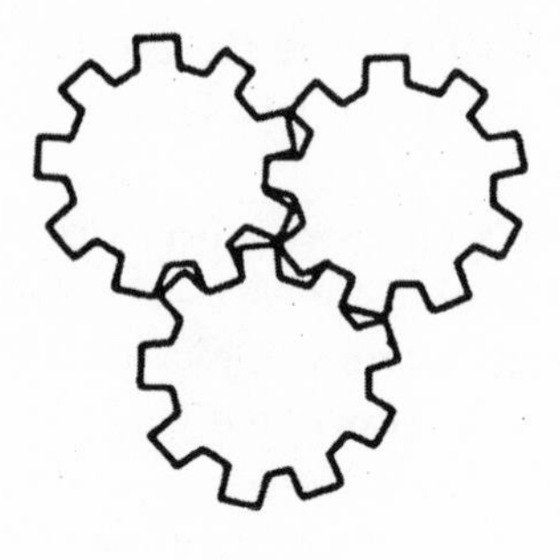

Fig. 16.1

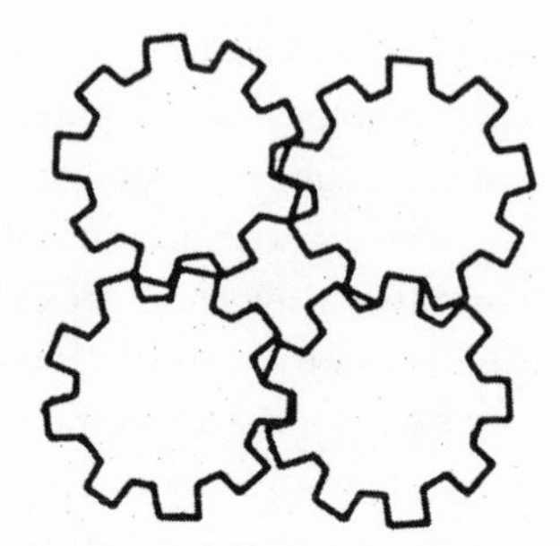

Fig. 16.2

being, then that computer is a thinking machine. If you are a silicon robot that is doing exactly what my carbon-based readers are doing, then you are reading my book and having thoughts about Pascal's arithmetic machine (one of your earliest ancestors).

Those with lingering sympathy to Descartes believe that Turing's emphasis on behavior is refuted by the possibility of zombies: mindless creatures who are functionally indistinguishable from people with minds. Since a zombie is not conscious but can do anything its minded counterpart can do, consciousness does not depend solely on input-output relations. Although the zombie thought experiment is intuitively persuasive, functionalists reply that our imaginations are faulty guides to what is possible. Suppose Pascal's mechanical calculator had three gears aligned as in figure 16.1. It is easy to imagine the gears all spinning. But they are actually gridlocked.

Perhaps you have now rerun the gear thought experiment and have spotted the subtle jam. Now focus your mind's eye on a scenario involving four interlocked gears (fig. 16.2). Still jammed?

The right answer is that the four-gear assembly can turn. In general, an even number of interlocked gears can turn but an odd number cannot. This principle dictates gridlock for the nineteen-gear circuit that is depicted on the silver-gold, two pounds coin introduced by the Royal Mint on June 15, 1998. Brute inspection cannot overturn the impression that this large assembly of gears can all spin. The gridlock is too sensitive to the small difference of whether the large number of gears are odd or even. We need theory to overrule imagination's verdict. Similarly, the functionalist can insist that theory is needed to correct the impression that a functional equivalent of you can be free of consciousness.

## EXPERIMENTS ON NOTHING

During Descartes's visit, Pascal tried to convince him that vacuums exist. Descartes believed that reality had to be a plenum. He wrote Christian Huygens that Pascal "had too much vacuum in his head."

Pascal began thinking about vacuums in 1646 when he learned of Evangelista Torricelli's experiment with a barometer. This involved placing a tube of mercury upside down in a bowl of mercury. Everybody wondered what kept the mercury suspended in the tube. The received view was that the "empty space" in the tube was filled with rarefied and invisible matter. Following Aristotle, they believed that nature abhors a vacuum. Pascal regarded the issue as empirical rather than conceptual. He conducted a series of experiments that dramatically supported the vacuum hypothesis. His conclusion was that there really was nothing holding up the mercury. Nor is there anything pulling liquid through a siphon. Instead the ocean of air that surrounds the earth presses down on the liquid except where there is a vacuum. In his 1653 "Treatise on the Equilibrium of Liquids," Pascal states his law of pressure: "Pressure applied to a confined liquid is transmitted undiminished through the liquid in all directions." When you suck on a straw, you decrease the pressure in the tube leading to your mouth. The liquid on the other end of the straw is no longer being so strongly pushed down and so rises to your lips.

In the age of rocket travel, we know empty space is a killer. But only in virtue of what it *fails* to do. If you were to step into the void without protection, your blood would boil. But not because empty space is hot. You would die because the void fails to exert pressure on your body. But what caused the death? Nothingness? Sheer space? Or must we suspend the requirement that effects have causes?

Physicists have not answered these questions with much more success than philosophers. However, physicists are at home with vacuums. They regard voids as part of the basic furniture of the universe.

Voids bubble more uncomfortably through common sense. The central stanza of Bette Midler's "Wind Beneath My Wings" gratefully praises a selfless friend who quietly assists the outgoing singer in her ascent to fame: "Did you ever know that you're my hero? You're everything I would like to be. I can fly higher than an eagle, for you are the wind beneath my wings." In light of Pascal, aerodynamicists now know that flight is made possible by the *vacuum* formed *above* moving wings. Thus, the refrain should be "I can fly higher than an eagle, for you are the void above my wings."

## THE STRUCTURE OF DISORDER

Laws governing a vacuum seem impossible because there is nothing for the law to be about. Chance also seems law-resistant. Randomness is absence of order. Pascal was stimulated by the conceptual tension. In his 1654 "Address to the Academie Parisienne de Mathematiques," Pascal concludes: "Thus, joining the rigor of demonstrations in mathematics with the uncertainty of chance, and conciliating these apparently contradictory matters, it can, taking its name from both of them, with justice arrogate the stupefying name: The Mathematics of Chance."

Pausanias mentions a picture painted by Polygnotos in the fifth century which shows Palamedeo and Thresites playing dice. According to Greek tradition, Palamedo invented dice to entertain bored Greek soldiers waiting for the battle of Troy. But dice go back to the first dynasty in Egypt. Randomizing devices, fashioned from symmetrical animal bones, date back to the Paleolithic era.

Despite this long history, the first book on dice is Gerolama Cardano's *De Ludo Aleae*, which was published in 1663, one hundred years after it was written. Cardano systematically addresses conflicts between theoretical predictions about how dice should behave and observations about how they actually behave. For instance, gamblers knew that with two dice, 9 and 10 can be made up in two different ways from 1, 2, 3, 4, 5, 6 namely, $9 = 3 + 6 = 4 + 5$ and $10 = 4 + 6 = 5 + 5$. They inferred that 9 and 10 should result with equal frequency. Yet experience indicates that 9 is more frequent.

Cardano accepts the observational evidence and amends the theory. He notes that the *order* of the cast is relevant. 9 can be made up by four permutations: $9 = 3 + 6 = 6 + 3 = 4$

+ 5 = 5 + 4. But 10 can only be made in three permutations: 10 = 4 + 6 = 6 + 4 = 5 + 5.

To a modern reader, this problem seems too easy to qualify as a paradox. But "paradox" should be relativized to the thinker in question. The earliest recorded use of "paradox" in 1616 states: "Paradox, an opinion maintained contrary to the commonly allowed opinion, as if one affirms that the earth doth move round and the heavens stand still." (Bullokar's *Chapbook*) What had been hailed as the "Copernican paradox" is no longer a paradox because Copernicus's arguments in favor of the earth orbiting the sun are no longer held in check by Aristotle's objections (that dropped objects would fall far from point of release, that wind would blow trees down, that we would see stars whoosh by). Just as news stops being news and becomes history, some solved paradoxes stop being paradoxes and become orthodoxies. "This was sometime a paradox, but now the time gives it proof." (Shakespeare, *Hamlet* III.i.114–15)

People who have yet to distinguish between combinations (groupings in which order is irrelevant) and permutations (groupings in which order is relevant) will be baffled by the apparent misbehavior of dice. It will take a Cardano to fight his way up to the vantage point that makes the paradox seem like a trivial mistake.

Cardano was serious about making observation fit with theory. Cardano cast a horoscope predicting the hour of his own death. When that day dawned and he found himself healthy and safe, Cardano killed himself rather than falsify the prediction.

## THE MONTY HALL PROBLEM

Recall the television game show "Let's Make a Deal" hosted by Monty Hall. A contestant selects one of three doors and wins whatever prize is behind the door. Behind one door is a valuable prize while the other two contain prank prizes, such as a goat. Suppose that you are a contestant and have picked door number 1. To increase the suspense, Monty shows you what is behind door 2. You expect to see no prize behind the door Monty shows because you know that he always reveals a *losing* door. He then offers you the chance to trade your claim on what is behind door 1 for what is behind door number 3. Should you switch?

In the September 1991 issue of the *Parade* magazine column "Ask Marilyn," Marilyn vos Savant advised switching. Many mathematicians scolded Marilyn for committing a fallacy.

But Marilyn was right. Most people infer that switching is pointless because you already know that Monty will reveal a losing door. And indeed, the two remaining doors would have an equal chance of being winners if Monty Hall had *randomly* revealed a door. However, Monty only reveals losing doors. Monty's revelation that door 2 has a goat cannot raise the probability that door 1 has the prize because you already knew that Monty was going to either reveal 2 as a loser or reveal 3 as a loser. However, Monty's revelation that door 2 is a loser does increase the probability that 3 is the winner. Prior to this news, door 3 only had a 1/3 chance of holding the prize. After learning that door 2 is a loser, the probability that the prize is behind door 3 rises to 2/3 because the probability of door 1 winning is not affected.

Nearly everybody gets the Monty Hall problem wrong. Many resist the correct answer even when it is explained to them. Despite Monty's extensive roster of victims, I am reluctant to describe "Should you switch doors?" as a paradox. True, there are conflicting good answers if brute persuasiveness is the standard. But might does not make right. The goodness of answers must be ranked by an objective standard (consistency with observation, common sense, scientific principles, etc.). After all, the point of grading answers is to figure out what we *should* believe. The Monty Hall problem was never a theoretical anomaly. The only professional controversy has been between rival psychological theories as to why this fallacy is so powerful. At the level of refereed journal articles, there has always been total consensus on the correct answer to *Should you switch doors?*—including among philosophers (who supposedly disagree about everything).

There is looseness in what counts as the best available perspective. Consequently, there will be looseness in what counts as a paradox. If we relativize the phrase to ideal thinkers, few surprises will count as a paradox. If we relativize to an amateur's perspective, then too many surprises will count as paradoxes. To keep *paradox* a discriminative term, we relativize to the perspectives of contemporary, well-functioning experts. For questions that lack experts, we relativize to the perspective of reasonable, intelligent people.

As illustrated by the circumnavigator's paradox, systems of intellectual division of labor can change. In a society that did not defer to statistics professors, the Monty Hall problem would qualify as a paradox—as would the dice puzzles resolved by Cardano.

## THE DIVISION PARADOX

The French gambler Chevalier de la Méré introduced Blaise Pascal to the division paradox. Suppose two gamblers have agreed that whoever wins six rounds gets the whole prize.

Each round is determined by chance, say, in accordance with the flip of a coin. The game is cut short after the first player has won five rounds and the second player has won three rounds. How can the prize be divided fairly?

The question was inconclusively discussed in the later middle ages as a problem of proportions. Pascal and his correspondent Pierre Fermat approached it as a problem of probabilities: from their fresh perspective, the players should divide the prize in accordance with the likelihood they would have won it had the game continued. The second player would win if and only if he won all of the next three rounds. The chance of that happening is $\frac{1}{2} \times \frac{1}{2} \times \frac{1}{2} = \frac{1}{8}$. Therefore, the second player should receive $\frac{1}{8}$ of the prize and the first player should receive $\frac{7}{8}$. Pascal and Fermat generalized this solution, independently of each other, in 1654. The origin of probability theory is frequently traced to this date.

Probability theory was suddenly thriving in the 1660s. The revolutionary prospect of putting gambling and insurance on a mathematical basis intrigued entrepreneurs. By 1688 London business circles knew of the existence of an insurance company that was run within Edward Lloyd's Thames-side coffeehouse on Tower Street. Hazardous maritime ventures could be undertaken without fear of utter ruin because one could hedge the risk by, in effect, betting that the cargo would be lost. The underwriters needed evidence about the probability of setbacks. However, the early underwriters made little meaningful use of probability theory. In practice, they fell back on ancient techniques for decreasing risk such as distributing cargo among several ships. Mainly, they used just the sort of heuristics that contemporary psychologists urbanely ridicule. These traditional businessmen were more prosperous than those who prematurely applied probability theory. After all, there was a critical lack of organized data and statistical techniques.

Anyone who could build the infrastructure needed for sound statistical inferences still stood to make a fortune in the insurance industry. To meet the demand for information about human life spans, mortality tables were compiled. These tables generated paradoxes similar to the dice enigmas discussed by Cardano. Edmond Halley showed that the average life span is 26 years and yet the chance of surviving beyond age 8 is ½. He was puzzled why the average age of the population is not 8.

Practical Englishmen were discouraged by the ease with which conflicting probabilities could be calculated. The statisticians often resembled those who prophesied by anagrams. The religious fanatic Lady Eleanor Davies (died 1652) discovered that the letters of her name, with an *L* substituted for the final *S*, could be rearranged as "Reveal, O Daniel." When brought before the Court of High Commission, she cited this anagram as evidence that she was possessed by the spirit of the prophet Daniel. The bishops thought she was mad but she had replies to all their objections. Finally, one bishop, who had been writing furiously during the proceedings, announced that he had irrefutable proof that Lady Eleanor was insane. He read out the anagram "Dame Eleanor Davies—never so mad a ladie!"

## PASCAL'S WAGER

"From around 10:30 until about 12:30 in the morning" on November 24, 1654, Pascal had a mystical experience. Eight years later, an inscription was discovered sewn into the jacket that clothed his corpse: "FIRE. God of Abraham, God of Isaac, God of Jacob, not of the philosophers or of the learned. Certainty. Certainty. Feeling, Joy, Peace.... Total Submission to Jesus Christ and to my director. Eternally in joy for one day of exercise on earth.... " Following that November morning, Pascal withdrew from scientific research and devoted himself to religious activities.

Blaise Pascal retained an interest in converting his libertine acquaintances to Christianity. In his *Pensées*, Pascal argues that, *from a nonbeliever's perspective*, it is prudent to acquire a belief in God: There is at least an outside chance that God exists. The implications are tremendous because God rewards believers with heaven and punishes unbelievers with hell. Since any fraction of the infinite is itself infinite, the expected value of theism is infinite. However much finite good accrues from secular living, the religious life is infinitely more prudent.

If belief were voluntary, as Descartes assumed, then the issue is simply a matter of deciding what to believe. But incentives for a belief do not directly cause beliefs in the way that evidence does. I hereby offer you a hundred dollars to believe that this book will ignite in ten seconds. Now you have a reason to believe this book will ignite. However, this incentive is not the sort of reason that makes you believe that this book will ignite. To believe, you need a reason that bears on the truth of the proposition that this book will ignite. So even if Pascal has given you a reason that you should believe that God exists (by pointing out the incentive of heaven), he has not given you the sort of reason (evidence) that produces belief that God exists.

Pascal's *Pensées* contains remarks that show the wager is not derailed by the distinction between incentives and evidence. He advises the libertine to *indirectly* acquire a belief in God. Since belief is contagious, an unbeliever can gradually become a Christian by socializing with Christians and participating in rituals. At first, the libertine will be just going through the motions. Eventually, beliefs catch up with behavior. Once a Christian, the former libertine will disapprove of his original profit motive for becoming a Christian. But the selfish motive that precipitated his Christianity is not needed to continue his faith. Once the wager argument has done its work, the new Christian can jettison the crass calculations.

Pascal cannot get his foot in the door if the atheist believes he *knows* that God does not exist. To pry open the minds of dogmatic atheists, Pascal adapts Sextus Empiricus's techniques. Pascal's goal is to demonstrate that reason is a cul-de-sac. He humbles the reader's intellect with a steady plip-plop of antinomies. The paradoxes descend from man's unique recognition of his finitude. All animals are finite but only man appreciates the contrast with infinity. Life is short for all animals. But man alone dreads death and perceives the menace it poses to the significance of his life. All creatures are specks in a vast cosmos but only man can recognize himself as a speck.

> What sort of freak then is man! How novel, how monstrous, how chaotic, how paradoxical, how prodigious! Judge of all things, feeble earthworm, repository of truth, sink of doubt and error, glory and refuse of the universe!
>
> Who will unravel such a tangle? This is certainly beyond dogmatism and scepticism, beyond all human philosophy. Man transcends man. . . .
>
> Know then, proud man, what a paradox you are to yourself. Be humble, impotent reason! Be silent, feeble

> nature! Learn that man infinitely transcends man, hear from your master your true condition, which is unknown to you.
>
> (1966, No. 131)

Pascal feels it is dangerous to explain how much man is an animal without also pointing out his greatness. Pascal wields an emotional analogue of Sextus Empiricus's method of equipollence:

> If he exalts himself, I humble him.
> If he humbles himself, I exalt him.
> And I go on contradicting him
> Until he understands
> That he is a monster that passes all understanding.
>
> (1966, No. 130)

Voltaire and Fermat were disturbed by Pascal's new polemics. They interpreted the wager as an effect of declining health. Pascal's "Prayer to Ask God for the Good Use of Illnesses" suggests that Pascal might have agreed! As Pascal suffered through the final stages of stomach cancer, he expressed fear of *recovery* rather than of further illness or death: "Don't pity me! Illness is the Christian's natural state. We all ought always to be like the sick man, suffering from the privation of every good and of all sensual pleasures, exempt from every passion . . . , without ambition or greed, constantly awaiting death." (Cole 1995, 249) The sick Christian, Pascal continues, should be *thankful* when forced to be just as he ought to be.

The main objections to Pascal's wager focus on the argument rather than the man who devised it. In 1746, Denis Diderot declined the wager with the observation that "An

Imam could reason just as well this way." Pascal has left out the possibility that there is a Baal or a Moloch or a Zeus or some other claimant of faith. In the absence of doctrinal constraints, we must also include inversions such as the possibility that God rewards the doubters and punishes believers. To narrow the field of contenders, Pascal must revert to the theologizing that initially seemed bypassed by the wager.

## THE ST. PETERSBURG PARADOX

Pascal's wager is also challenged by economists who reject the possibility of infinite utility. Their finitism emerged in discussions of a problem that was first stated in a letter written by Nicholas Bernoulli and published in 1713. A fair coin will be tossed until a head results. You will then be paid $\$2^{n-1}$ where $n$ equals the number of tosses. So the expected return is: $(\frac{1}{2} \times \$1) + (\frac{1}{4} \times \$2) + (\frac{1}{8} \times \$4) + \ldots :+ (\frac{1}{2}n \times \$2^{n-1}) +$ . . . . Since each addend equals a half dollar, and there are infinitely many of them, the sum is infinite. Thus, someone who maximized expected money should be willing to pay any amount of money for this bet. Yet few people would pay $100 for the deal.

Jean d'Alembert named this puzzle the St. Petersburg paradox because the first article on the paradox was published by the Imperial Academy of Sciences at St. Petersburg. The author was Nicholas Bernoulli's cousin Daniel Bernoulli. He pointed out that doubling one's cash holdings from a million to two million does not really double its value to you. Each new dollar tends to have less influence on your welfare than the preceding dollar. Daniel Bernoulli's insight is enshrined in contemporary economics as the law of the diminishing marginal utility of money. The rate of diminution resists precise calculation, but Daniel Bernoulli inferred that it is a logarithmic function. This would preclude infinite sums.

In economics, the most popular solution to both the wager and the St. Petersburg paradox is evaluative finitism. Following Daniel Bernoulli, economists formulate the axioms of decision theory in a way that ensures value is *necessarily* finite. This limit on desire grates against several economic themes. Economists tell us that desire is insatiable, that ends cannot be irrational, and that what counts are people's beliefs about what they can acquire rather than what actually exists. Right or wrong, Pascal seeks the infinite reward of heaven and flees from the infinite punishment of hell. Indeed, most people have religious hopes and fears of infinite proportion. Whether or not infinite value can be actually secured, the economist seems obliged to model the choices of those who *believe* in infinite value.

Economists try to enforce their finitism by peppering doubters with the puzzles that accrue from allowing nearly any infinite aspect into decision theory. Take the possibility of infinite time. In *Foundations of Statistics*, Leonard Savage notes that the longer you save, the more you have. So it seems an immortal should save forever! Savage sidelines the enigma by stipulating that his theory only applies to finite quantities. But the puzzle does not require infinite *value*. Suppose a bottle of Everbetter wine improves endlessly but only to the limit set by the quality of a moderately nice wine. (Pollock 1983) This finitely good wine gets better only in the way $1/n$ gets closer to 0. When should an immortal connoisseur drink the wine? Not now because it will be better later. Not at any particular time later because the wine would be even better if the connoisseur waited. Yet it now seems that he never drinks the wine!

Alternatively, we can imagine the *probability* undergoing an infinite improvement. Suppose a bookkeeper is eternally lodged in limbo. Limbo is a neutral state, neither good nor bad. The bookkeeper has a single opportunity for a vacation to another state somewhat better than limbo, say, two weeks in Florida. Since the bookkeeper's odds of failing to get the vacation equal $1/n$ for each year spent in limbo, the bookkeeper should definitely wait more than one year. But the numbers seem to doom him to an unbroken stay in limbo.

## THE TWO ENVELOPE PARADOX

Economists also use their finitism to solve paradoxes that initially do not appear to involve infinity. Consider the two envelope paradox: You are offered a choice between two envelopes, A and B. You are informed one envelope contains twice as much as the other. You pick A. The organizer of the event then asks you whether you want to switch envelopes. Should you switch?

Go ahead, peek inside your envelope. You find $10. Now you know envelope B either contains $5 or $20. Since each alternative is equiprobable, the expected value of switching to B is (½ × $5) + (½ × $20) = $12.50. Since that is a gain of $2.50, you should switch. The same argument works regardless of how much money you find in the envelope. Therefore, you are justified in switching even if you do not bother to look inside envelope A.

The argument against switching is that envelope A is just as likely to contain twice as much as B as B is as likely to contain twice as much as A. So A and B are of equal value. Anti-switchers also note that the argument for switching has a weird implication. Suppose envelope B was given to another contestant. The switching argument would apply equally to him and so would advise him to trade his envelope for yours!

Commentators on the two envelope paradox agree that the question of whether to switch is resolvable if you know there is a limited supply of cash. For instance, if you know that the game organizers have at most $1,500 to distribute, then you would not want to switch if you found $1,000 in your envelope. Nor would you want to switch if the amount were close to $1,000. If you find $1, then you should definitely switch. Ditto for amounts close to $1. When you know how much money is available, the amount of money in your envelope becomes a clue as to how much money is in the other envelope.

But what should you do if the money supply is infinite? Now the problem resembles the St. Petersburg paradox. Economists who follow Nicholas Bernoulli complain that the two envelope paradox overlooks the diminishing marginal utility of money. They will toss the two envelope paradox in the same wastebasket that contains the Saint Petersburg paradox and Pascal's wager.

I personally think that a complete economic theory (or ethical theory) must allow for some decision problems that involve infinite value, infinite time, and infinite populations. Possibly, physics or metaphysics will one day exclude these infinities as objectively impossible. But this only seems relevant when we overlook the subjective nature of decision theory. What counts for the decision theorist are people's *perceptions* of their situation, not the situation itself. Therefore, a decision theory that does not take Pascal seriously cannot itself be taken seriously.

The strangeness of Pascal's opinions has been surpassed by other gifted mathematicians—sometimes to the ruin of other mathematicians. In the course of researching the two envelope paradox (which has recently become a hot topic in economics and philosophy), I discovered that the prolific Edmund Landau introduced it in 1912 (Kraitchik 1930, 253). This is the same Edmund Landau who was fired by the University of Göttingen in 1934 for a Jewish definition of $\pi$. Landau's textbook characterized $\pi/2$ as the value of x between 1 and 2 for which cosine x vanishes. Nazi students were incensed by such abstraction. The prominent number theorist Ludwig Bieberbach published a defense of the dismissal on the grounds that Landau was imposing his racial style on sensitive young Germans.

SEVENTEEN

# Leibniz's Principle of Sufficient Reason

According to Pascal, we are wise enough to appreciate our contradictions but not wise enough to resolve them. He winds up using probability calculations as a ladder to heaven—a ladder that is kicked away after religious conversion.

The philosophers in these next three chapters are more optimistic about our ability to solve the paradoxes. Their basic strategy is conservative. Each identifies some successful area of human thought and holds it up as a model of how we ought to think. Paradoxes are diagnosed as failures to absorb the lessons the model tacitly demonstrates. For rationalists, the model is mathematics and logic. The traditional problem with this model is application. How can lofty a priori reasoning instruct us about the nitty-gritty empirical world? This gap was widened by increasing reluctance to view the world of the senses as having a lesser degree of reality than the world of triangles and frictionless planes.

## LEIBNIZ'S PRINCIPLES

Gottfried Leibniz (1646-1716) interpreted probability theory as a new way to link pure deduction to the empirical realm. For him, probability theory is a branch of logic. Whereas deductive logic handles arguments that aim to make the conclusion *certain* given the premises, inductive logic deals with arguments that aim to make the conclusion *probable* given the premises. As a diplomat, Leibniz hoped that the mathematics of chance would become a tool of conflict resolution. The contending parties would pool their evidence and then calculate the probabilities of rival hypotheses. Although calculation need not yield the truth of the matter, it would produce agreement.

There has been some progress toward this ideal. In a well structured experiment, the scientists turn over their data to statisticians. Some parts of the job of assigning probabilities are so mechanical that they can be delegated to computers. Computer simulations have been used to demonstrate the correct solution to the Monty Hall problem. Perhaps computers will one day solve some deep paradoxes.

In 1678 Leibniz was the first to define probability as the ratio of favorable cases to the total number of equally possible cases. If equal possibility is understood as equi*probability*, then Leibniz's definition is circular. Pierre-Simon de Laplace (1749-1827), who is often mistakenly credited with inventing the definition, occasionally lapsed into this circularity.

But Laplace normally wielded an epistemic criterion: outcomes are equiprobable if there is no more reason to expect one event rather than another. Laplace's criterion is satisfied by a coin that is biased in an *unknown* direction. Since you have no more reason to expect H(eads) than T(ails), H and T are equipossible. Although you know the coin does not have an equal propensity to come up heads or tails, you must assign the same probability. Probability is a measure of our ignorance. Laplace next invites us to consider the case in which the biased coin is to be tossed twice. There are four possible outcomes: HH, HT, TH, TT. Is the event of getting two homogeneous tosses (HH or TT) equipossible with the mixed outcomes (HT or TH)? No, because the bias makes a homogeneous outcome easier to produce than a mixed result. Laplace emphasizes that here the criterion of equipossibility is violated: when the coin is biased, the uniform possibility (HH or TT) is easier to bring about than the mixed result (HT or TH).

Many people think that Laplace's biased coin illustrates the ambiguity of "probable." In the objective sense, H and T are not equally probable outcomes for the biased coin. The equiprobability is only subjective: each outcome receives the same degree of credence. This subjective sense invites a further division between the probability we actually assign and the probability we *ought* to assign. A man who is less astute than Laplace might wrongly assign the same probability we *ought* to (HH or TT) as to the (HT or TH) outcome. The probability we ought to assign can be fleshed out by intellectual norms. Surprisingly, the requirement of consistency is enough to ensure conformity with the probability calculus. Your probability assignments are consistent just in case there is no way for anyone to make a "Dutchbook" against you. (A Dutchbook is a collection of individually fair bets that guarantees a net gain for the bookie.)

Leibniz had metaphysical views about equipossiblity that mix objective probability with subjective probability. He has the objective sense of "probable" in mind when explaining which possibilities succeed at becoming actual. Many possibilities are not co-possible. The possibility that conflicts with the fewest other possibilities becomes actual. Thus, simplicity and harmony are guides to empirical truth.

This objective picture of possibilities requires a limbo where nonexistent entities battle to enter the realm of existence. How can nonexistent things do anything? Perhaps this difficulty motivated Leibniz's subjective account of equipossiblity: possibilities start out as God's thoughts. These thoughts are complete plans for a universe. Each of these possible worlds is a consistent and complete way that things could be. Since there are many ways things could have been, the actual world is just one of many possible worlds. Those backed by better reasons have a stronger tendency to become actualized by God.

The subjective side of Leibniz's philosophy assigns God a large role. When one concentrates on the objective side, God looks like a hanger-on, perhaps even an ornament to put Leibniz's royal patrons at ease.

Leibniz's system is founded on two principles. The principle of contradiction says that anything that involves a contradiction is false and whatever is opposed to a contradiction is true. At first blush this principle seems to exclude only trivial falsehoods such as "Leibniz was a secretary of the Rosicrucian Society and was not a secretary of the Rosicrucian Society." But Leibniz believes that it excludes all falsehoods. According to Leibniz, statements always have a subject-predicate form. A statement is true if the predicate is contained in the subject. For instance, "Each man is male" is true because the subject, man, is defined as "male adult human being"; the subject term contains the predicate "male." For individuals, the subject term consists of a complete description of the individual. Thus, if one could exhaustively analyze the subject term "Gottfried Leibniz," one would find *born in Leipzig* on the infinite list of predicates. To an infinite mind, "Gottfried Leibniz was born in Leipzig" is therefore an a priori truth. Since Leipzig is part of the meaning of "Gottfried Leibniz," a full understanding of Leibniz implies a full understanding of Leipzig. The subject term 'Leipzig' in turn involves the residents of Leipzig, relations with other cities, and so on. To fully know anything is to know everything. Each individual mirrors all the other individuals in the universe.

Despite this holism, each individual is "windowless" in that the truths about the individual do not depend on anything else. The internal nature of a thing completely determines its history. The apparent influence of shears upon a shrub is not really an intrusion on the shrub. There is a preestablished harmony between the blades and the twigs. Our actions are an unfolding of our inner natures, so we are free.

Finite minds cannot perform an infinite analysis. Often we limited thinkers can only know the truth by using empirical means—just as accountants must resort to calculators to confirm that $111,111,111 \times 111,111,111 = 12,345,678,987,654,321$. But this does mean that this equation is made true by the gears of the calculator or any other contingent thing.

Leibniz's principle of sufficient reason says that everything must have a reason. Leibniz says that we use this principle constantly in our inferences. He cites Archimedes' reasoning: a scale with equal weights must be balanced because there is no more reason for one side to go up rather than the other.

Leibniz uses the principle of sufficient reason to prove that God exists. A possible world is a complete, alternative way things might be. There are many possible worlds. Why is our world the actual world? There can be a reason only if God exists.

Leibniz believes God chose our world because it is the best of all possible worlds. In *Candide* Voltaire lampooned Leibniz's optimism as wishful thinking. But try to sketch out a *complete* alternative that is better. In Harry McClintock's "The Big Rock Candy Mountain," a hobo wistfully sings,

> In the Big Rock Candy Mountain, You never change your socks, And little streams of alkyhol, Come trickling down the rocks, O the shacks all have to tip their hats, And the railway bulls are blind, There's a lake of stew, And gingerale too, And you can paddle all around it in a big canoe, In the Big Rock Candy Mountain

The hobo's paradise is not idyllic for the blind police with wooden legs, nor for the hens that lay soft-boiled eggs (not to mention the jerk who got hanged for inventing work). The hobo's improvements over the actual world are relative to his limited perspective.

## LEIBNIZ'S PREDICTIONS

Don't expect a perfect world to be perfect *for you.* The world is perfect in the objective sense of being better over all (as a *world*). Since variety is good, Leibniz predicted that there are animals of every size, including ones that are too small for us to detect with unaided vision. He also predicted, contrary to Aristotle, that there are intermediate species, including organisms that are borderline cases between animal and plant. Darwin was to later echo Leibniz with his favorite motto "Nature does not make jumps."

Leibniz also inferred from the principle of sufficient reason that nature cannot make perfect duplicates. For God would have no more reason to put one duplicate here and the other duplicate there. If $x$ is indiscernible from $y$, then $x$ is identical to $y$. Leibniz deployed this principle of the identity of indiscernibles against atoms. Since atoms are simple things, they cannot differ qualitatively. There is at most one atom. Yet atomists say that there are many atoms. Therefore, the atomists are refuted by the principle that indiscernible things are identical.

A pair of vacuums would also be excluded by the identity of indiscernibles. One empty space is indiscernible from any other. Even a single vacuum constitutes a gap in nature. That is ruled out by the principle of continuity. God would not wish to forego the opportunity to fill every part of space with something good.

Leibniz put his metaphysics into empirical practice. One of his favorite anecdotes concerns the principle that

> There is no such thing as two individuals indiscernible from each other. An ingenious gentleman of my acquaintance, discoursing with me in the presence of Her Electoral Highness, the Princess Sophia, in the garden of Herrenhausen, thought he could find two leaves perfectly alike. The princess defied him to do it, and he ran all over the garden a long time to look for some; but it was to no purpose. Two drops of water or milk, viewed with a microscope, will appear distinguishable from each other. This is an argument against atoms, which are confuted, as well as the void, by the principles of true metaphysics. (1989, 333)

Leibniz uses the principle of the identity of indiscernibles to rescue the principle of sufficient reason. At first glance, Buridan's ass is a counterexample to the principle of sufficient reason. Consider someone who attempts to starve an ass by presenting it with two equally appealing bales of hay. This is an unpromising method for killing asses. Wouldn't the ass just arbitrarily choose one bale over the other? Leibniz responds by insisting that there will inevitably be a small difference between the two bales of hay.

This solution is incomplete because the identity of indiscernibles does not guarantee that the difference is a relevant difference. Leibniz concedes that two eggs can be completely similar *in shape*. He just denies that the two eggs can be completely similar in all respects. So what prevents the bales from being completely similar *in desirability*? And since we are really talking about *perceived* similarity, why can't the ass just have equal desires for the distinct bales? Empirically, perceived similarity is easier to achieve than actual similarity.

One may also accuse Leibniz of exaggerating the precision of his predictions. Although the principle of the identity of indiscernibles implies that no two leaves are exactly alike, it does not predict that human beings can always detect those differences. If the gentleman had found two leaves that looked exactly alike, Leibniz would have retreated with the clarification that "indiscernible" must be relativized to God. For only God perceives all properties.

Scientists share Leibniz's tendency to overestimate the precision of their theory's predictions. When a prediction is confirmed, they do not draw attention to the role of background assumptions and the many inductive leaps needed to connect a theory with a prediction.

## GEOMETRICAL PROBABILITY

Games are usually organized into artificially discrete elements: the equal sides of a die, the uniformly shaped cards in a deck, etc. This encouraged the belief that probability always reduces to questions about combinations and permutations. The theory of combinations was first presented in Leibniz's *Ars Combinatoria*.

In 1777, the French naturalist Georges Louis Leclerc, Comte de Buffon, showed that combinations cannot be a complete foundation for probability. His incompleteness argument was inspired by a popular game that involved continuous outcomes. Gamblers throw a coin at random on a floor tiled with congruent squares. They bet on whether the coin would land entirely within the boundaries of a single square tile. Buffon realized that the coin would land within the tile exactly if the center of the coin lands within a smaller square, whose side was equal to the side of the tile minus the diameter of the coin. The probability of winning is simply the ratio of the area of the small square to the area of the tile.

This was the beginning of the study of "geometric probability," where probabilities are determined by comparing measurements, rather than by identifying and counting alternative, equally probable discrete events. Buffon went on to consider cases involving more complex shapes. In his famous Needle Problem, a needle is thrown at random on a floor marked with equidistant parallel lines. When the spacing of the lines equals the length of the needle, the probability of striking a line equals $2/\pi$.

This unexpected appearance of $\pi$ as a measure of probability illustrates the interrelatedness of mathematics. People were impressed by how $\pi$, an irrational number, could reliably percolate up through a random process. In 1901, M Lazzerini reported making 3,408 tosses and getting a value of $\pi$ equal to 3.1415929, a figure which is only off by 0.0000003 from the true value of $\pi$. (Although a famous result, it is too good to be true. The few mathematicians who bother to probe the details conclude that there was either a methodological error or fakery).

Lazzerini was following the tradition of stochastic simulation inaugurated by Buffon. Buffon encouraged his readers to verify his calculations by repeatedly dropping a needle on a chessboard. In the same article, he reports a simulation used to establish the value of $n$ in the St. Petersburg game. He had a child toss a coin until it appeared heads. The child did this 2,048 times. The results suggested that the value of the game is 5 despite the infinite expected value.

Laplace and Buffon solved the needle problem by extending the principle of indifference to cases involving an infinite number of events (corresponding to a point on a line and lines on a plane). The basic idea is to find a fair way of comparing the favorable region to the total area of possibilities. As a rationalist, Leibniz would have been very pleased to see the principle of indifference generate such an interesting, experimentally testable, precise result.

## BERTRAND'S PARADOX

In 1889 Joseph Louis Bertrand published a collection of probability paradoxes that challenged the principle of indifference. His best known is like Buffon's except that the needle is tossed on a small circle. Here is Bertrand's mathematically pristine formulation: "A chord is drawn *ran-*

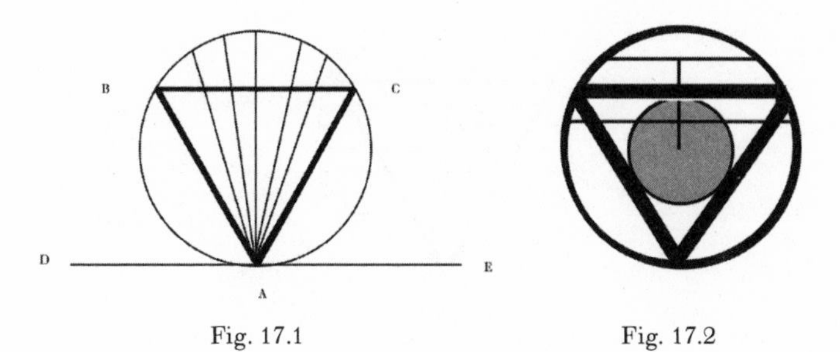


Fig. 17.1

Fig. 17.2

*domly* in a circle. What is the probability that it is longer than the side of the inscribed equilateral triangle?" (1889, 4-5) Bertrand gives three conflicting but apparently cogent answers to this question.

First solution: A chord of a circle is any straight line touching two points of its boundary. For convenience, consider all the chords emanating from point A at a vertex of the equilateral triangle, as in figure 17.1. (The argument can be adapted to points other than at this vertex.) There are chords emanating in every direction 180 degrees from A. Any chord lying within the angle BAC, the "shaded" region, is longer than the sides of the triangle. All the others that start from A must be shorter. Since the inscribed triangle is equiangular, angle BAC is 60 degrees. Therefore, $60/180 = 1/3$ of the chords are longer than the sides of the inscribed triangle. Therefore, the answer is 1/3.

Second solution: A chord is uniquely identified by its midpoint. Now consider the chords that have their midpoints within the small circle. This shaded circle (fig. 17.2) has a radius half of the big circle. Exactly those chords with midpoints within the shaded circle are longer than the side

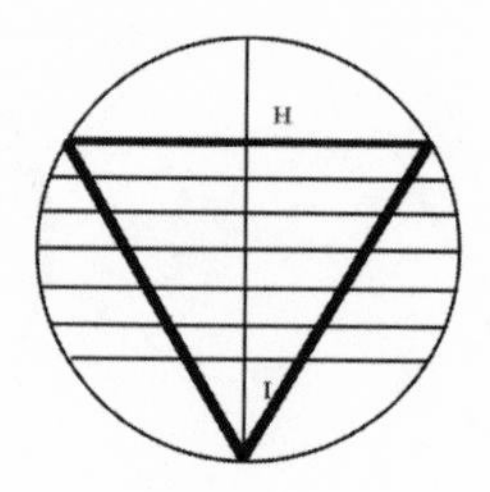


Fig. 17.3

of an equilateral triangle. The small circle has an area ¼ of the big circle. Therefore, the answer is ¼.

Third solution: Consider a line bisecting the triangle and circle, as in figure 17.3. The chords longer than the sides of triangles have their midpoints closer to the center than half the radius, i.e., below H and above I. If the midpoints are distributed uniformly over the radius (instead of over the area, as was the case in the second solution), the probability becomes ½.

Bertrand has presented us with an embarrassment of riches. Each answer is acceptable on its own, both in its reasoning process and its conclusion. The paradox lies in the incompatibility *between* the deductions rather than *within* the deductions themselves. The *deductions* are individually plausible but jointly inconsistent.

The paradoxes of geometrical probability are trouble for theorists who classify each paradox in terms of an argument with an unacceptable conclusion. Bertrand's three-armed antinomy has *three* individually acceptable conclusions.

Those who identify paradoxes with surprising conclusions might reply as follows: Bertrand's paradox uses the separate calculations as the basis for separate subconclusions, which are then recruited into a superargument with three premises: "The probability is ⅓. The probability is ½. The probability is ¼. Therefore, the probability is ⅓ and ½ and ¼." Under this analysis, the paradox is the superconclusion "The probability is ⅓ and ½ and ¼."

This superargument approach cannot be generalized to a case in which there are infinitely many rival calculations. On mathematical grounds, Bertrand believes that there are infinitely many calculations of the above sort. An argument can only have finitely many premises. Therefore, an antinomy with infinitely many arms cannot be compressed into a single argument.

An antinomy is a collection of arguments rather than an argument. Collections can be infinitely large and therefore may contain infinitely many premises and conclusions. There can also be collections of antinomies. As we shall see in chapter 20, Immanuel Kant believed that the Antinomy of Pure Reason was a collection of antinomies that lurk beneath an epochal debate between Leibniz and Samuel Clarke. In principle, antinomies can be ordered in an infinite ascending hierarchy.

In addition to this formal problem, the superargument strategy is strained because simple inspection of the premises is enough to show that the superargument is unsound. We do not need to peek at the contradictory conclusion. Superarguments are not paradoxes for the same reason that jumble arguments (discussed in chapter 8) are not paradoxes.

Bertrand's resolution of his paradox is skepticism: "Among these three answers, which one is proper? None of the three is incorrect, none is correct, the question is ill-posed." (1889, 5) Bertrand belonged to a finitist school of mathematicians who questioned the meaningfulness of questions about infinite choices.

But is the matter so hopeless? E. T. Jaynes acknowledges that Bertrand's paradox "has been cited to generations of students to demonstrate that Laplace's 'principle of indifference' contains logical inconsistencies." (1973, 478) But why not let Mother Nature dictate the right solution to the paradox? Accordingly, Jaynes and a colleague conducted an experiment. One of them tossed broom straws onto a five-inch-diameter circle drawn on the floor. His results suggest that the correct answer is ½.

Bas van Fraassen (1989, chap. 12) is willing to accept Jaynes's experiment as providing the right answer but regards it as a Pyrrhic victory for the principle of indifference. According to van Fraassen, the principle of indifference is supposed to provide initial probabilities without evidence. The idea is that we can always avoid a probability gap (not having any probability to attach to a proposition) by using our very lack of evidence as the basis for assigning probabilities. Jaynes's experiment only solves the problem by accumulating data.

Van Fraassen believes that the principle of indifference manifests the rationalist's dream of getting something from nothing. He thinks Leibniz's correct predictions about the empirical world are like the predictions of self-professed clairvoyants. Some of the accuracy of their predictions is an illusion; clairvoyants make many vague predictions and forget about most of the predictions that are so badly wrong that they cannot be reinterpreted as correct. If the clairvoyant's prediction embodies any genuine knowledge, that is knowledge acquired through surreptitious reliance on observation and experiment. The rationalist may not realize that good old-fashioned perception is the real source of his grand insights into the nature of our world. But if he wants to really understand how he understands the world, he should confine himself to observation and experiment. Or so say van Fraassen's empiricist forefathers. In the next chapter, we will see how well they manage to steer clear of the paradoxes that bedeviled rationalism.

EIGHTEEN

# Hume's All-Consuming Ideas

David Hume (1711–1776) looked more "like a turtle-eating alderman" than a philosopher. When this cheerful Scot became popular in the French salons, the *philosophes* poked fun at his stoutness. Once, as Hume entered a room, d'Alembert quoted from the beginning of St. John's Gospel: "And the word was made flesh." A lady admirer of *le bon David* riposted "And the word was made lovable."

After Hume achieved his ambition of literary fame, his friends urged him to update his best seller, *History of England*. "Gentlemen, you do me too much honor, but I have four reasons for not writing: I am too old, too fat, too lazy, and too rich." Hume preferred supper parties. At one he hosted, a guest complained about the spitefulness of the world. Hume replied "No, no, here am I who have written on all sorts of subjects calculated to excite hostility, moral, political, and religious, and yet I have no enemies, except, indeed, all the Whigs, all the Tories, and all the Christians." (Fadiman 1985, 293)

Hume thought reason offered almost-zero support to common sense and subzero support to religion. Empiricism is about setting limits. Rationalists claim that pure reason can demonstrate substantive facts about the world. Empiricists say that only experience can reveal what exists and how it works. Pure reason can only tell us what follows from what. The revolution in physics seemed to vindicate empiricism by requiring all claims about nature to be backed by observation and experiment.

Starting from these scientific, no-nonsense premises, Hume organizes a feast of paradoxes. First, just as there is no arguing over taste, there is no arguing over ultimate ends. "Ought" judgments are always relative to some stipulated goal. Reason and experience tell us only which means secures which ends. "Reason is and ought to be the slave of the passions, and can never pretend to any other office than to serve and obey them." (1739, 415). A cannibal can rationally prefer to eat his children rather than feed them.

Turning our attention to the main course of nature, we cannot justify the belief that the knife *forces* the flesh to separate from the lamb's thigh bone. We only observe correlations, never causation. Nor can we observe the future. Thus, we have no basis to believe that the future will resemble the past. Yes, bread has nourished in the past. But in the yet-to-be-sampled future, bread is just as apt to be poisonous.

Hume's bad news does not relent if we remain cautiously in the present: We cannot justify beliefs that our ideas faithfully portray the nature of external objects. We cannot even demonstrate that the bowl of cherries continues to exist when everyone leaves the room to sip sherry. Indeed, we have no basis to believe that there are things that exist independently of thoughts.

What goes for objects goes for subjects. The thinkers supposedly responsible for thoughts are no more observable than plates and pudding. Consequently, the belief in substantive selves is a mere prejudice. Descartes's "I think, therefore I exist" overinterprets the data. He is only entitled to observe "There are thoughts."

At the end of this heady evening, all that remains are ideas. Ideas have gradually consumed what they were assigned to represent—including their thinkers.

Hume was pleased by the power of skeptical arguments to damp down superstition and temper religious fanaticism. However, like many circumspect individuals, Hume partly envied the credulous. He regularly attended church services led by a sternly orthodox minister. When Hume was reproached for being inconsistent, he answered, "I don't believe all he says, but *he* does, and once a week I like to hear a man who believes what he says." (Fadiman 1985, 293)

Hume believed that even a master skeptic such as Sextus Empiricus can have only a fleeting effect on ordinary convictions. Common sense and perception are essential to survival. Nature ensures that reason cannot suppress them. While in the study, the philosopher may entertain doubts about whether there are external objects. But once he returns to the company of his friends and society, nature and custom reassert themselves. Aside from religion, the aspiring skeptic winds up believing what his neighbors believe.

Hume's bemused solidarity with the great herd of humanity did not appease his enemies. They perceived Hume as abdicating his responsibility as a philosopher. Instead of justifying our central convictions or extending our knowledge, Hume said that we must content ourselves with psychological explanations. Questions about what we *ought* to believe were to be replaced by a description of how we in fact form beliefs.

David Hume was provocatively slow to distinguish between sages and madmen. This led the ministers and town council to vote against Hume's appointment as a professor of moral philosophy at the University of Edinburgh in 1745. He had to instead become the tutor of a nobleman—who turned out to be insane. Henry Thomas relishes the poetic justice:

> The philosopher and the lunatic lived together in a secluded house. The laird's moods were unpredictable. One day he pressed Hume to his heart. The next day he drove him out of the room. He purred like a kitten and barked like a dog. He leaped over the sofas and scrambled down the banisters. He crept stealthily over the carpets and sprang upon his tutor with a ghostly laugh. Finally they locked him up. He begged to see his tutor and discussed with [him] the perplexing questions of human reason.
>
> (1965, 124)

What a twisted ending! Let's try to understand what went wrong by retracing the steps of British empiricism.

## LOCKE

John Locke (1632-1704) inaugurated the British tradition of empiricism with *An Essay Concerning Human Understanding*. He had earlier discussed human understanding with five or six friends. But they bogged down in verbal disputes, untestable assertions, and circular reasoning. Locke concluded that "before we set our selves upon Enquiries of that Nature, it was necessary to examine our own Abilitys, and see, what Objects our Understandings were, or were not fitted to deal with." (1975, 7:14–33) Instead of aspiring to be one of the master-builders of physics or chemistry, Locke resolves to work as an "Under-Labourer . . . clearing the rubbish that lies in the way of knowledge." (1975, 9:34–10:26)

Locke is an anti-authoritarian who thought it was demeaning "to live lazily on scraps of begg'd Opinions." His guiding principle was that *everything* we learn about the world is through experience. If you have never tasted a pineapple, you cannot have a just idea of how it tastes. Experience is essential for the formation of concepts and therefore for knowledge of the propositions expressed with concepts. He notes that when rationalists have trouble finding any observations to support a principle or to account for our possession of the concept, they do not surrender. Instead, they say the concept or principle is innate. This is a lazy man's method of philosophizing. Locke denies that we have any innate ideas. Babies do not believe that parallel lines never meet. The New World Indians are innocent of the principles touted as universal by the rationalists.

Locke believed that we enter the world as blank slates. As the moving finger of experience writes, we note repetitions of the same type of thing (the fire of a candle and the fire of the hearth) and correlate the occurrence of different types of things (fire and smoke). The rationalists noted that we need general concepts to make these judgments. Thus, they inferred that conceptual knowledge is logically prior to empirical knowledge. Locke tried to simultaneously solve this paradox of inquiry and the problem of universals with a theory of abstraction. According to Locke, we derive the general idea of a cat from a particular idea of a cat by deleting features that are not shared by other cats. The result is a kind of schema that is the meaning of "cat."

You learn that there is a cherry in front of you when light bounces off the cherry and into your open, healthy eyes. The stimulation causes your brain to form an image of the cherry. Since the image can exist without the cherry, you must *infer* the cherry. Illusions and hallucinations show that we never directly perceive external objects. This point was also reinforced by the discovery that light has a finite speed. There is a time lag between the cause of perception and its effect. The Andromeda nebula is visible to the naked eye but the light has taken two million years to reach us. Since the perceiver can only be directly seeing what he is now seeing, he is only *indirectly* perceiving the external causes of his perceptual images.

Locke's theory of perception is known as representative realism: the perceiver must infer external reality from his internal stock of intermediate entities. The "way of ideas" gives rise to the problem of the external world. How can I tell how well my representation of a cherry corresponds to the cherry? This is a serious question of physics. When Galileo constructed his telescope, he had to test the fidelity of its images. At a port, he had a delegation of leading citizens look at distant ships through his telescope. When the ships docked, the citizens could verify that the ships had the details conveyed by the telescopic images two hours before. Telescopic images are mildly distorted. Microscopic images were very distorted. Observations based on microscopes were long subject to reservations that were not extended to telescopes.

Physicists were already suspicious of the fidelity of our visual images. Robert Boyle introduced a distinction between primary and secondary qualities. Primary qualities (shape, mass, distance, motion) are really possessed by objects. Secondary qualities (color, warmth, beauty) are produced by a combination of the object's primary qualities and the psychological makeup of the observer. The cherry is not intrinsically tasty or pretty. The cherry does have an objective chemical constitution that interacts with a tongue to produce the sensation of sweetness. Physicists study primary qualities and so frame their laws in terms of mass and shape, not beauty and sweetness.

Many physicists were (and are) prepared to attribute a massive illusion to human observers. For most of them regard color as a secondary quality. The cherry reflects light in a way that gives rise to a red visual image, but that redness is not a property of the cherry itself. The physicists invidiously compare this deceptiveness to our idea of the roundness of the cherry. Cherries really are round, and our visual image of the cherry faithfully portrays that roundness.

Locke eventually notices that he has trouble vindicating the distinction between primary and secondary qualities. Doubts about the objectivity of secondary qualities seem to spill over to the primary qualities. I can tell how well an engraving of a hippopotamus corresponds to the hippopotamus by visiting the creature itself. But I cannot compare my ideas of a hippopotamus with the hippopotamus itself. I am confined inside a "veil of ideas." While in this claustrophobic mind-set, I am ripe for more radical worries. How do I know whether others experience the world as I do? Perhaps my neighbor experiences colors exactly opposite to my colors (where I see green, she sees red, and so on all around the color wheel). This systematic inversion would not be revealed by how my neighbor sorts ripe tomatoes from green tomatoes—or anything else she does or says.

Locke responds to the problem about the external world by stressing the involuntary nature of perceptual ideas. When a daydreamer envisages a tree in the college quadrangle, he can dictate the size and species of the tree. But when seeing the tree, the images are not under his control. The best explanation of the visual pattern is that it is caused by features of the tree out there in the quad. Physicists engage in the same kind of inference when inferring entities from experimental data.

Locke did become progressively uncomfortable with substances. A substance seems like a vague "something I know not what." Accordingly, he preferred to analyze important concepts in psychological terms—without relying on substances. For instance, Locke analyzed "$x$ is the same person as $y$" as $x$ having the same memories as $y$. If a prince awoke with the memories of a cobbler, then the prince would be that cobbler. Locke's worries about substance were to be dramatically elaborated by subsequent empiricists.

## BERKELEY

The Irishman George Berkeley (1685–1753) believed that Locke's materialistic empiricism deprived God of any explanatory role. This weakens empiricism's ability to withstand skepticism and inadvertently promotes godlessness. Yet, Berkeley was drawn to the intellectual honesty of empiricism. He suspected that Locke had adulterated empiricism with science worship. Locke tried to make empiricism serve as a foundation for the corpuscular physics of his era. Berkeley believed the two were incompatible. True, empiricism is roughly suggested by Newton's physics. But after clarification, Berkeley believed that this same empiricism condemns important elements of Newton's physics: material objects, absolute space, infinitesimals, subvisible matter, atoms, vacuums, etc. The Newtonians' persistent loyalty to these transcendental, mysterious, and downright incoherent objects shows that unscientific Christians have no monopoly on dogmatism.

Berkeley is especially troubled by Locke's theory of abstract ideas. Locke says the general idea of a cat is of an animal that has a color but no particular color, weight but of no particular weight, gender but is neither male nor female. This indeterminacy is unimaginable. What cannot be conceived cannot exist. There is no abstract idea of a cat. The illustrious Locke is babbling.

There are only particular ideas that are used abstractly. Consider a woman who has moved into an empty house and is deciding where to deploy her furniture. Instead of moving the furniture around, she places rags on the floor to represent respectively her sofa, cabinet, chair, clock, and mirror. She compares various layouts by attending only to the locations of the rags, not their size or shape or colors. Her abstract reasoning is evident from the manner in which she handles particular rags, not her possession of entities that are intrinsically general.

Berkeley directs equal suspicion against Locke's "ideas" of material objects. There certainly are sofas and mirrors and cherries. We sit in sofas, gaze into mirrors, and eat cherries. But material objects are supposed to be things that underlie these experiences. According to Locke's distinction between primary and secondary qualities, the cherry looks red but is not red. It tastes sweet but is not sweet in itself. The cherry itself only has the primary qualities of mass, shape, etc. But Berkeley objects that ideas can only resemble other ideas.

When Galileo compared telescopic images of the ship to the ship as viewed close up, he was comparing images with images. Arguments for the mind-dependence of color apply and are equally effective in showing the mind-dependence of shape, size, and distance.

Berkeley also opposed the distinction between primary and secondary qualities on the more radical grounds that the idea of a material object is incoherent. Our idea of a cherry is necessarily of something that is sweet and red. The true spirit of empiricism is to go with appearances. Hence, an empiricist should reject material reality as a fabrication of philosophers. To be is to be perceived.

Berkeley could not fail to realize that his idealism seems to fly in the face of common sense. A bishop condemned young Berkeley for his vain pursuit of novelty. Upon reading Berkeley's *Principles of Human Knowledge*, a physician diagnosed the author as insane. Even one of Berkeley's great allies, the satirist Jonathan Swift, instructed his servants not to open the door for the visiting Berkeley on the grounds that Berkeley believed that he could walk through doors.

Since one of the ideas associated with the door is impenetrability, Berkeley had a ready explanation of why he could not pass through a door. He could also explain why all was not a dream by appealing to the orderliness of waking experience.

Berkeley was more heavy-handed when asked why objects continue to exist when we no longer perceive them. Berkeley's answer was that *God* continues to perceive objects that no human being observes.

Critics insisted that Berkeley's slogan "To be is to be perceived" must be mistaken because they could imagine an unobserved tree. What can be conceived, can possibly exist.

So the existence of the tree does not imply the existence of a perceiver.

Berkeley characterized this thought experiment as self-defeating. The person who claims to be imagining an unperceived tree envisages it from a particular angle and in color. In any case, the very act of imagination is a kind of perception.

Is it? In 1827 the pious Swiss painter Leopold Robert offended some viewers of his "Two Girls Disrobing for Their Bath." He assured them that "I have placed the figures in a completely secluded spot so that they would not possibly encounter any observation from onlookers." (Fadiman 1985, 471) The embarrassed artist Robert is reaching for a genuine distinction between observing a depiction of disrobing girls and depicting the observation of disrobing girls. A rejoinder to Berkeley can be fashioned in the same syntax: Someone can imagine a tree without imagining someone imagining the tree.

Berkeley presents himself as the defender of common sense. It is his opponents who are postulating unobservable entities that skulk beneath the ordinary world of appearances. Occasionally, Berkeley concedes that even ordinary people believe in material objects: "It is indeed an opinion strangely prevailing amongst men, that houses, mountains, rivers, and in a word all sensible objects have an existence natural or real, distinct from their being perceived by the understanding." (1986, 1, 4)

If there is no idea corresponding to "material object," how can people form the belief that mountains are material objects? How can Locke mistakenly believe that there are abstract ideas if he cannot even conceive of them? Berkeley poked fun at Newton's notion of an infinitesimal. But how could he joke about Newton's notion if the idea does not exist to be ridiculed?

## HUME AGAIN

David Hume accepts the bulk of Berkeley's criticisms of Locke. As an admirer of Cicero's mix of skepticism and Stoicism, Hume has no interest in fighting skepticism (especially if reason is to be suited in the armor of theology). Hume is willing to let the chips fall where they may. He accepts empiricism as a distillation of the only resources for justifying beliefs. If a belief cannot be put in accord with the way of ideas, then Hume is not willing to engage in heroic measures to save it. The Stoic empiricist must be detached enough to accept bad news. If the belief is still ambulatory after public decapitation, Hume concludes that its presence never depended on reason.

Hume began his career with comparative optimism. He hoped to do for the mind what Newton did for the physical universe. He increased the empiricist's resources by characterizing Locke's opposition to innate ideas as a confused overreaction to rationalist excesses. The empiricist is free to admit that we are born with many ideas. He need only deny that these ideas *justify* any beliefs. Hume distinguished between concept empiricism (all our ideas come from experience) and judgment empiricism (all justified propositions are justified by experience). The empiricist can further admit that children mature in stages. Thus, their cognitive development need not be characterized as a continuous accumulation of experience. When the child's ability to process experience suddenly expands, so will his empirical knowledge.

Hume liberalized ethics and aesthetics by allowing more room for emotion and feelings. The empiricist does not need to construe moral justification as the product of observation and experiment. Right and wrong come down to what would please an ideal judge. This mild idealization takes away prejudice and ignorance but is intended to preserve the humanity of the judge. The ideal judge is still animated by emotions—just untainted emotions.

Hume enforces this emotive approach by contending that there is an is/ought gap. Past ethicists began from premises describing empirical realities and then moved on to claims about what ought to be the case. According to Hume, moral arguments require moral premises. These premises about what *ought* to be the case cannot be deduced solely from premises about what *is* the case. Consequently, ethicists cannot answer "Why be moral?" For Hume, the question of moral motivation never arises because morality is a matter of feeling.

He argues that there is also a gap in inductive reasoning. How do we know that the sun will rise tomorrow? True, the sun has risen repeatedly in the past. But that does not entail the sun will rise tomorrow. We can conceive of the earth standing still or the sun exploding. Thus, there is no *deductive* justification for "The sun will rise tomorrow." Could there be inductive justification? Only if we are justified in believing that the future will resemble the past. We can imagine this proposition being false, so it cannot be established deductively. But any inductive argument for "The future will resemble the past" will rely on that principle itself and so be circular. For instance, some say the future will resemble the past because past futures have always resembled past pasts. But this does nothing to remove the possibility that there is a discontinuity between past futures and future futures.

Hume realized that the empiricist has trouble inferring causes from correlations. We can observe that when a moving billiard ball strikes a stationary billiard ball, then the ball that was at rest begins to move. But we do not witness the first ball *forcing* the second ball to move. The common sense notion of causation includes this notion of natural necessitation. Thus, the empiricist is not in a position to save the initially plausible idea that people observe some things causing other things.

To make this verdict more palatable, Hume offered a psychological explanation of why we mistakenly believe ourselves to directly perceive the first billiard ball causing the second ball to move. When we see an event of type A followed by an event of type B, *force of habit* leads us to expect B. We project this inner sense of necessity onto the event.

One consolation of banishing causality is that it no longer menaces free choice. If natural necessitation is a myth, then one is not compelled to do anything. Hume thinks of freedom negatively, as freedom from duress and obstacles. Thus, we can be free regardless of how thickly scientists weave their web of correlations.

Hume thinks another kind of projection occurs when our perception is interrupted. If I am viewing Edinburgh's mountain, Arthur's Seat, and then briefly shut my eyes, Arthur's Seat looks the same after I open them. This steadiness of appearance leads me to a steady expectation of the same appearance. I project the continuity onto the mountain itself. A more complicated interpolation occurs with things that change in predictable ways. I know how a log will appear as it burns down. This pattern of alteration in my expectations gets projected onto the log itself. "The imagination, when it is set into any train of thinking, is apt to continue even when its object fails it, and, like a galley put in motion by the oars, carries on its course without any new impulse." (1739, 198) We feign a continuous existence even though we are not justified in these interpolations.

The empiricist who has such trouble establishing the external world might be expected to find a welcome contrast when searching for the self. What could be more accessible to you than your own self! But Hume reports that, as far as his own case is concerned, his harvest only yields more ideas.

The best empirical sense Hume can make of the self is that it is a bundle of ideas. The bundle theory has the virtue of forestalling some paradoxes about substance. If, as Aristotle believes, substances have priority over properties, then we can ask what the world would be like if Julius Caesar had all the properties of Mark Antony and Mark Antony had all the properties of Julius Caesar (even to the extent of Caesar being called by "Mark Antony" and vice versa). This world would look exactly like ours. The indistinguishability inclines many to deny that we have described a distinct possible world. We have only described our own world in different language. Leibniz solves this paradox with the principle of the identity of indiscernibles: no two substances have exactly the same properties. But Hume's bundle theory solves the theory at a more radical level by saying that there are no substances of the sort that have priority over properties. If one pictures substances as cushions into which one can plunge pins (properties), then it makes sense to ask what pure substances are. It also makes sense to exchange every pin from one cushion with every pin of another cushion. But if substances are just collections of pins, then these questions about substance cannot arise.

But the bundle theory has its own paradoxes. The basic problem is that bundles are too arbitrary to sustain intuitive distinctions about selves. What makes one bundle of ideas *me* and another bundle *you*? Not the fact that *I* thought of the ideas constituting my bundle. For that reintroduces a substance that has priority over its properties. Not the implications between the ideas in my bundle. For ideas are "loose and separate"; the existence of one idea never necessitates or precludes the existence of another idea. Given that there are only ideas, there is no justification of my conviction that there has been only one self associated with my stream of ideas rather than a succession of momentary selves, one for each idea. Hume concedes that he is "invol'd in such a labyrinth, that, I must confess, I neither know how to correct my former opinions, nor how to render them consistent."

> In short, there are two principles, which I cannot render consistent; nor is it in my power to renounce either of them, viz. *that all our distinct perceptions are distinct existences, and that the mind never perceives any real connexion among distinct existences.* Did our perceptions either inhere in something simple and individual, or did the mind perceive some real connexion among them, there would be no difficulty in the case. For my part I must plead the privilege of a sceptic, and confess, that this difficulty is too hard for my understanding.
>
> (1739, 636)

NINETEEN

# The Common Sense of Thomas Reid

War and civil unrest became increasingly prominent in European consciousness after the Protestant Reformation. Paradoxes became described in militaristic terms. Rationalists defended themselves from atop a citadel of mathematics and pure reason. The empiricists retreated to the growing fortress of physics. Thomas Reid takes the battle out to the plains of common sense.

Reid prefaces his *Inquiry into the Human Mind: On the Principles of Common Sense* by remarking,

> that I never thought of calling into question the principles commonly received with regard to the human understanding, until the "Treatise of Human Nature" was published in the year 1739. The ingenious author of that treatise upon the principles of Locke—who is not sceptic—hath built a system of scepticism, which leaves no ground to believe any one thing rather than its

> contrary. His reasoning appeared to me to be just; there was, therefore, a necessity to call in question the principles upon which it was founded, or to admit the conclusion.
>
> (1764, 1)

Reid actually traces the principles to Descartes. If you believe that you directly perceive only ideas, then any beliefs you have about things outside this private realm must be justified by an inference. If you can show that a proposition cannot be proved from premises about our ideas, you have shown that it is not held on rational grounds.

Descartes characterized ideas as supremely knowable. They have no hidden properties. Ideas are exactly as they appear to be. They set the standard for certainty. Truths about ideas are Archimedean points that allow reason to pry out myths from the otherwise immovable earth of common sense. Given Descartes's Way of Ideas, reason operates as a tribunal that oversees the deliverances of all other faculties. Reid wrote:

> The defects and blemishes in the received philosophy concerning the mind, which have most exposed it to the contempt and ridicule of sensible men, have chiefly been owing to this—that the votaries of this Philosophy, from a natural prejudice in her favour, have endeavored to extend her jurisdiction beyond its just limits, and to call to her bar the dictates of Common Sense. But these decline this jurisdiction; they disdain the trial of reasoning, and disown its authority; they neither claim its aid nor dread its attacks.
>
> (1764, I, iv)

Reid's project is to restore the dignity of philosophy. Hume has inadvertently demonstrated the absurdity of the way of ideas. Reid's negative task is to diagnose why this doctrine seems so attractive and why it fails. His positive task is to replace the Way of Ideas with an alternative theory of perception and knowledge that conforms with common sense. Although I am a convert to Reid's causal theory of perception, I shall concentrate on his account of common sense.

## NATURE OF COMMON SENSE

Reid characterizes common sense as a body of beliefs that issues from a faculty that nearly all human beings exercise daily. Since the source is the same, common-sense beliefs are universal and coeval with the origin of mankind. Unlike science, common sense is immutable and so does not make progress. Aside from infants and lunatics, there is massive agreement about our environment and each other. These propositions are compulsively believed because they are essential to health and safety. Since children also need to survive, common-sense beliefs "appear so early in the minds of men that they cannot be the effect of education or of false reasoning." They are reflected in the distinctions present in all natural languages: male/female, substance/quality, active/passive, past/present/future, etc.

The universality of common-sense beliefs make them too trite to articulate. However, this does not stop them from having the status of first principles. Common-sense beliefs are self-evident. There is no searching for evidence, no consulting of authorities, no chains of deduction. The negations of common-sense beliefs are immediately recognized as false:

> We may observe that opinions which contradict first principles, are distinguished, from other errors, by this:— That they are not only false but absurd; and, to discountenance absurdity, Nature hath given us a particular emotion—to wit, that of ridicule—which seems intended for this very purpose of putting out of countenance what is absurd, either in opinion or practice.
>
> (1764, VI, iv)

The emotion fitted to paradox is amusement. A conclusion that runs contrary to common sense would be dangerous to take seriously.

Given the compulsive nature of common sense, people who oppose it generally lapse into inconsistency. General doubts are never consummated with particulars. If you stroll with a skeptic, he will deny that he is justified in believing that he is approaching a post. But he will gingerly walk around it. This gives him away as a hypocrite. Thus, paradoxes often provide a secondary source of amusement—the conflict between the paradox-monger's words and deeds.

Is this *argumentum ad hominem*? Yes, says Reid, but it is a "good *ad hominem*, if it can be shewn that a first principle which a man rejects, stands upon the same footing with others which he admits: for, when this is the case, he must be guilty of an inconsistency who holds the one and rejects the other." (1764, VI, iv)

The judgments of common sense are overlapping axioms from which reason can prove theorems that are not self-evident. Reid believes that these axioms are consistent with each other. Thus, he disagrees with those who think some paradoxes are built from internal conflicts within common sense. Reid also rejects Hume's frequent diagnosis of the paradoxes as arising from a conflict between reason and common sense. The job of common sense is to judge what is self-evident. The job of reason is to draw conclusions that are not self-evident from those that are. Therefore, reason must always coincide with common sense.

Geometers prefer that axioms be independent of each other. This helps reduce the number of axioms. One price of this economy is that deductions tend to be longer. Common sense needs to be fast, so it has a large number of axioms that are organically connected to each other. When it comes to common sense, we cannot pick and choose. We must accept the entire root system.

Reid admits that there is vagueness about the boundaries of common sense. He does not attempt to exhaustively list all of its principles. However, he specifies the principles pertinent to philosophy. Many of these are contingent truths. Reid tends to couch them as premises that can be readily marshaled against Hume's skepticism:

1. That the thoughts of which I am conscious are thoughts of a being which I call MYSELF, my MIND, my PERSON.
2. That those things did really happen which I distinctly remember.
3. That we have some degree of power over our actions, and the determinations of our will.
4. That there is life and intelligence in our fellow men with whom we converse.
5. That there is a certain regard due to human testimony in matters of fact, and even to human authority in matters of opinion.

6. That, in the phaenomena of nature, what is to be, will probably be like what has been in similar circumstances.

Other principles of common sense concern necessary truths. Some concern grammar, such as, Every complete sentence must have a verb. Yet others concern logic: every proposition is either true or false; none is both truth and false; circular reasoning proves nothing; whatever is affirmed of the genus may be affirmed of the species. Hume had claimed that we cannot form any idea of geometrical figure (such as a straight line) which is not a copy of an earlier impression. Reid counters with common-sense geometry.

Reid did not forget how Hume got his foot in the door of ethics by noting that there is no arguing over taste. Reid confronts Hume at the top of this slippery slope with first principles concern matters of taste. He thinks judgments of beauty can be rational and true. Morality also has first principles; for example, no one is to be blamed for what he has no power to hinder. Reid resists Hume's view that moral judgments express feelings rather than judgments.

Reid's list also includes metaphysical first principles: for instance, thoughts must have a subject (a thinker) and anything that begins to exist must have a cause. Defenders of the design argument for the existence of God will find uses for this principle: "That design and intelligence in the cause may be inferred, with certainty, from marks or signs of it in the effect." The universe is so orderly that it is readily described as a giant, intricate machine. Where there is an artifact, it is reasonable to infer a maker of powers and foresight proportional to the effect.

Reid's common sense looks like an impression left by Hume; concave where Hume is convex, convex where Hume is concave. One explanation is that common sense is reactive. We do not bother to defend (or even think about) the proposition that the future resembles the past until David Hume formulates the problem of induction. Paradoxes illuminate common sense by provoking bits of it into consciousness. As more paradoxes are discovered, more of common sense becomes visible. Without a provocateur, common sense is faceless.

## COMMON SENSE AND PHILOSOPHICAL ARGUMENT

Like Reid, Sydney Smith was a Scottish clergyman. Smith helped found the *Edinburgh Review*. One day Smith and a friend encountered two women screaming insults at each other from second-story windows at the opposite sides of a narrow Edinburgh street. "Those two will never resolve their differences," remarked Smith, "They are speaking from separate premises." (Fadiman 1985, 514)

Reid thought debate with skeptics was futile because of a lack of shared premises. The first principle of common sense is that the natural faculties are not fallacious. Any proof of this principle would be circular because reason is itself a faculty. If anyone were to reject this principle, "it would be impossible by argument to beat him out of his stronghold; and he must even be left to enjoy his scepticism." (1764, VI, 5)

Reid is too pessimistic. Incompatible premises can imply the same conclusion. When my watch says it is 1:10 and yours says it is 1:15, they conflict. Yet each entail that it is past 1:00. You can change your adversary's conclusion by reasoning from *his* premises and *his* inference rules. In 1684, the British playwright

Nathaniel Lee was confined in the London asylum Bedlam. A friend, who had heard Lee was suffering one of his bouts of insanity, visited him. To his relief, he found Lee calm and reasonable. Lee took his friend on a tour around the asylum. His friend's hopes soared. When they eventually reached the roof of the asylum, Lee suddenly gripped his friend's arm and excitedly exclaimed, "Let us immortalize ourselves; let us leap down this moment!" Lee's friend coolly responded: "Any man could leap *down*, so we should not immortalize ourselves that way. But let us go down and try if we can leap *up*." Nathaniel Lee was delighted by this counterproposal and ran down the stairs to see if he could put it into practice. (Fadiman 1985, 348)

Although Reid sometimes harshly characterizes his adversaries as "metaphysical lunatics," he distinguishes them from the institutionalized variety. Metaphysical lunatics only have fleeting departures from common sense.

> We are born under a necessity of trusting to our reasoning and judging powers; and a real belief of their being fallacious cannot be maintained for any considerable time by the greatest Sceptic, because it is doing violence to our constitution. It is like a man's walking upon his hands, a feat which some men upon occasion can exhibit; but no man ever made a long journey in this manner. Cease to admire his dexterity, and he will, like other men, betake himself to his legs.
>
> (1785, VI, 5)

## FOLLOWING THE ARGUMENT

Reid compared the power of reason to walking. It is acquired and sustained by exercise. Nature prompts our first steps.

"After repeated efforts, much stumbling, and many falls, we learn to walk; and it is in a similar manner that we learn to reason." Philosophers tend to arbitrarily elevate reason above the other faculties of perception and common sense. Reid thinks reason can never override common sense:

> The sceptic asks me, Why do you believe the existence of the external object which you perceive? This belief, sir, is none of my manufacture; it came from the mint of Nature; it bears her image and superscription; and, if it is not right, the fault is not mine: I even took it upon trust, and without suspicion. Reason, says the sceptic, is the only judge of truth, and you ought to throw off every opinion and every belief that is not grounded on reason. Why, sir, should I believe the faculty of reason more than that of perception?—they came both out of the same shop, and were made by the same artist; and if he puts one piece of false ware into my hands, what should hinder him from putting another?
>
> (1764, VI, xx)

Philosophers who follow the Way of Ideas are guilty of a double standard. They meekly accept the deliverances of introspection, yet they eye the deliverances of perception and memory with suspicion. In truth, the deliverances of introspection seem *more* doubtful. We have trouble attending to the workings of our own minds. After all, sensations are designed to aid perception. They are not designed to be objects of perception in their own right.

Socrates said that we should follow the argument wherever it leads. Descartes supports Socrates with an analogy. If a traveler is lost in a forest, then he should continue to walk as straight as he can in one direction. The traveler may not end up where he wished, but he will probably be better off than in the middle of the forest.

True, when people are bereft of landmarks, they tend to walk in circles. But is philosophy typically a journey with no clues along the way? At the very least, says Reid, philosophers can use information about where they end up to assess the correctness of their route: "A traveller of good judgment may mistake his way, and be unawares led into a wrong track; and, while the road is fair before him, he may go on without suspicion and be followed by others; but when it ends in a coal-pit, it requires no great judgment to know that he hath gone wrong." (1764, introduction, VIII) Any conflict with common sense is a sure sign that there is a mistake somewhere. We do not need to wait for a diagnosis of the error before rejecting the argument.

## CRITICISMS OF REID'S CONCEPTION OF COMMON SENSE

In a letter to Hugh Blair dated July 4, 1762, Hume objects to Reid's oversophistication of common sense:

> The Author supposes, that the Vulgar do not believe the sensible Qualities of Heat, Smell, sound, & probably Colour to be really in the Bodies, but only their Causes or something capable of producing them in the Mind. But this is imagining the Vulgar to be Philosophers & Corpuscularians from the Infancy. You know what pains it cost Malebranche & Locke to establish that Principle. There are but obscure Traces of it among the Ancients viz in the Epicurean School. The Peripatetics maintained opposite Princi-

> ples. And indeed Philosophy scarce ever advances a greater Paradox in the Eyes of the People, than when it affirms that Snow is neither cold nor white: Fire hot nor red.
>
> (Aberdeen University Library MS 2814/139)

Subsequent philosophers share Hume's suspicion that Reid gerrymanders the constituency of common sense to ensure that it is never defeated. The American pragmatist C. S. Peirce (1839-1914) thought that common sense courts this illicit support because it is so vague. It is common sense that there is some order in nature, but only more specific descendants precisifications of that amorphous conviction are open to refutation.

Peirce agrees with Reid that common-sense beliefs are indubitable. Hume only had "paper doubts." Peirce characterized strong thinkers as great breath-holders. Holding your breath against a belief is not doubting it. But unlike Reid, Peirce denies that indubitability implies truth. As a fallibilist, Peirce thinks any of our beliefs could be mistaken. Still, Peirce does not think *all* of our beliefs could be false.

Henry Sidgwick maintained that science and philosophy "continually at once corrects and confirms crude Common Sense." (1905, 425) This great mass of ore must be smelted by philosophers to remove "inadvertencies, confusions, and contradictions." (1905, 428) His *Methods of Ethics* (1874) shows how the morality of common sense incorporates awkward compromises between conflicting ideas, how it trails off into vagueness and vicious incompleteness. He presents utilitarianism as a moral theory that conservatively streamlines common sense.

Many philosophers believe common sense has a self-amendment clause. G. F. Stout (1860–1944) conceived of common sense as less a matter of specific beliefs and more a matter of general tendencies to form beliefs. He viewed science and philosophy as polishing away the animistic rough edges of common sense ("the tendency to find Mind in Nature generally"). Stout thought common sense always has the last word because philosophical and scientific challenges only succeed when they use common sense to overcome the presumption not to change common sense.

Bertrand Russell denies that common sense must always be accommodated. He quipped "Common sense implies physics and physics refutes common sense." As vague as common sense is, it still makes falsifiable claims.

The most famous common-sense philosopher of the twentieth century, G. E. Moore, admitted that common sense underestimates the distance from the earth to other heavenly bodies. G. E. Moore makes no attempt to define common sense but he is generous with examples: the earth has existed for many years past; inhabitants of the earth have been in contact with one another; they have also been at various distances from each other; and all this is common knowledge. As tame as these truisms may seem, philosophers propose theses that conflict with them. Parmenides did deny the reality of time and this conflicts with the statement, The earth has existed for many years.

Moore's specimen box also contains propositions that must be expressed with the demonstratives *here, now*, and *that.* In his lecture "A Proof of the External World," Moore held up one hand to support the premise "Here is a hand," then another hand in support of "And here is another," and concluded "Therefore, there are at least two material things." Moore refutes philosophical theses by bringing the abstract into unadorned conflict with the concrete. This style of argument is backed by a principle of weighted certainties. He thought the propositions of common sense were far more evident than the philosophical premises used by idealists and skeptics. So even if common sense is fallible, *philosophy* cannot hope to overturn it.

This special restriction on philosophy is suspicious in light of Moore's concession that astronomy has overturned common-sense beliefs about the distance to the stars. There is ample historical evidence that parts of philosophy develop into science. If philosophy leads to science and science overturns common sense, then philosophy must at least have an indirect ability to overturn common sense.

Moore also neglects the extent to which philosophers prompt a change of mind by pointing out conflicts (and convergences) that are independent of their own philosophies. Logicians are especially fond of being neutral commentators who point out that the claimants for our credence are operating at cross-purposes.

## THE SCIENTIFIC STUDY OF COMMON SENSE

Computer scientists initially tried to manufacture intelligence by getting computers to perform tasks that human beings find intellectually challenging: calculating missile trajectories, breaking codes, winning at chess. Progress was rapid after the first electronic computers were developed in World War II. The achievements of these electronic brains were humbling: problems that are hard for people are easy for computers. Was there anything computers could not do?

Computers do have trouble coping with combinatorial explosions. Consider a traveling salesman who wants to know the shortest route connecting a number of cities. As the number of cities increases, the number of possible routes grows exponentially. A computer that is programmed to solve the problem by brute force will rust out before examining all the possible paths that exist between 100 cities. Computer scientists respond by giving up the goal of finding the shortest route in favor of the more tractable goal of *probably* finding a route that is *close* to the shortest. This scaled-back objective allows the computer to focus on promising routes.

In 1969, John McCarthy and Patrick Hayes published their discovery of a *general* combinatorial explosion: the frame problem. How can a computer update knowledge of a changing situation? The objects and properties that make up a situation are interdependent. Thus, the number of possible side effects grows exponentially with the number of objects and the number of properties they may possess. Suppose my plan is to illuminate a room by walking over to the light switch and flipping it on. How do I know that my first step will not break the light bulb? How do I know that my second step will not make the light switch scurry to a new location on the wall? These are silly questions. Their philosophical air is due to an absence of common sense. But unlike human beings, computers do not develop common sense on their own. To solve the frame problem, researchers must artificially instill common sense. They must introduce "frame axioms" analogous to Reid's first principles. The computer scientists are guided by the sort of paradoxes that Reid relies upon in his pioneering efforts.

Psychologists who study common sense have been influenced by both computers and evolutionary theory. Reid thought common sense was created by God, so Reid could easily explain its perfections. The hypothesis of divine design has much more trouble accounting for imperfections. Accordingly, Reid is reluctant to admit any flaws in common sense.

The evolutionary account of common sense easily explains the imperfections of common sense but has more trouble accounting for its perfections. If common sense is an adaptive trait, then we cannot depend on God's foresight.

Evolution cannot take one step back to take two steps forward. Natural selection develops traits short-sightedly, with each step forward requiring an immediate payoff. It is a blind hill-climber. In a terrain with many hills, it will arrive at a summit but almost certainly not the highest summit. For once natural selection climbs to the top of a small hill, the rule "Always go up!" vetoes a precondition for moving to a higher hill. Common sense is a collection of local optima. Little wonder that people, with the benefit of foresight, can artificially do better than common sense.

Evolution cannot afford to put all its eggs in one basket. Common sense must be a diversified collection of judgmental tendencies. One part must be permitted to fail without a catastrophic collapse of the corporate body. If God had designed common sense in one omniscient swoop, then it could be the sort of all-or-nothing package Reid envisaged. But common sense must have more of the modular character that computer scientists will inevitably confer on their common-sense computers (if the frame problem is soluble).

Reid says that only infants and lunatics lack common sense. The contrasts are more nuanced than this. Developmental psychologists have shown that children develop common sense in stages. For instance, naive physics is acquired before naive psychology. The ability to attribute desires matures before the ability to attribute beliefs. Three-year-old children operate under the assumption that others believe what they do. Consequently, they have trouble attributing *false* beliefs.

Mental disorders are also more diverse than Reid assumed. The mental disorder of autism suggests that the acquisition of naive physics is not invariably followed by the acquisition of naive psychology. Other mental disorders suggest that common sense is composed of modules that can be selectively incapacitated. Philosophers have an interest in these diseases of common sense; they show paradoxes operating in a genuinely pathological manner.

Developmental psychology and abnormal psychology are "philosophical" areas of psychology. Like philosophy, they illuminate common sense by studying what happens when common sense fails to operate.

TWENTY

# Kant and the Antinomy of Pure Reason

Dr. Jean-Christophe Marchand conjectures that the *Critique of Pure Reason* was produced by a brain tumor. Until the age of forty-seven, the scientist Immanuel Kant wrote clearly. Astronomers recognize him as the inventor of the nebular hypothesis: planets, stars, and galaxies formed from dust that swirled together under the force of gravity. In the *Natural History and Theory of the Heavens* Kant writes, "Millions and whole myriads of millions of centuries will flow on, during which always new worlds and systems of worlds will be formed. . . . The creation is never finished or complete."

Kant (1724-1804) had an active social life that consisted mostly of dinner parties. There are a few hints at romance. In one letter, dated June 12, 1762, Frau Maria Charlotta Jacobi sends Kant a kiss from her and her girlfriend. She suggests that Kant "may wind her watch" the next time they meet.

Kant continued to publish steadily until 1771. Then he fell into his silent decade. In 1781, Kant emerged with the

*Critique of Pure Reason.* The topics are dizzyingly abstract. Sentences, tottering with jargon, soldier on for a whole page. German students prefer to read Norman Kemp Smith's English translation; The *Critique of Pure Reason* loses something in the original.

Kant's explorations of our innate cognitive architecture allow little role for emotions. This is salient in his subsequent ethical writings. Kant insists that morality is a matter of rigorous consistency. Cutting in line is wrong because you cannot consistently will that all members of the queue be permitted to occupy any position. Lying is wrong because you would fall into a contradiction if you willed that all testimony can be insincere. Kant explicitly forbids any exceptions. You cannot lie to save an innocent man from a murderer!

Kant emphasizes duty over kindness. Consider a lifeguard who rescues a boy. The less she likes the boy, the surer we can be that her motivation is *moral.* Rightness is a matter of following the appropriate rule. Like William of Ockham, Kant denies the moral relevance of consequences. The lifeguard deserves no more praise for a successful rescue than an unsuccessful rescue. What matters is following the correct maxims, not securing benefits that accrue from this obedience.

Granted, Kant stresses respect for persons. But often this is expressed negatively, as revulsion toward treating people as objects instead of free agents. He thinks our sensual side leads us to treat others as sexual objects. Kant compares womanizers to cannibals. Kant opposed birth control. He viewed sexual relations even within marriage as unsavory.

Many people are turned off by Kant's loathing of our sensual side, by his stiff subordination of emotion to reason, and above all, by his inhumane writing style. They suspect something is wrong with Kant. The neuroscientist Michael Gazzaniga backs Marchand's *argumentum ad cranium*:

> Kant began to complain of headaches and other maladies and gradually lost vision in his left eye. Dr. Marchand deduced that Kant had a left prefrontal lobe tumor—growing slowly, but there. Damage to this area affects language ability and the ability of our emotional system to cue us toward good cognitive strategy. Is it possible that all those Kantians have saluted a man who was writing nonsense—a philosophy for those who do not have a normal cognitive and emotional system?
>
> (1998, 121)

I think Gazzaniga's query is answered by the continuity of Kant's private correspondence. Kant's letters from age 40 to 60 do not reveal any change in his linguistic competence. When addressing nonphilosophers, Kant abstains from technical terms and streamlines his syntax. His letters evince the normal emotional range of a busy Prussian academic. If Gazzaniga did not harbor antecedent doubts about the value of Kant's philosophy, he would no more challenge Kant's talk of the "transcendental unity of apperception" than he would challenge the cant of quantum mechanics.

Gazzaniga intimates that Kant's disciples were so cowed that they could not detect a lapse into nonsense. Severely retarded sufferers of "chatterbox syndrome" have normal, even overdeveloped, linguistic faculties that enable them to pass as hypersophisticated conversationalists. They love big words. Listeners eventually detect empirical errors and a general failure to connect words with deed. Since philosophy professors are not expected to connect their esoteric discourse with practical affairs, it is more difficult to convict them of speaking nonsense.

However, after Kant entered his seventies, his followers were the first to detect cognitive decline. As Kant inched toward senility, acquaintances grimly joked that he was being "de-Kanted." Even Kant's dull-witted servant of forty years, Martin Lampe, began to exploit his master's growing confusion. A former student, who was then overseeing Kant's affairs, had to pension off Lampe. Kant continued to call his new servant "Lampe." To compensate for his disintegrating short-term memory, Kant wrote himself copious notes. One of these resolves that "the name Lampe must now be completely forgotten." In *Kant: A Biography*, Manfred Kuehn writes, "This kind of performative contradiction is perhaps more indicative of his condition than any of the other anecdotes that are told about the old Kant." (2001, 417-18)

Augustine regarded vulnerability to paradox as a sign of fallen reason. And before Augustine, Sextus Empiricus pioneered the analogy between paradoxes and diseases. Kant breaks from this negative tradition by construing "the antinomies" of theoretical reason as a sign of mental *normality*.

## THE FOUR ANTINOMIES OF PURE REASON

In the *Critique of Pure Reason*, Kant presented the four "antinomies of pure reason" as overextensions of reason's pursuit of completeness. By antinomy, Kant means a pair of apparently impeccable arguments for opposite conclusions. His formulation of the arguments was affected by a recent, titanic debate between Gottfried Leibniz and Samuel Clarke (a spokesman for Isaac Newton). After discussing the four transcendental ideas that underlie the antinomies, Kant presents the pros and cons side by side.

**THESIS**

The world has a beginning in time, and is also limited as regards space.

**PROOF**

If we assume that the world has no has no beginning in time, then up to every given moment an eternity has elapsed, and there has passed away an infinite series of successive states of things. . . .

**ANTITHESIS**

The world has no beginning, and no limits in space; it is infinite as regards both time and space.

**PROOF**

For let us assume that it has a beginning. Since the beginning is an existence which is preceded by a time in which the thing is not, there must have been a preceding time in which the world was not, i.e.an empty time. . . .

Each competing proof takes on the air of a *reductio ad absurdum*. Instead of directly deducing the conclusion, the arguments suppose the opposite of what they are designed to prove and then deduce a contradiction.

In this first antinomy, Kant supposes, for the sake of contradiction, that there is an infinite past. He then infers there must have been an infinite wait to reach the present moment. An infinite wait cannot be complete. Yet here we are at the present moment. So the wait must have only been finite.

The antithetical arm of the antinomy supposes that the world has a beginning. Prior to the commencement of time, there must have been a stage in which there was no time. Change implies time. Nothing can happen in a timeless era. History would be stalled at the starting line!

These arguments about time have implications for space. To conceive of the universe as containing infinitely many things, you must imagine an inventory being made of all the objects. But if you only have finite time to make a list, that survey can only be finitely long. Therefore, a universe that contains infinitely many things is inconceivable.

To establish that the totality of things in space is infinite, we extract an absurdity from the supposition that this totality is limited within infinite space. Consider the region of space in which there are no longer any objects. This region is a vacuum. But a vacuum is nothing and nothing cannot limit anything.

Something has gone wrong! It is possible for there to be two valid *direct* arguments for incompatible conclusions, for one of the arguments could have a false premise. But an indirect argument has no premises. In particular, a *reductio ad absurdum* just supposes a proposition, deduces a contradiction without the help of further premises, and then infers the negation of that conclusion. Any pair of valid *reductios* must yield compatible conclusions. If both arguments really are *reductios*, then the problem cannot be a false premise. The problem must be purely logical.

The riddle behind the second antinomy is, Does everything divide up into discrete atoms or is there some continuous "gunk" that is infinitely divisible? The thesis of the second antinomy is atomism: every composite object is composed of simple parts. If there were no simple things, then there would have to be infinitely small things. But to be infinitely small is to be of no size. A collection of nothings, even infinitely many nothings, cannot add up to something. Since there is obviously something rather than nothing, there must be a limit to how far things can be divided.

The antithesis is that everything is infinitely divisible. If there were simples, then we would have something in space. Space is continuous. Given this infinite divisibility of space, we *can* divide the simple thing into different parts. There will always be a difference between, say, the left side of the object and its right side.

The riddle behind the third antinomy is the classic dilemma of freedom or determinism. The thesis is that there are some uncaused causes, in particular, acts of freewill. Think of the difference between raising your arm and your arm rising. When you raise your arm, a free choice enters the causal order. That intervention does not itself have a cause. If your arm passively rises, then you look for a cause such as involuntary contraction of your arm muscles. This cause must itself have a cause. The explanation is open to continuation by a third cause. On and on we go down the chain. We can arbitrarily break off the inquiry because of limited resources. But the only principled way of completing the inquiry is to anchor the chain of events in a decision by a free agent. Thus, it is incoherent to suppose that the world could be composed solely of passive causes. By calling the chain of passive causes a "world," you imply it is a *complete* collection of events. But to be an uninterrupted story, there must be at least one active cause to originate the series.

You are not merely a passive puppet that moves because of an action instigated by a puppeteer. You are an autonomous *agent*. Most things are mere patients whose behavior must be totally explained by causes outside of them. You know by introspection that you are one of the rare exceptions.

Could there be world that never had any agents? There could be a puppet whose strings are pulled by another puppet. And that puppet could in turn be manipulated by another puppet. But we cannot continue this series indefinitely. Sooner or later, we must postulate a puppeteer—at least in the past. Only free actions have the self-explanatory nature that can halt an infinite regress.

The antithesis denies that there is freewill. There is only the passive kind of causation in which each event wholly depends on some earlier cause. If agents introduced new energy into causal order, there would be something coming from nothing. An absolutely free act would violate the principle of sufficient reason: there must be a reason for every event.

Gottfried Leibniz illustrated the principle of sufficient reason with Archimedes' deduction: a scale with equal weights must be balanced because there is no more reason for one side to go up rather than the other. Samuel Clarke agreed that the scale must be at rest because it only involves passive objects. If an agent is confronted by equally balanced alternatives, he can arbitrarily choose one over the other. (In the 1950s, existentialists amplified this point: we sometimes choose the less weighty alternative because of weakness of will—or sheer defiance. Freedom is the silver lining in every irrational cloud.)

Leibniz denies that an arbitrary choice would differ from mere behavior. If your body moves randomly, the "act" is not yours. If you try to make it your act (rather than one of your effects) by claiming it is caused by your character, then you are no longer conceiving of the act as an uncaused cause.

Clarke admits that the self-motion associated with freewill is somewhat mysterious. But so is gravity. The movement of falling objects appears to require action at a distance. That is so strange we would be quite skeptical of gravity if it were a rare phenomenon. But falling apples are common. So are free choices. We should accept both without pretending to understand their deeper natures.

Kant thinks the proofs for freedom and determinism are equally forceful. He cites side motives to explain why people accept one argument rather than the other. Freewill is a requirement for being morally responsible. Freewill is also an asset in building a case for the existence of God. Suppose we follow Isaac Newton in picturing the universe as a big machine. Given that we also accept the requirement that every explanation be anchored with an act of freewill, we are poised to infer that there is a maker of the machine.

Leibniz complained to Clarke that acts of freewill have the same stupefying effect as miracles. If God can intervene anywhere and at anytime, why should we push our inquiry through the anomalies experience presents? It is self-defeating to rescue the natural order by postulating supernatural causes.

Kant regards the moral and religious aspects of freewill as potent distractions. The steadiness of our convictions as rationalists or empiricists is traced to the steadiness of our biases: "If men could free themselves from all such interests, and consider the assertions of reason irrespective of their consequences, solely in view of the intrinsic forces of their grounds, and were the only way of escape from their perplexities to give adhesion to one or other of the opposing parties, their state would be one of continuous vacillation." (1965 A475-B503) What matters in the third antinomy is the transcendental aspect of freewill. Reason is stymied because agency seems to block the quest for completeness and yet also seems essential to this quest.

The riddle behind the fourth antinomy is whether there is a necessary being or just an endless chain of contingent beings. If all beings were contingent, then each thing would depend on something that depended on yet a third thing. There would be no bottom to the sequence.

The antithesis argues against the existence of a necessary being. Only a field of contingent beings can form a unified whole. If the necessary being is part of the empirical universe, then it is the sort of thing whose existence is open to empirical confirmation or refutation. But only contingent beings satisfy this condition of possibly not existing. If the necessary being is outside the empirical realm, then it is not the sort of thing that explains an empirical sequence of events. Once you start an explanation within the empirical realm, you cannot hit an eject button and whoosh up to the realm of necessary beings.

Might the necessary being be the whole sequence of contingent events or the fusion of all the contingent beings? No, reasons Kant, the whole can be necessary only if one of its parts is necessary.

## ORIGIN OF THE ANTINOMIES

Kant formulates the antinomies in the technical vocabulary of his grand architectonic system. But he thinks these paradoxes arise from natural, universal thought patterns. Even children think, What happened before that? This can be asked of any event. One does not need to be a philosopher to think, What is beyond that? This makes sense whenever asked of a point in space.

The concepts originating the four antinomies are; *before*, *part of*, *caused by*, and *depends on*. Each of these can be driven to a "logical conclusion" in two absurd ways. We argue for the thesis by showing how the antithesis generates a vicious infinite regress. We argue for the antithesis by showing how the thesis implies a viciously *ad hoc* stopping point (a first moment, an indivisible part, a spontaneous cause, a causer who cannot have failed to exist).

We drive the concepts onward because the ideals regulating inquiry command completeness. You achieve your goals by always reaching further, endlessly expanding the application of each of the four powerful ideas *before*, *part of*, *caused by*, and *depends on*. An antinomy is "not arbitrarily invented but founded in the human reason as such." (1950, 337–38)

The dialectical origin of each idea arises from a combination of technical proficiency and selective attention. Logic professors teach us how to construct arguments. That skill has been applied to articulate each arm of the antinomies. By focusing on one intrinsically attractive alternative, you can mine evidence favoring just one side of the debate. If you do this systematically across a wide range of antinomical issues, the result is a sweeping metaphysical system.

Kant believes that rationalism flowered by defending the thesis of each antinomy. In reaction, empiricism developed by refining arguments for each antithesis. The rationalists believed that central features of nature could be ascertained by reason alone. They built upon our cognitive geography in one direction. The empiricists believed that all knowledge of nature relied on experience. They built in an opposed direction. Rationalism, taken alone, would be decisively proven. But the same could be said for empiricism. Thus, their powerful arguments cancel out.

This mega-application of Sextus Empiricus's method of equipollence first occurred to Kant as he analyzed the public correspondence between the rationalist Gottfried Leibniz and the empiricist Samuel Clarke. Each of these scholars argued masterfully from their classic perspectives. But "there arises an unexpected conflict which never can be removed in the common dogmatic way; because the thesis as well as the antithesis, can be shown by equally clear, evident, and irresistible proofs. . . . " Rationalists and empiricists try to pull each other down through ever more intricate debate. Kant regards these tactical refinements as futile: "all the metaphysical art of the most subtle distinction can not prevent this opposition. . . . " (1950, 337-38, 339–40)

The rationalists and empiricists were like two evenly matched teams in a tug of war. Ironically, the competing parties are kept standing by their opposing efforts. Kant's strategy is to cut the rope.

## KANT'S COPERNICAN REVOLUTION

As a scientist, Kant had a sleepy sympathy with empiricism. He was shaken by David Hume. Kant believed Hume drove empiricism to its logical conclusion: the skepticism of Sextus Empiricus. As a scientist, Kant also thought we have plenty of knowledge. He was so confident in scientific progress and common sense that his inquiry just presupposes that we know about as much as the scientists of his era believed we knew. To avoid skepticism, Kant swung to rationalism. Rationalists correctly believed that there are synthetic a priori propositions. But Kant believed Hume had also demonstrated that there is no reason why a mind-independent reality must live up to expectations of reason. The best we can expect from a world we did not create is indifference.

When Copernicus had trouble accounting for the movements of stars with the hypothesis that they are all moving around the observer, he tried the reverse hypothesis: The observer is moving and the stars are at rest. Kant was encountering parallel difficulties accounting for a priori knowledge on the hypothesis that our ideas of objects must conform to the objects. His Copernican revolution was to try the reverse hypothesis that objects must conform to ideas of objects. From this inverted perspective, experienced reality is a collaboration between our minds and external causes. As the empiricists emphasized, we cannot check the faithfulness of our ideas by comparing them with what they represent. We are trapped in the circle of our own ideas. Traditional metaphysics aims at studying a mind-independent world. But all we can know about things in themselves is that they exist and have some causal influence over our perceptions. Therefore, traditional metaphysics is a hopeless enterprise.

Should ordinary people be shocked that the external world is so intransigently unknowable? Kant believed that we are normally concerned with "phenomenal reality"—the world as it appears to us. Plato dismissed the realm of appearances as mere shadows of the real world of the forms. But the introspective Augustine made appearances a world of their own. The Augustinean reads "There appears to be a square in figure 20.1" as a correct description of an appearance rather than a hedged report of a square that is actually not there. Even after we realize that we are projecting the square into a sequence of bars, we still "see" the square. Similarly, Kant continues to see the objects in his room configured in space even though he believes he is just projecting spatial relations onto objects.

Fig. 20.1

René Descartes's meditations further persuaded philosophers that this world of appearances provides our only available premises for conclusions about noumenal reality (the mind-independent realm of things in themselves). We must excogitate the external world from inner certainties. George Berkeley boldly disagreed on both the need and possibility of this escape to the external world. Although Berkeley believes that there are cherries and fireplaces, he thinks "material object" is an incoherent philosopher's term. If you take away how the cherry tastes and feels and sounds, you take away the cherry. Kant does not go that far. He believes the noumenal realm is real. He just insists that we are radically overopinionated about it. We can know virtually nothing about things in themselves.

The feeling that we know much about noumenal reality is due to the "transcendental illusion" of construing a subjective condition of our conceptual scheme as an objective feature of reality. We are a bit like the astronomer Percival Lowell. When peering at Venus through his giant telescope, he regularly claimed to see "spokes." It turns out that he was seeing shadows cast by the blood vessels in his own eye. Astronomers speculate that a physician might have been able to diagnose Lowell's hypertension by studying his diagrams of Venus.

Kant has a stronger version of the projection thesis than scientists accept. They grant that secondary qualities such as color are projected onto the world. But they believe that objects really have primary qualities such as weight, solidity, and electric charge. Physicists take pride in telling us how things are in themselves. Kant thinks this is metaphysics masquerading as physics. Observation and science only inform us about phenomenal reality.

In addition to yielding particular facts, phenomenal reality is also open to the more abstract kind of investigation that we associate with the theory of perspective. Since the Renaissance, artists have worked out principles of representation. Their aim was simply to draw better pictures, but they were actually engaged in a mathematical enterprise. Kant portrays number theorists as unconsciously working out the structure of time and geometers as working out the structure of space.

External things contribute to the content of experience, but the mind regulates the form those experiences must take. Appearances are situated in an arena of space and time. For material things, it is always proper to ask what is next to an object, what is the left side, and where was it before. By conceiving of something as a substance, one acquiesces to the legitimacy of questions about its parts, questions about its location, and so on. Material things also must fit into a unified casual order. Your left shoe did not just pop into existence. It had to be cobbled into existence. The raw materials must have themselves been brought into existence by other causes.

Just as Euclid perfected geometry by articulating the inner rules for constructing spatial experience, Aristotle perfected logic by articulating the inner rules of inference. In the preface to the second edition of the *Critique of Pure Reason*, Kant says that after Aristotle, logic has not needed "to retrace a single step, unless, indeed, we care to count as improvements the removal of certain needless subtleties or the clearer exposition of its recognized teaching, features which concern the elegance rather than the certainty of the science." (1965, B viii) The status of the logical paradoxes had declined to such a low level that Kant's optimism could be taken seriously. The liar paradox, the paradoxes of identity, and the problem of negative existentials were not even regarded as anomalies. They were stale sophistries with no more significance than parlor tricks.

## KANT'S CONFLICTING SOLUTIONS

One mark of a paradox is that different thinkers "solve" it in incompatible ways. A stronger mark of a paradox is that one and the same thinker "solves" it in incompatible ways.

Kant's older and simplest solution takes a cue from Aristotle: the antinomies confuse a potential infinity with an actual infinity. Although the chain of temporal order (or division or causation or dependence) can be continued without end, we cannot infer that it ever actually reaches infinity. The imperative to extend the domain of the concepts is a regulative ideal. Unfortunately, these ideals have been reified into impossible limit-objects. Thus, each antinomy rests "on a mere delusion by which they (the conflicting dogmatists) hypostatize what exists merely in thought, and take it as a real object existing, in the same character, outside the thinking subject." Under this solution, all of the arguments composing the antinomies are sound. Each antinomical issue is analogous to the riddle "What happens if an irresistible force meets an immovable object?" The two answers to this "antinomy" appear to be contradictory:

*Thesis:* If an irresistible force meets an immovable object, then the immovable object moves.

*Antithesis:* If an irresistible force meets an immovable object, then the immovable object does not move.

Yet each side can be soundly argued. Proof of the Thesis: An irresistible force can move *anything*. So if there is an immovable object, it is an object and so it must move. Proof of the Antithesis: An immovable object cannot be moved by anything. So if there is an irresistible force, even that cannot move it. The conclusions of the proofs are compatible because they are conditionals with impossible antecedents. It is possible for there to be an irresistible force and it is possible for there to be an immovable object. But they are not *co-possible.* The riddle tricks you into assuming that the confrontation could take place. Anything follows from an impossibility. Even contradictory consequences. Garbage in, garbage out! If you do not realize what is going on, you will try to defend one of the consequences. You will slant the evidence so that it seems to confirm your answer and disconfirm the "contrary" answer. But both thesis and antithesis are true.

Although Immanuel Kant never retracts this solution, he becomes nervous. If the necessary being is a limit-object and limit-objects are delusions, then Kant is heading toward atheism. Kant rejects all metaphysical arguments for God's existence, but he is eager to leave room for God as a possibility. Indeed, he softens the impact of criticisms of the ontological argument and of the cosmological argument by claiming that these destructive points clear the way for faith.

There is more bad news if freewill is a limit-object. For then Kant gets all the pain of hard determinism without the cold satisfaction of putting everything in its place.

To rescue the *possibility* of God and the *possibility* of freewill, Kant suggests that the phenomenal/noumenal distinction affects the third and fourth antinomies. On this softer, second solution, there are two kinds of causes. In addition to phenomena causing other phenomena, noumena cause phenomena. Thus, it is possible that your noumenal self causes phenomenal effects. (The self you see in the mirror and experience through introspection is your phenomenal self, your noumenal self is what lies beneath these appearances.) Freewill is possible because noumenal causation might spontaneously originate effects. Similarly, Kant rescues the possibility of a necessary being with a distinction between *noumenal* dependence and phenomenal dependence. God could be the being that rests at the bottom of a *noumenal* chain of dependence.

So on this second solution, the arguments composing the third and fourth antinomies are not sound. If the phenomenal-noumenal duality is understood as forcing different senses of "cause," then the arguments commit the fallacy of equivocation. If that duality is understood as revealing that there are two species of causation, then the arguments have false premises or embody an invalid inference.

Kant suggests that we can accept freewill and accept determinism as a principle that applies to phenomenal causality. Similarly, we can accept the necessary being and respect a prohibition against accepting phenomenal stopping points.

Although Kant does not think freewill and God can be proved, he does think they can be articles of faith. Indeed, he thinks practical reason makes them part of a "rational faith."

Kant's *Critique of Pure Reason* continues to inspire. I leave you with V. Alan White's "Antinomy" (sung to the tune of "Chimchiminey" from the film *Mary Poppins*):

Antinomy, antinomy, antinomy—
it's not merely one but it's two QEDs—
antinomy, antinomy, antinomy—
contradictory results from the same premises!
(Despite what one thinks—both can't be believed!)

Immanuel Kant said the world can't begin
then thought better of it, and said it can't end;
how better adjoin separate theses as these
but publicize them as Kant's antinomies?

Old Zeno thought space a remarkable thing
(somewhat as we think of a pig on the wing);
Achilles could not catch a Testudines
if burdened by so many antinomies!

We search for the truth till the end of the day—
but closer approaching seems farther away—
an infinite effort our destiny be—
the lover of wisdom's own antinomy!

TWENTY-ONE

# Hegel's World of Contradictions

Georg Wilhelm Friedrich Hegel (1770-1831) accuses Immanuel Kant of contradicting himself. Kant opens by announcing that things in themselves (noumena) are unfathomable causes of appearances (phenomena). But Kant later says that we actually impose a causal scheme on phenomena. Experience must take place within a constructed arena of space and time. If the noumenal self is unknowable and other noumenal things are unknowable, then how could Kant know what is solely contributed by the noumenal self? It is self-defeating, writes Hegel, to judge that one cannot make judgments about noumena:

> It argues an utter want of consistency to say, on the one hand, that understanding only knows phenomena, and, on the other, assert the absolute character of this knowledge, by statements such as "Cognition can go no further"

> . . . No one knows, or even feels, that anything is a limit or a defect until he is at the same time above and beyond it.
> (1959, section 60)

Hegel rejects the idea that reality is something which *underlies* appearance. He says that reality is manifest *in* appearance. Characteristics that we normally think apply only to our representations of reality actually apply to reality itself. For instance, we tend to think that vagueness is a property of our descriptions of clouds. But Hegel insists that the clouds are themselves vague. The difference between the word "cloud" and a cloud in the sky is less drastic than "precise" philosophers contend. The affinity between an object and its representation is ensured by Hegel's retention of Kant's theme that reason constructs appearances. Reason dictates the structure of reality. Since reason is the ground for what is real, the real is what is rational.

Kant believed there were only four antinomies because he thought there were only four ways to misapply transcendental ideas to phenomenal reality. Hegel rejects Kant's assumption that the contradictions are products of transcendental illusion. Hegel takes them to be accurate perceptions of an inconsistent reality. It is possible to view the Penrose triangle (fig. 1.2) and other impossible figures as consistent patches of ink. But the correct way to see them is inconsistently. "Square circle," "many-sided circle," and "straight curve" are self-contradictory. Yet geometers regard circles as polygons composed of very short sides. In an era when arithmetic was taken to be the science of quantity, mathematicians struggled to explain the usefulness of negative numbers and imaginary numbers such as $\sqrt{-1}$. If multiplying a negative with negative number yields a positive number, then -1 cannot have a square root. Yet applied mathematicians were finding all sorts of uses for $\sqrt{-1}$. Hegel was not mystified. If a judgment is true when it corresponds to the facts, then when the facts are inconsistent, a true judgment of those facts must be inconsistent. If we keep an open mind, we discover that contradictory phenomena are wrongly dismissed as illusions.

> According to Kant, . . . thought has a natural tendency to issue in contradictions or antinomies, whenever it seeks to apprehend the infinite. But Kant . . . never penetrated to the discovery of what the antinomies really and positively mean. The true and positive meaning of the antinomies is this: that every actual thing involves a coexistence of opposed elements. . . . The old metaphysic, . . . when it studied the object of which it sought metaphysical knowledge, went to work by applying the categories abstractly and to the exclusion of their opposites. Kant, on the other hand, tried to prove that the statements issuing through this method could be met by other statements of contrary import with equal warrant and necessity.
>
> (1880, section 48)

Hegel therefore accepts the contradictions. His idealism makes this less shocking. Hegel has no direct quarrel with the principle that all mind-independent things are free from contradiction. He just thinks the principle misleadingly suggests that there are mind-independent things. If everything is mind-dependent, then things are free to have properties that at first seemed limited to representations of things.

Our beliefs shape up under the prodding of inconsistencies. If reality is idea-like, then this developmental pattern should extend to history. Hegel's popularizers simplified the logic of history as a triadic progression of thesis, antithesis, and synthesis: History is a dialogue in which thesis confronts antithesis. This conflict is resolved by a synthesis which incorporates the elements of truth in the thesis and antithesis. This synthesis constitutes a new thesis that comes to be opposed by a new antithesis. A yet higher synthesis occurs and the dialectic continues. Although each thesis and antithesis fails to be fully true, the syntheses are more comprehensive and so have a higher degree of truth. Thus, there is progress toward the absolute truth.

Progress is hard to see from a local perspective. Up close, events seem to meander through our lives without purpose. But this is because reason often accomplishes its ends through indirect means. This does not mean that the historian can predict the future. We can only appreciate "the cunning of reason" in hindsight.

At times, Hegel seems to even express doubt about that. Echoing the Socratic contradiction that he knows only that he knows nothing, Hegel says, "We learn from history that we learn nothing from history." But whether we realize it or not, everything fits in with the absolute truth.

Hegel's preferred reaction to a paradox is to acquiesce to the contradiction. Just as a judo master redirects his opponent's blows instead of blocking them, Hegel merely shifts Zeno's point of impact. In the case of Zeno's paradox of the arrow, Hegel concedes that

> If we wish to make motion clear to ourselves, we say that the body is in one place and then it goes to another; because it moves, it is no longer in the first, but yet not in the second; were it in either it would be at rest. Where then is it? If we

> say that it is between both, this is to convey nothing at all, for were it between both, it would be in a place, and this presents the same difficulty. But movement means to be in this place and not to be in it, and thus to be in both alike; this is the continuity of space and time which first makes motion possible. Zeno, in the deduction made by him, brought both these points into forcible opposition.
>
> (1892, 274)

Zeno's only mistake was his assumption that contradictory phenomena cannot be real. Zeno thought he was supporting Parmenides' conclusion that all is one. But if becoming is more basic than being, Zeno's paradoxes of motion really demonstrate the pervasiveness of change.

Hegel associates rest with the principle that everything is identical with itself. Change comes from the principle of contradiction. A cherry develops from a bud in the same manner that an amended theory develops from the refutation of an earlier view. "He who claims that nothing exists which carries in it a contradiction as an identity of opposed determinations is at the same time claiming that nothing alive exists. Indeed the force of life and, even more, the power of the Spirit, consists in positing the contradiction in itself, in enduring and overcoming it." (1970, 162) With the exception of Heraclitus, the major Greek philosophers regarded permanence as real and change as illusory. This bias is clear from their use of *reductio ad absurdum.* They treat contradiction as a mark of unreality. Hegel thinks contradictions are more real because they control development:

> But it is one of the fundamental prejudices of logic, as hitherto understood and of ordinary thinking, that contradiction is not so characteristically essential and immanent

> a determination as identity; but in fact, if it were a question of grading the two determinations and they had to be kept separate, then contradiction would have to be taken as the profounder determination and more characteristic of essence. For as against contradiction, identity is merely the determination of the simple immediate, of dead being; but contradiction is the root of all movement and vitality; it is only in so far as something has a contradiction within it that moves, has an urge and activity.
>
> (1969, 429)

Everything changes and so everything is ultimately contradictory. Zeno's great discovery is that

> There is *nothing at all* anywhere, in which contradiction—i.e., opposed determinations—cannot and should not be exhibited. The abstracting activity of the understanding is a clinging on to one determinacy by force, and effort to obscure and remove the consciousness of the other one that is contained in it.—But if the contradiction is exhibited and recognized in any object or concept whatever, then the conclusion that is usually drawn is: "*Therefore* this object is *nothing*." Thus Zeno first showed that movement contradicts itself, and that it therefore *is* not; likewise the Ancients recognized *coming to be* and *passing away*, the two kinds of becoming, as unique determinations, by saying that the *one*, i.e., the Absolute, does not come into being or pass away.
>
> (1880, 89)

The fundamental law is that everything is inherently contradictory.

Many of Hegel's countrymen viewed his logic as the culmination of two thousand years of thought. Reason was becoming self-conscious at the University of Berlin. Government ministers welcomed Professor Hegel's nationalistic theme that Germany was at the apex of civilization. They rewarded his organic theme that the state has more reality than its citizens (just as a man is more real than his organs and his organs are more real than its cells). With the metaphysical primacy of the state came moral primacy; rights evaporated into the lofty state above, duties rained down on its sea of constituents.

But even some of Hegel's friends suspected that his logic was a conjuring trick. Johann Goethe feared that Hegel was kicking up a dust storm of syllogisms that disinterred pre-Kantian metaphysics. Goethe probably had Hegel's logic in mind when he has Mephistopheles recommend the *Collegium logicum* to an enthusiastic student:

> Unseen the threads are knit together,
> And an infinite combination grows.
> Then, the philosopher steps in
> And shows, no otherwise it could have been:
>
> (Faust I, lines 1922ff.)

Philosophers generally regard the principle of contradiction as a core rule of debate. Once you drive your adversary to a contradiction, he is obliged to give up. But there is Hegel assuring us that a contradiction is "not, so to speak, an imperfection or a defect in something . . . On the contrary, every determination, every concrete thing, every notion is essentially a unity of different and distinctive moments, which by virtue of their clear and essential differences pass over into contradictory moments." (1969, 422) This struck many of Hegel's colleagues as more alarming than poor sportsmanship. If contradictions were permitted (indeed celebrated), then people could not be rationally criticized. Dangerous thinking could not be brought to heel by a *reductio ad absurdum*. When reason is no longer restrained by fear of contradiction, anything can be "justified." Kantian loyalists worried that the Enlightenment would be rolled back by this debased reason. In 1795, Kant had argued eloquently in "Perpetual Peace" for an international federation that would eliminate war. Hegel spoke up for war:

> War is not to be regarded as an absolute evil and as a purely external accident, which itself has some accidental cause, be it injustice, the passions of nations or the holders of power, etc., or, in short, something or other which ought not to be. . . . War is the state of affairs which deals in earnest with the vanity of temporal goods and concerns. . . . War has the higher significance that by its agency, as I have remarked elsewhere, the ethical health of peoples is preserved in their indifference to the stabilization of finite institutions; just as the blowing of the winds preserves the sea from the foulness which would be the result of a prolonged calm, so also corruption in nations would be the product of prolonged, let alone "perpetual" peace.
>
> (1973, 324)

Hegel adopts Heraclitus's theme that war is a catalyst of change integral to the human condition. How does one argue against Hegel if he regards his inconsistencies as signs of a dynamic reality?

Hegel's junior colleague, Arthur Schopenhauer, denied that Hegelianism should be dignified with a rebuttal. Schopenhauer tried to expose Hegel as a charlatan. Schopenhauer felt Hegel was robbing Germans of their Kantian heritage. Instead of honestly conveying critical reason's bad news for metaphysics, Hegel treated Kant's doctrines as periscopes to a more splendid metaphysical realm.

Hegel's reactionary rationalism was epitomized by his 1801 dissertation *De Orbitis Planetarum*. He criticized Newton and tried to find an a priori justification for Kepler's laws. On numerological grounds, Hegel supports Plato's opinion in the *Timaeus* that there could be no planet between Mars and Jupiter. But in the beginning of 1801, astronomers discovered the asteroid Ceres between the two planets—and subsequently a few other such anti-Hegelian asteroids. Instead of abandoning a priori astronomy, Hegel tried to show that these asteroids fill a gap that would have otherwise been unreasonable.

Astronomers who try to debunk astrologists with more science are often chagrined by the astrologer's ability to incorporate counterexamples into a super-pseudoscience. Schopenhauer believed that Hegel was coopting Kant in the same fashion. Kant's strictures about the inaccessibility of noumena were being used to frame a "little window opening into the supernatural world." Hegel's abuse of Kant put Schopenhauer in mind of the Greek custom of enacting farces over the graves of the great.

To oppose this massive fraud, Schopenhauer scheduled his lectures to compete with Hegel's. Students would be forced to choose between Schopenhauer's independent, clear, consistent development of Kant and Hegel's state-sanctioned, obscure, unabashedly contradictory debasement of the great master.

Schopenhauer lectured to nearly empty rooms. Hegel's students overflowed large lecture halls. Disgusted, Schopenhauer left the academic field to the peddlers of sophistry and rhetoric. As Heraclitus said, "Asses prefer garbage to gold."

Alone in his boarding room, the brooding Schopenhauer continued to oppose Hegel. Hegel's optimism was countered with Schopenhauer's pessimism. Hegel's acceptance of contradictions was countered by Schopenhauer's claim of perfect consistency: "To seek contradictions in me is completely idle: all is from one gush." (Letter to Johann August Becker, March 31, 1854) Whereas Hegel said history is the unfolding of *reason*, Schopenhauer made blind *will* the central force of the universe. Schopenhauer's emphasis on irrational forces may have been precipitated by awareness of his susceptibility to irrational fears and compulsions. He took excessive precautions against disease and always slept with a loaded pistol nearby.

Schopenhauer accepted Kant's verdict about the inaccessibility of noumena but thought man's hunger for general explanations was too strong to be put aside. Man is an *animal metaphysicum*, who compulsively raises questions about the fundamental nature and significance of the world. Religion attempts to meet this need but not in a fashion that can be rationally justified. Philosophers try to meet this demand for rational certification. Inevitably they overstep. The human intellect is designed to serve the will. Thus, it is "a quite abnormal event if in some man's intellect deserts its natural vocation . . . in order to occupy itself purely objectively. But it is precisely this which is the origin of art, poetry and philosophy, which are therefore not produced by an organ intended for that purpose." (1970, 127) Whereas Hegel objectifies paradoxes, Schopenhauer subjectivizes them. Paradoxes are symptoms of intellectual perversion. This clinical revulsion wafts through German literature. In *The Magic Mountain*, Thomas Mann writes "Paradox is the poisonous flower of quietism, the iridescent surface of the rotting mind, the greatest depravity of all." (1955, 221-222)

The Stoics associated what is natural with what is good. Schopenhauer thinks what is natural is bad. Nature is a stupid clash of wills. Schopenhauer's only point in describing something as unnatural is to raise a doubt about its effectiveness. Our minds work in a largely automatic, unconscious fashion shaped by a drive to survive and reproduce. When we find ourselves puzzled by questions we cannot imagine how to answer, we have reason to doubt that the question is well formed. Even if the question is well formed, we should still doubt that we are competent to answer the question.

The Turks have many stories about the thirteenth-century character Nasreddin Hodja. As a judge, he was obliged to listen to a man who had come to his house to complain of a neighbor. After listening carefully, Hodja said "You are right." The man left happily. But the news of Hodja's judgment angered the accused neighbor; he marched to Hodja's house and gave his side of the story. Hodja again listened carefully and said "You are right." The second man left happily. Hodja's wife had been listening to all this: "But Hodja, they both can't be right." Hodja listened carefully and said "You are right."

If Hegel accepts contradictions, then mustn't he be as agreeable as Hodja? Anything follows from a contradiction.

As noted in chapter 8, paraconsistent logicians try to engineer brakes for these runaway deductions. Classical logicians reply that the meaning of "contraction" is intimately connected with rules of inference such as *reductio ad absurdum*. You can only deviate from these rules of inference by changing the very meaning of contradiction. And if you change the meaning, you are just changing the topic. If Hegel does not mean what we mean by contradiction then his claim that there are true contradictions is just misleading advertising.

My own opinion is that Hegel uses "contradiction" in a conventional way; he just has an unconventional view of reality. Given idealism, reality is like a body of beliefs or a work of fiction. Such systems contain contradictions. We can consistently describe a contradiction in Thomas Hobbes's belief system by saying "According to Hobbes's political philosophy, citizens have an obligation to submit to the death penalty and yet the state has no right to require the citizen to submit to the death penalty." The qualifier "According to Hobbes's political philosophy" prevents the contradiction from infecting the description of the contradiction.

Contradictions are often inaccurately attributed to theoretical systems and movie plots. Hegel thinks that some of his followers make this sort of error; they lard reality with contradictions it does not possess. Hegel also thinks his students sometimes inconsistently describe reality and confuse the inconsistency of their description with an inconsistency they are describing. It is even possible to inconsistently describe inconsistency. In *Hegel: A Reexamination*, J. N. Findlay writes,

> . . . a contradiction is for the majority of logical thinkers, a self-nullifying utterance, one that puts forward an assertion and then takes it back in the same breath, and so really says nothing. It can readily be shown that a language system which admits even *one* contradiction among its sentences, is also a system in which *anything whatever* can be proved. . . .
>
> (1958, 76)

But a statement that says nothing cannot imply everything. Hegel has no more interest in these inconsistencies than other thinkers. For Hegel, the deep contradictions are the ones embedded in the realm of ideas constituting reality itself.

When we describe contradictions in a story, we sometimes leave the "In the story" qualifier unstated. That omission makes our description sound contradictory. Hegel often drops the qualifier in this way. However, Hegel has stronger grounds for dropping it than a concern for brevity. Hegel's qualifier ultimately boils down to "In reality." If he says "In reality, *P* and not *P*," then he does not get the insulation afforded by "In the story, *P* and not *P*." This loss of insulation is the real source of instability in Hegel's philosophy.

Well, that is *my* interpretation. Many other scholars have tried to understand Hegel's talk of contradiction as metaphorical or as a synonym for irony or as an equivocal allusion to opposed forces. Most are just puzzled as to what Hegel did mean. Hegel was disappointed by this incomprehension. There is a report that on his deathbed Hegel complained, "Only one man ever understood me." Hegel fell silent for a while and then added, "And he didn't understand me."

TWENTY-TWO

# Russell's Set

When the mathematics student Bertrand Russell (1872–1970) entered Cambridge University, he subscribed to the empiricism of his godfather, John Stuart Mill. However, the younger generation of philosophers believed that Mill had been superseded by Hegel. A recent graduate of Cambridge, John McTaggart, told the young Russell that although he did not believe in God, he did believe in immortality and a harmony between human beings and the universe. McTaggart claimed that the unreality of space and time could be proved with mathematical rigor. This colorful mixture of logic and spirituality contrasted with the black-and-white calculating of mathematicians.

Russell's conception of philosophy was inspired by McTaggart's *Studies in the Hegelian Dialectic.* After his graduation, Russell expressed an ambition to write "a dialectic logic of all the sciences and an ethic that should apply to politics." He hoped that something like Spinoza's religion could be rigorously demonstrated.

## THE HEGELIAN HUNT FOR CONTRADICTIONS

Part of Russell's project was to show how contradictions led from mathematics to physics and from physics to metaphysics, and then onto the Absolute. Russell thought the contradictions would be most easily revealed in geometry, especially with respect to continua. Mathematicians were in danger of forgetting "that philosophical antinomies, in this sphere, find their counterpart in mathematical fallacies. These fallacies seem, to me at least, to pervade the Calculus, and even the more elaborate machinery of Cantor's collections." (1990, 52)

In *An Essay on the Foundations of Geometry*, Russell claimed to find contradictions related to the "relativity, infinite divisibility, and unbounded extension of space." (1897, 177) For instance, a point must be spatial and yet must not contain any space. After all, any finite extension is capable of further analysis. Russell thought geometry's contradictions are inherited from the nature of space. As such they are innate and inescapable. To solve the paradoxes endemic to "empty space" and "point," one must introduce the concept of "matter." That is, one must transcend geometry with kinematics.

Russell's book on geometry was well received. He planned to next write a book on the foundations of physics. However, dynamics proved recalcitrantly empirical.

Russell shifted to the more familiar terrain of arithmetic. He was interested in Georg Cantor's attempt to treat number as a continuous quantity. As a Hegelian, Russell rejected Cantor's transfinite numbers on the grounds that infinity would have to be "a quantity larger than any assignable quantity." If 1, 2, 3, . . . , *n*, . . . is unlimited, how could Cantor find a place for a number that would follow all these numbers?

Eventually Russell concluded that his criticism rested on two mistakes: treating infinity as an infinite number and treating all infinities as being equal. This retraction was partly precipitated by Alfred North Whitehead's suggestion that Russell actually read Hegel's books on logic. Russell had been reading mathematically literate interpretations of Hegel. Once he read Hegel in the original, Russell was shaken. The master was committing "ignorant and stupid" mistakes.

This was probably just the reaction Whitehead was hoping for. As Russell's opinion about Hegel sank, his opinion of mathematicians rose. At Cambridge, the vast majority of mathematicians seemed narrow and uncultured. Students crammed to pass the Tripos examination, a marathon of tricky mathematics. To make a respectable showing, you had to train intensively. So teachers and students focused on competitive, time-sensitive problem-solving. This shallow regime did not encourage ruminations on the philosophical difficulties posed by infinitesimals, continua, and infinity.

But when Russell encountered mathematicians in France, Germany, and Italy, he no longer pictured the whole profession as hurriedly sweeping its contradictions under a rug. True, the usual reaction to George Berkeley's criticisms of infinitesimals was some foot shuffling and a reminder that infinitesimals led to the right answers. But Karl Weierstrass showed how the right answers could be obtained through an alternative, epsilon-delta notation (which follows the linguistic strategy we saw pioneered by Peter of Spain). Since this avoided infinitesimals, mathematicians were now free to concede to Berkeley that infinitesimals were incoherent.

Georg Cantor was persuading more and more mathematicians that his transfinite arithmetic solved Zeno's paradoxes. Giuseppe Peano had axiomitized arithmetic. All of this showed that an effective cadre of mathematicians did take contradictions seriously. There were far fewer unsolvable contradictions than implied by Hegel. By 1899, Russell felt the number of contradictions had dwindled to one: "The number of finite numbers is infinite. Every number is finite. These two statements seem indubitable, though the first contradicts the second, and the second contradicts Cantor." (Russell 1994, 123) But even this paradox seemed to disappear when Russell became persuaded that mathematics was not really the science of quantity. Once mathematics was pictured more abstractly, as a study of symbol manipulation, all contradictions appeared to evaporate. Mathematics looked increasingly like a body of secure tautologies.

## THE SECOND ANALYTIC PHILOSOPHER

Russell's empty catch made him ripe for defection. His colleague at Cambridge University, G. E. Moore, was developing an analytic alternative to Hegelianism. Moore attacked idealism with a combination of conceptual analysis and appeals to common sense. Nowadays, many philosophy students regard Moore's writings as a pedantic defender of the status quo. But at the beginning of the twentieth century, Moore's writings were electrically dissident. Idealism was in magisterial hegemony in Europe and the Untied States. Moore countered with a charismatic naiveté.

Moore admitted that he could not pinpoint the missteps of many idealist arguments. He just knew that they were wrong because their conclusions contradicted everyday certitudes. One job for philosophers is to find the fallacy in such paradoxical arguments. In contrast with Russell, Moore did not think the philosopher was in the business of correcting or refining common sense. Like Reid, he thought philosophical challenges to common sense were insincere and self-defeating. Philosophers should instead analyze what common-sense statements mean. Unlike Reid, Moore accepted the Way of Ideas. He thought that statements such as "I see a hand" should be analyzed in terms of sense data. Analyses of common sense are not themselves common sense.

Russell felt Moore liberated him. As a realist, Russell could now see the grass as really green. He could construe science as having an ever-tightening grip on an objective world. Russell summarized his defection in "Why I took to Philosophy":

> Hegel thought of the universe as a closely knit unity. His universe was like a jelly in the fact that, if you touched any one part of it, the whole quivered; but it was unlike a jelly in the fact that it could not really be cut up into parts. The appearance of consisting of parts, according to him was a delusion. The only reality was the Absolute, which was his name for God. In this philosophy I found comfort for a time. As presented to me by its adherent, especially McTaggart, who was then an intimate friend of mine. Hegel's philosophy had seemed both charming and demonstrable. . . . In a rash moment, however, I turned from the disciples to the Master and found in Hegel himself a farrago of confusions and what seemed to me little better than puns. I therefore abandoned his philosophy.
>
> (1956, 21)

Russell now pictured the universe as a pile of buckshot. Like Hume's ideas, Russell's "atomic facts" were independent units that could be logically compounded into molecular facts. The role of the philosopher was to show how complex statements could be analyzed into simpler statements and how atomic statements manage to be true or false. Like Leibniz, Russell assigned a central role to logic in his metaphysics.

Ordinary language was unsuited for this project because it is larded with ambiguity, vagueness, and redundancy. What Russell needed was a logically perfect language; a language in which each object has a single name and each name has a single object; a language in which each concept is expressed by one and only one predicate; a language in which every sentence has clear rules for its construction. Paradoxes cannot arise in this language. Equivocation is impossible because all ambiguity has been removed. The sorites paradox cannot be expressed because there is no vagueness. Puzzles about nonexistence disappear because there are no empty names. Puzzles about identity are forestalled because no object goes around under different names. Finally, meaninglessness is prevented because each atomic sentence is meaningful and all other sentences are molecules that are meaningfully assembled from meaningful atoms.

In addition to rendering the negative service of preventing spurious issues from arising, the logically perfect language positively informs the metaphysician about the nature of reality. The language shows that the world is a collection of facts rather than a heap of objects. "Bertrand Russell was descended from Prime Minister John Russell" and "Prime Minister John Russell was descended from Bertrand Russell" are about the same individuals and employ the same concept.

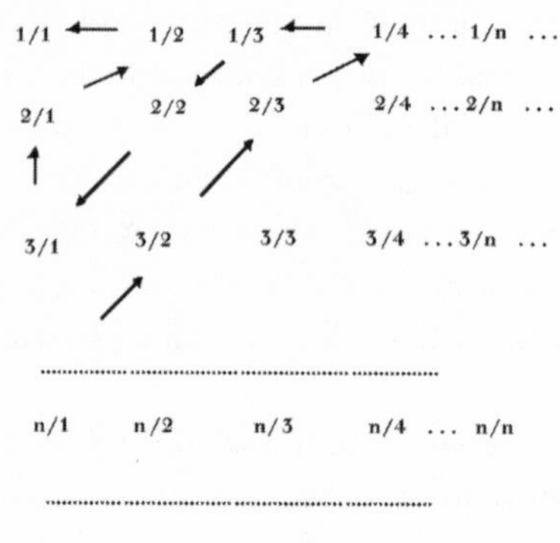


Fig. 22.1

But only one of them is made true by the fact that the Prime Minister John Russell was Bertrand Russell's grandfather.

This logically perfect language would have the same structure as reality itself. It would reflect all and only genuine possibilities. The role of science is to figure out which possibilities are actual. The role of the philosopher is to construct the framework. In this way, the scientist is spared the trouble of eliminating hypotheses that could not possibly be correct. The scientist would also benefit from this clear picture of what implies what. Although a philosopher lacks any special expertise as to which possibilities are actual, he would be able to say, "If this possibility is actual, then that possibility must also hold."

## LOGICISM AND CANTOR

One important part of an ideal language would be mathematics. Rationalism is supported by our knowledge that $1 + 1 = 2$. There is no causal link between us and numbers, so we appear

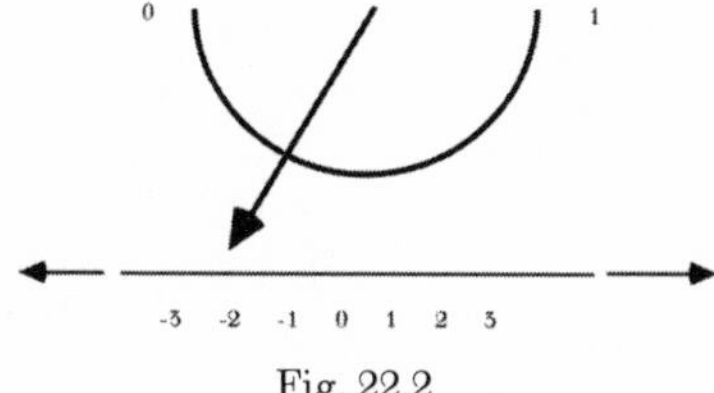


Fig. 22.2

to have nonempirical access to the truths of arithmetic. Empiricists suggested that our knowledge of arithmetic is like our knowledge of tautologies. This is logicism, the view that mathematics reduces to logic. Russell believed that Cantor's conception of a set presented an opportunity to work out this reduction of mathematics to logic in rigorous detail. The size of a collection, its cardinality, is what is left after we abstract away the nature of its members and their order. One is the cardinality of a unit set composed of a single individual, say, the planet Mercury. The union of Mercury with the set of that set yields a set with two members. Adding the set of that set with the two previous members gives us three. All the natural numbers can be represented by continuing this progression.

Rational numbers are just those numbers that can be represented as a ratio of integers. These "fractions" can be put into a one-to-one correspondence with the natural numbers (fig. 22.1). Cantor was interested in proving that not all cardinalities are equal. After failing to prove that the set of all real numbers is greater than the set of real numbers between 0 and 1, Cantor surprised himself by demonstrating that all the real numbers could be put into a one-to-one correspondence with the real numbers in the interval between 0 and 1 (fig. 22.2). More importantly, Cantor devised the diagonal argument to show that there is no one-to-one

| | | | | | | | | |
|---|---|---|---|---|---|---|---|---|
| 1/3 | = | **3** | 3 | 3 | 3 | . | . | . |
| 1/2 | = | 5 | **0** | 0 | 0 | . | . | . |
| $\sqrt{.1}$ | = | 3 | 1 | **6** | 2 | . | . | . |
| $\sqrt{.5}$ | = | 7 | 0 | 7 | **1** | . | . | . |
| . | . | . | . | . | . | . | . | . |

Fig. 22.3

correspondence between the real numbers and the natural numbers. Suppose there were a one-to-one correspondence. We would then be able to list all the real numbers in an infinite square. Each real number between 0 and 1 corresponds to an infinite decimal expansion. For instance, 1/3 = .333333. . . . So the list would look like something like figure 22.3. Now consider the sequence corresponding to the diagonal of the list: 3061. We can construct a new decimal expansion by letting the *n*th digit equal 1 if the diagonal digit is 0 and 0 for any other digit: That antidiagonal, .0100 . . . , cannot be on the list, for it differs from any number on the list by at least one digit.

The diagonal argument can be used to show that the power set of the natural numbers (the set of all its subsets) is bigger than the set of natural numbers. We can describe any set of natural numbers by just writing true or false depending on whether the *n*th natural number is a member of the set. For instance, the set of even numbers is <False, True, False, True, . . . >. A one-to-one correspondence between the set of natural numbers and its power set would look like figure 22.4. The diagonal sequence is <False, False, True, True, . . . >.

| | | | | | | | | |
|---|---|---|---|---|---|---|---|---|
| *Evens* : | **False** | True | False | True | . | . | . | . |
| *Odds:* | True | **False** | True | False | . | . | . | . |
| *Primes*: | False | True | **True** | False | . | . | . | . |
| *Squares:* | True | False | False | **True** | . | . | . | . |
| . . | . | . | . | . | . | . | . | . |

Fig. 22.4

Now consider the sequence that results by reversing all those truth values: <True, True, False, False, . . . >. The sequence defined by this antidiagonal cannot be on the list. It diverges at least once with each sequence on the list.

Cantor went on to prove that the power set of any set (the set of all subsets of that set) always has a higher cardinality than the set. It follows that there is an infinite hierarchy of transfinite numbers.

Cantor's proof that there is no highest transfinite number was controversial. Henri Poincaré thought there was a set of real numbers only if its elements could be paired off with the natural numbers. Since the diagonal argument proved there was no pairing, Poincaré inferred that there is no *set* of real numbers. Luitzen Brouwer construed the diagonal argument as a recipe for constructing *new* real numbers. C. S. Peirce argued similarly that there is no completed whole of real numbers. For any real number, there is a higher real number. But the infinity is potential, not actual.

When Russell was calculating how many things are in the universe, he was led to a set that included everything. The number of things in this set must be the largest number because there is nothing further to add! Russell therefore suspected that the diagonal argument committed some subtle fallacy.

Cantor's correspondence with Richard Dedekind suggests that Cantor was aware of how the universal set was an anomaly for the conclusion of the diagonal argument. If the power set of a set is always bigger than the set, then the universal set would be bigger than itself. Cantor was only mildly concerned. He was a religious man who believed that God had granted him a special gift to work out the nature of infinity. He had seen anomalies come and go in his development of transfinite arithmetic. From the history of number theory, he knew irrational numbers, negative numbers, and imaginary numbers had each faced trials. Why should transfinite numbers be different? Cantor flirted with the idea that some infinities are immeasurable: "manies too big to be regarded as one." These "inconsistent multiplicities" inspired Cantor's mystical awe: "The Absolute can only be acknowledged and admitted, never known, not even approximately." (Hallet 1984, 13)

Russell was in no position to partake in Cantor's ad hoc equanimity. Why didn't the set of real numbers count as an immeasurable infinity? The diagonal argument for higher order infinities would be reduced to the status of revealed theology.

Like the editors who turned down the diagonal argument for publication, Russell noticed that the antidiagonal resembled the liar paradox. When evaluating "This statement is false," you are forced to endlessly change true to false and false to true. The construction of the antidiagonal takes the same oscillating path.

This objection to the diagonal argument boomerangs. In May of 1901, while finishing *Principles of Mathematics*,

Russell realized that the liar paradox bears a more damning resemblance to a slight variant of this universal set. A set that contains everything must contain itself. Now consider a set that includes all and only those sets that do not include themselves as members. If this set contains itself as a member, then it does not contain itself as a member. But if it does not contain itself as a member, then it does include itself as a member.

Russell at first thought this derivation of a contradiction was sophistical. He was not the first to have run across this type of argument. In 1889 an assistant to Peano, Cesare Burali-Forti, was working on the theory of ordinal numbers. Ordinals measure size like the ticket counters at butcher shops measure the length of the queue. Ordinals do not convey information about the distance that lies *between* the members of the sequence. When three customers are ranked by first, second, third, the sequence is well ordered because there is a first member and a unique next position in line. To extend the concept of well-ordering to infinite counters, we are careful not to require that there be a last member of the sequence. For instance, <0, 1, 2, 3, . . . > is well ordered. But there must be a first member: < . . . , -2, -1, 0, 1, 2, . . . > is not well ordered. The sequence of non-negative rational numbers <0, . . . , ¼, . . . , ½, . . . , 1, . . . , 2, . . . > singles out a first number but fails to single out the second. The nonstandard ordering of the integers <0, 1, 2, . . . , . . . , -3, -2, -1> is not well ordered because it does not single out which whole succeeds all the natural numbers. However, a sequence that stacks all the evens before the odds, <0, 2, 4, . . . , 1, 3, 5, . . . >, is well ordered. The accelerated sequence so popular in Zeno's paradoxes <½, ¾, ⅞, . . . , 1> is well ordered. Burali-Forti notes that the sequences constituting ordinals can be ranked in size. First comes <1>, second comes

<1, 2>, then <1, 2, 3> and so on. That is to say, the set of ordinals is well ordered. Any set that is well ordered has an ordinal number. Therefore, it must have an ordinal. However, this ordinal must be greater than every element in the set and so cannot be in the set!

Nowadays, this is called the Burali-Forti paradox. But Burali-Forti regarded his reasoning as a *reductio ad absurdum* of the trichotomy law. This law says that given any pair of ordinal numbers A and B, either A; = B, A < B or A > B. Burali-Forti was shocked when Cantor later offered a proof of the trichotomy law. It turns out that Burali-Forti had misread Cantor's definition of well ordering. After Burali-Forti renamed his concept "perfect ordering," he concluded that both proofs were correct.

For Burali-Forti and most others, Cantor's theory was too fluid to serve as the backdrop for paradoxes. Those sympathetic with Cantor construed surprising deductions from Cantor's theory as intriguing conjectures. Those hostile to Cantor viewed such results as disconfirming implausibilities. Only after Cantor's work hardened into mainstream mathematics did the surprises become commonly described as paradoxes.

Russell stands apart from the other set theorists in his refusal to put these anomalous sets on the back burner. At first he invested time in the puzzles just because they looked like resolvable sophistries. Time lost on "the contradiction" made the deadline for his book *Principles of Mathematics* more pressing. The systematic nature of the book made it difficult to dodge the question whether his set contained itself.

Russell became more and more fretful. He sought advice from fellow logicians. Once he telegraphed Alfred North Whitehead reporting that he had found a solution. After

Whitehead congratulated him, Russell's "indescribable relief" collapsed under the weight of a minor variation of the original paradox.

Still unsure whether "the contradiction" was an important discovery or a failure of ingenuity, Russell wrote Peano. Peano did not reply.

On June 16, 1902, Russell decided to turn to a logician he had read about in a review by Peano: Gottlob Frege. Russell had recently discovered that Frege was also working on the logicist program and had made much progress. Perhaps Frege could solve the paradox. Russell's letter arrived just as the second volume of Frege's *Basic Laws of Arithmetic* was in press. Whereas Russell had suffered pinprick by pinprick, Frege absorbed the lesson in a single stab. He quickly realized that his fifth law must be a contradiction. (This axiom permits the construction of Russell's set by claiming that two sets are equal if and only if their corresponding functions coincide in values for all possible arguments. An expression such as $f(x)$ must then be considered both a function of the argument $f$ and a function of the argument $x$.) In a rapidly drafted appendix, Frege starts to ask the right questions: "Is it always permissible to speak of the extension of a concept, of a class? And if not, how do we recognize the exceptional cases? Can we always infer from the extension of one concept's coinciding with that of a second, that every object which falls under the first concept also falls under the second?"

On June 22, Frege candidly replied to Russell:

> Your discovery of the contradiction has surprised me beyond words and, I should like to say, left me thunderstruck, because it has rocked the ground on which I meant to build arithmetic. . . . I must give some further thought

> to the matter. It is all the more serious as the collapse of my law V seems to undermine not only the foundations of my arithmetic but the possible foundations of arithmetic as such. . . . Your discovery is at any rate a very remarkable one, and it may perhaps lead to a great advance in logic, undesirable as it may seem at first sight.
>
> (Frege 1980, 132)

Russell was much impressed with Frege's dedication to truth: "upon finding that his fundamental assumption was in error, he responded with intellectual pleasure clearly submerging any feelings of personal disappointment."

Actually, Frege never again published anything significant. Depressed by the paradox, Frege feared that his whole life's work had been shown to be nearly worthless.

Frege had thought that we have infallible access to logical truths by intuition. The abstraction axiom says that any coherent condition may be used to determine a set. What could be clearer? Yet, Russell's paradox shows that this intuition is a contradiction.

Analogues of the abstraction axiom are common in semantics. We seem to define certain things into existence. During the heyday of American unionism, L. S. Johnston (1940) had a secretary who was annoyed by organizations that excluded their secretaries. The secretary wished there was a union for secretaries who could not be members of the organization they worked for. Since Johnston was a mathematician familiar with Russell's set paradox, he was primed to notice that the secretary was asking for the impossible. Suppose there was a union that could be joined just by secretaries who were excluded from membership in an organization that employed them. The union grows so big that it hires a secretary. She is not excluded by any other organization. Is this secretary eligible to join the union for excluded secretaries? If she is eligible to join the union, then no organization excludes her. This makes her ineligible to join the union. But if she is ineligible, then she is excluded by the union and is therefore eligible!

We have fallen into a contradiction because we assumed that it is possible for such a secretary to exist. This result is paradoxical because we think that groups are *defined* into existence. If we want to form a chess club, we can do it by *declaring* ourselves to be members of the club. Gottlob Frege had the same intuition about sets: any condition that can be described is sufficient for defining a set.

## AFTERMATH

Russell's first effort to restrict the abstraction principle occurs at the end of *Principles of Mathematics.* In "Appendix B: The Doctrine of Types," he suggests that we ban references to the paradoxical set. The sentences used to define sets need to be assembled into a hierarchy. At the lowest level are sentences about individuals. At the second level are sentences about sets of individuals. Third comes sentences about sets of sets of individuals, and so on. A predicate holds of "all objects" only when they are at the same level. According to Russell's "vicious circle principle," the meaning of a term cannot be specified until one specifies the exact range of objects that are candidates for satisfying it. Self-reference is meaningless.

But what about the previous sentence? Is that meaningless? Attempts to state the theory of types violate the theory. Russell struggles with this problem of self-defeat in the more mature version of the theory in his 1908 article "Mathematical Logic as Based on the Theory of Types" and in his monumental *Principia Mathematica*, co-authored with Whitehead.

After the gravity of Russell's paradox was appreciated, there was a spate of paradoxes by Jules Richard, Kurt Grelling, Julius Konig, and Ernst Zermello. G. G. Berry was one of the first individuals to produce new semantic paradoxes. Berry's paradox was presented by Russell in the following sentence: "'The least integer not namable in fewer than nineteen syllables' is itself a name consisting of eighteen syllables; hence the least integer not namable in fewer than nineteen syllables can be named in eighteen syllables, which is a contradiction." (Russell 1908, 223)

Berry is a curious figure. He had a humble job as a librarian in the Bodleian library at Oxford. To introduce himself, Berry presented Russell with a visiting card. On one side was written, "The statement on the other side of this card is true." On the other side was written, "The statement on the other side of this card is false." (There is a myth that this looped liar was the invention of Philip Jourdain.)

Berry's correspondence with Russell reveals that Berry was gifted at mathematical logic. But he never published theorems. As Leibniz wrote of Berkeley, Berry may have been "one of that class of men who wish to be known by their paradoxes." (Russell 1900, 72)

TWENTY-THREE

# Wittgenstein and the Depth of a Grammatical Joke

> The problems arising through a misinterpretation of our forms of language have the character of *depth*. They are deep disquietudes; their roots are as deep in us as the forms of our language and their significance is as great as the importance of our language.—Let us ask ourselves: why do we feel a grammatical joke to be *deep*? (And that is what the depth of philosophy is.)
>
> (Wittgenstein 1958, 111)

The logician and mathematician, Reverend Charles Dodgson, better known by his pseudonym, Lewis Carroll, is famous for his linguistic humor. In *Alice's Adventures in Wonderland*, the Duck inquires in vain for the referent of "it" in the Mouse's lecture: "Stigand, the patriotic archbishop of Canterbury, found it advisable . . . to go with Edgar Atheling. . . . " The Duck assumes the "it" should be something particular such as a frog or a worm. But the Mouse is using "it" as a dummy pronoun; it is inserted to appease a grammatical hunger for an object term. If David Hume is correct, Descartes may be like the Duck when searching for the referent of "I" in "I think, therefore, I exist."

Dodgson's whimsy carried over to his recreational mathematics. Interestingly, he believed these riddles could serve the serious purpose of spiritual protection. In his introduction to *Pillow Problems*, he writes, "There are sceptical thoughts, which seem for the moment to uproot the firmest faith: there are blasphemous thoughts, which dart unbidden into the most reverent souls; there are unholy thoughts, which torture, with their hateful presence, the fancy that would fain be pure. Against all these real mental work is a most helpful ally." The puzzles should be challenging but not *too* difficult. Veterans of sensory deprivation chambers recommend that you pass the time by posing intellectual challenges: reciting the alphabet backwards, listing all the prime numbers less than a hundred, etc. They caution that the problem must be definitely soluble. If you have the misfortune of picking a question that you cannot answer, you will not be able to switch the topic. You will come to hate the question but will not be able to stop thinking about it.

Paradoxes parasitized the attention of Bertrand Russell's protégé, Ludwig Wittgenstein. Wittgenstein (1889-1951) was repulsed by philosophers who had actually grown fond of the Eternal Questions. He philosophizes only in the hope of ending his compulsion to answer.

## WITTGENSTEIN'S THERAPY

When Leo Tolstoy was a boy, his older brother challenged him to stand in the corner until he stopped thinking about a white bear. The more little Leo tried to stop thinking about a white bear, the more he thought about it. He only stopped thinking about the white bear when he became distracted. People who are plagued by obsessional thoughts cannot simply decide not to think those thoughts. Relief comes involuntarily. At best, the obsessive thinker can cultivate a lapse of attention by altering his circumstances.

Wittgenstein distracted himself by watching American movies, preferably westerns. He would sit in the front row eating pot pies, completely engrossed. He also read detective stories (as do many philosophers—perhaps out of a hunger for resolution). However, such diversions only supplied a few hours of relief to Wittgenstein. His only sustained period of peace came after the publication of his *Tractatus* in 1921. Thinking that he had exposed all philosophical problems as violations of an ideal grammar, he retired from philosophy to become an elementary school teacher in the remote Austrian village of Trattenbach.

Eventually Wittgenstein became persuaded that this ideal language was itself delusory and so restlessly returned to Cambridge University in 1929. In the following decade, he pieced together "ordinary language philosophy." With much self-recrimination, Wittgenstein renounced his earlier demand that grammar meet the a priori requirements of logic. Instead of trying to think of how language *must* operate, he resolved to observe how speakers actually behave. From this anthropological perspective, a natural language such as

English resembles London—a living, growing city with ancient roots. There are modern sections laid out neatly in grids. But many other neighborhoods sprawl haphazardly. London cannot be defined in a day. It is a motley of overlapping institutions. All of the useful generalizations must be hedged and local. Paradoxes arise when we overextend analogies, when we lift expressions out of context, and when we disengage patterns of discourse from their practical (and impractical) purposes.

According to Wittgenstein, most paradoxes can be nipped in the bud by bringing words back into their natural settings, by studying how they are taught to children, and by noting the role they in play in larger practices. To avoid being overwhelmed by complexity, he also considers simplified language games. But these artificial specimens should not be treated as ideals that ordinary language imperfectly approximates. We easily slip on the ice of idealization. We steady our thinking by constantly returning to the rough ground.

In some circumstances, we may find that the rules of language really lead to a contradiction. Russell and Frege treated contradictions as crises. But Wittgenstein compared news of a contradiction to the discovery that a game has a loophole that would guarantee a trivial victory. If there is trouble, we may close the loophole on an ad hoc basis. If people do not actually exploit the loophole, then no repair is needed. We can *live* with some paradoxes. Perhaps some of them, such as the problem of freewill, will occasionally trouble us in a practical way. After all, we must sometimes judge hard cases involving addiction, compulsion, and duress. But the appropriate reaction is to make small adjustments. We should not replace the arthritis of common-sense with the prosthesis of metaphysics.

Sextus Empiricus tried to end philosophical inquiry by any means available, rational or irrational. If there were a safe antiphilosophy pill, Sextus would have prescribed it. Wittgenstein opposes noncognitive cures. He thinks that freedom from philosophical worries must proceed through insights into how language sets traps for us.

## PICTURING WORDS AS NAMES

The meaning of names seems especially simple. When Abraham Lincoln uttered "Fido" the word's meaning was its bearer: Lincoln's floppy-eared, rough-coated, yellowish dog of uncertain ancestry. In Plato's dialogues, Socrates naively extends the "Fido"/Fido model to terms such as "courage," "knowledge," and "good." Since there are no mundane bearers of these words, Socrates infers that there must be transcendental bearers: the forms of courage, knowledge, and goodness. This subliming of the language leads to a cluster of problems about universals. Can a universal exist without instances? Must each pair of universals be related by a higher universal? How can material beings know anything about these abstract entities?

Wittgenstein maintains that if we look at how we actually use words, we see there is often no feature that is common and peculiar to all uses. In the case of "game," there is only a network of overlapping similarities—a family resemblance. Thus, the Socratic demand for definition rests on the false presupposition that there is some common thread binding all uses of a term.

The "Fido"/Fido model also lurks behind key paradoxes in the philosophy of the mind. We presuppose that words such as "headache" have bearers. Since the bearer cannot be physical, we infer there is a mental bearer. On the one hand, this nonphysical entity seems elusive because it is not open to public view. Hence, there is no independent check on whether it is present. On the other hand, pain seems like the easiest thing to know. The sufferer of a headache cannot falsely believe he has a headache. And if he has a headache, he cannot fail to notice it. For pain, to be is to be perceived. This private realm of entities is easily seen as the best known realm for the person who hosts them. Thus, it becomes tempting to view the mental realm as the foundation of all other knowledge. The mental realms of other people are unavailable to your inspection, hence you seem particularly ill suited to judge whether others have the same sort of ideas as you do or even whether they have such ideas at all. The external world as a whole looks like something we must audaciously infer on the basis of our own ideas. At bottom, what you *know* best are your own ideas. At bottom, what you are *really* talking about are ideas that you are having or might have. Since these ideas are necessarily *your* ideas and ones about which *you* cannot be mistaken, each of us is really speaking a private language. Communication is impossible because our languages do not have any words or sentences that mean the same thing. We can neither agree nor disagree with each other.

Wittgenstein argues that a private language is impossible. A rule that only you can follow is a rule that cannot sustain the contrast between obeying the rule and violating the rule. If there is no way to get it wrong, there is no way to get it right. *Private rule* is a contradiction in terms. Private languages must be defined with private rules. Therefore, there can be no private languages.

Wittgenstein also challenges the assumption that "pain" refers to anything. He suggests that "I have headache" does not *report* a headache; it expresses pain like a groan. Instead of clutching your forehead in misery, you substitute a piece of verbal behavior. "The paradox disappears only if we make a radical break with the idea that language always functions in one way, always serves the same purpose; to convey thoughts—which may be about houses, pains, good and evil, or anything else you please." (1958, 304) Wittgenstein encourages the development of alternatives to his avowal theory of "pain." Wittgenstein's point is not to substitute a philosophical theory with another philosophical theory. He does not trace philosophy's problems merely to the choice of false premises. Wittgenstein thinks the real problem is that we feel compelled to choose premises.

## THE RELEVANCE OF LINGUISTIC ODDITY

The Scottish writer Robert Louis Stevenson was fond of a little girl who complained about being born on Christmas Day. Instead of receiving presents on two days of the year, she only received them on one. In his will, Stevenson bequeathed the girl his own birthday. He appended the following clause: "If, however, she fails to use this bequest properly, all rights shall pass to the President of the United States."

Stevenson's "bequest" shows that a birthday is not a possession that can be transferred. This moral resembles philosophical remarks about limits. A philosopher who is faced with the problem of other minds remarks, "I cannot feel your pain." It is helpful to compare the deep privacy of pain to the shallow privacy of birthdays.

Wittgenstein "once said that a serious and good philosophical work could be written that would consist entirely of *jokes* (without being facetious). Another time he said that a philosophical treatise might contain nothing but questions (without answers)." (Malcolm 1958, 29) In his *Philosophical Investigations*, Wittgenstein often blends jokes and questions:

> Why can't a dog simulate pain? Is he too honest?
> Why can't my right hand give my left hand money?
> Why does it sound queer to say: "For a second he felt deep grief?" (Only because it so seldom happens?)
> (1958, 250, 268, II, i)

Anthony Kenny, a methodical Wittgenstein scholar, reports that *Philosophical Investigations* contains 784 questions; 110 are answered and 70 of these answers are *meant* to be wrong.

Wittgenstein says his aim is "to teach you to pass from a piece of disguised nonsense to something that is patent nonsense." (1958, 464) For instance, one might compare "Where does an idea go after it has been thought?" with "Where does a flame go after it goes out?." Since jokes and riddles are succinct, acknowledged cases of patent nonsense, they are handy candidates for these logical analogies.

Other "ordinary language philosophers" tried to defuse philosophical problems by drawing analogies with manifest linguistic absurdities. Gilbert Ryle's *The Concept of Mind* frequently accuses René Descartes of committing "category mistakes."

> A man would be thought to be making a poor joke who said that three things are not rising, namely, the tide, hopes, and the average age of death. It would be just as

> good or bad a joke to say that there exist prime numbers and Wednesdays and public opinions and navies; or that there exist both bodies and minds.
>
> (1949, 23)

Wittgenstein thought similar limits are revealed by philosophical remarks such as "The colors green and blue cannot be in the same place simultaneously."

Ordinary language philosophy is an abridged descendant of common-sense philosophy. Contrary to the expectations of Thomas Reid, several common-sense beliefs have been overturned by post-eighteenth-century physics. Principles that hold for medium-size objects in familiar conditions break down at the scales studied by astronomers and microphysicists. To avoid encroaching on science, ordinary language philosophers only retain the linguistic aspect of Reid's philosophy. They restrict themselves to making remarks about how language operates. As native speakers of English, they have mastered its rules and can judge whether sentences are part of English. Sadly, we do not have direct access to the rules we are employing. We must infer the rules from data about which sentences belong to English. Statements of the rules of language are analytic. They are not remarks about the world. This explains why philosophy can be done from the armchair. Philosophy, like mathematics, is an a priori field.

In practice, ordinary language philosophers exploited empirical clues as to what the rules might be. We know that English cannot be composed of infinitely many independent rules because that would make the language unlearnable. Wittgenstein frequently appeals to functions of language when suggesting how conventions are organized. But this "peeking" is much like the informal testing geometers employ to guide their conjectures. The statements themselves are a priori even if we actually used an a posteriori mode of investigation. (What matters is that the statement *could* have been learned without experience.)

When we use language properly, our problems are well structured: there is always an answer even if it turns out that we cannot learn the answer. With philosophical questions, we fall into dazzled confusion as to what would even count as an answer. This sentiment dates back to Wittgenstein's *Tractatus* period:

> Most of the propositions and questions to be found in philosophical works are not false but nonsensical. Consequently we cannot give any answer to questions of this kind, but can only establish that they are nonsensical. Most of the propositions and questions of philosophers arise from our failure to understand the logic of our language.
>
> (They belong to the same class as the question whether the good is more or less identical than the beautiful.)
>
> And it is not surprising that the deepest problems are in fact not problems at all.
>
> (1969a, 4.003)

There are no answers to philosophical questions because there really are no such questions; there are merely pseudoproblems that masquerade as questions. A field makes progress only by answering questions, so philosophical progress is impossible. ("The riddle does not exist. If a question can be put at all, then it can also be answered.") At best, one can *dissolve* philosophical problems by showing how they arise from misunderstandings of how our language works.

## SARTRE AND THE SELF-DECEIVED

The later Wittgenstein never presents a definitive resolution of a paradox. He only hints and sketches, encouraging others to think for themselves. His followers did attempt to dissolve a paradox that Jean Paul Sartre popularized in the 1950s: Is self-deception possible? I suspect the ordinary language philosophers targeted this paradox partly out of envy and resentment. While the British philosophers were dismissed by bored book reviewers as "verbosophers," the French existentialists were lionized as beacons of culture. Sartre, Simone de Beauvoir, Albert Camus, André Malraux were celebrities. Like the Stoics, they offered an integrated vision of reality and the human condition. They honored character traits that give rise to philosophy. The existentialists met their public halfway by presenting their views in literature and plays. The cloistered Wittgensteinians were just curing each other.

In *Being and Nothingness*, Sartre observes that self-deception seems to be an all-too-common phenomenon. Yet, there is a compelling objection to its very possibility. To be a deceiver, one must not believe the deception, but the victim must believe the deception. Since it is impossible to both believe and not believe the deception, self-deception is impossible.

One popular way to disarm the contradiction is to divide the self into parts, homunculi, and say one homunculus is deceiving another homunculus. The danger of an infinite regress becomes apparent when we ask whether homunculi can themselves be self-deceived. Answering no is ad hoc: any creature that is sophisticated enough to deceive others is sophisticated enough to apply the same trick to itself. If the homunculi can deceive themselves, then we must postulate subhomunculi, and sub-subhomunculi, and so on.

Perhaps a metaphysical psychologist would welcome the implication that each self is composed of infinitely many selves. Wittgensteinians would recoil. Instead of postulating an infinite hierarchy of subselves, ordinary language philosophers trace the difficulty to misleading surface grammar. The statement "King George IV deceived himself into believing that he fought at Waterloo" looks like it uses "deceive" in the same sense as "King George IV deceived Princess Caroline of Brunswick into believing he fought at Waterloo." But the Wittgensteinians denied that the "deceive" in self-deception is used in the same sense as the "deceive" in other-deception. They compared "deceive yourself" to "invite yourself," "defeat yourself," and "teach yourself." You invite yourself to a party if you attend without an invitation. When you defeat yourself, you are not both victor and vanquished; you are just the main reason why someone else defeated you. We can feign a paradox for "Abraham Lincoln was self-taught" by modeling self-teaching on the teaching of others: As teacher, Lincoln knows the lesson. As student, Lincoln does not know the lesson. Therefore, Lincoln both knows and does not know the lesson!

Any puzzlement generated by this sophistry rests on a determination to model self-teaching on other-teaching. We should instead approach reflexive expressions with respect for the idiosyncrasies of language. Yes, reflexive expressions do suggest that they all have the logical form "*a* bears relation *R* to itself." But no, this surface grammar sometimes masks a very different depth grammar. In particular, " . . . we say when 'Jones deceives himself about *P*' is true, it is true that Jones believes *P* under belief-adverse circumstances, e. g., circumstances such that the evidence Jones has does not warrant belief in *P*." (Canfield and Gustavson 1962, 32) This paraphrase "self-deception" aims to condense a "cloud of philosophy into a drop of grammar."

As a byproduct of linguistic therapy, we may learn how language works. But this incidental progress in linguistics is not *philosophical* progress. Helpful philosophy is like medicine. The physician only offers the patient relief from a bad thing. He may make discoveries of scientific interest along the way, but these advances are not the aim of medicine. When the philosopher unties a conceptual knot, there is no positive *philosophical* residue.

## RULE FOLLOWING

Wittgenstein contrasts the way children learn to recite the alphabet with the way they learn to recite numerals: "There are two ways of using the expression 'and so on'. If I say, 'The alphabet is A, B, C, D, and so on', then 'and so on' is an abbreviation. But if I say, 'The cardinals are 1, 2, 3, 4, and so on', then it is not." (1976, 170-71) A child learns the alphabet by memorizing a complete list. If you give him the letters up to G, you cannot expect him to extrapolate to H, I, J, K. In contrast, a child cannot learn an endless list of number words by rote. He must learn to continue on his own.

How did you manage to master the rule for extending numerical sequences endlessly? Even simple continuations require adding. How did you learn "plus"? Saul Kripke (1982) credits Wittgenstein with the discovery of a skeptical paradox about rule following. Suppose you have never computed 68 + 57 before. You answer 125, confident that this corresponds to your past usage of "plus." A skeptic questions your certainty: perhaps your past usage requires that the answer be 5. After all, there are indefinitely many rules that could have yielded your past results. How do you know which rule you intended?

> This was our paradox: no course of action could be determined by a rule, because every course of action can be made out to accord with the rule. The answer was: if everything can be made out to accord with the rule, then it can also be made out to conflict with it. And so there would be neither accord nor conflict here.
>
> (1958, 201)

Kripke says Wittgenstein solves the paradox by denying that rule following involves self-interpretation. Instead, we are just trained to use words. Our mastery of a rule is a matter of being inducted into a linguistic practice.

Many philosophers think Kripke is perverting the aim of Wittgenstein's therapy. Wittgenstein had no interest in discovering new paradoxes. He only wanted to eliminate old ones. If Wittgenstein were right about paradoxes being pseudoproblems, then it should not be possible to solve them.

However, Wittgenstein regularly relapses into the kind of philosophizing he renounces. He is not immune to the charm exerted by an answer "which sets the whole mind in a whirl, and gives the pleasant feeling of paradox." (1976, 16) Like a fellow alcoholic, Wittgenstein identifies with Cantor when he giddily concludes that there are infinitely many infinitely large numbers. Wittgenstein thinks Cantor invented the transfinite numbers while under the influence of an alluring interpretation of "1, 2, 3, 4, . . . . " He speculates that "The dots introduce a certain picture: of numbers *trailing off* into the distance too far for one to see. And a great deal is achieved if we use a different sign. Suppose that instead of dots we write , then '1, 2, 3, 4, Δ' is less misleading." (1976, 170) Dr. Seuss's *On Beyond Zebra* opens with a young boy proudly writing on a blackboard. Conrad Cornelius o'Donald o'Dell, has demonstrated his exhaustive knowledge of the alphabet: A is for Ape, B is for Bear, . . . and Z is for Zebra. An older boy compliments Conrad. He breezily concedes to young Conrad that *most* people stop with Z. But *his* alphabet continues beyond Z. The extra letters let him spell new things. The older boy thus introduces Conrad to an otherwise inaccessible realm of exotic creatures. For instance, the Q-ish letter quan is for the vertically symmetric Quandary who lives on a shelf.

> In a hole in the ocean alone by himself
> And he worries, each day, from the dawn's early light
> And he worries, just worries, far into the night.
> He just stands there and worries. He simply can't stop . . .
> Is his top-side bottom? Or bottom-side top?

The tour given to Conrad would put Wittgenstein in mind of other never-never lands.

Wittgenstein insists that he does not wish to replace one philosophical theory with another. But he frequently does just that. He advances, albeit guardedly, the use theory of meaning, the avowal theory of pain, the doctrine of family resemblance, etc. Despite poking fun at the philosopher's preoccupation with limits and impossibility results, Wittgenstein is known for his refutation of private languages, for treating the limits of language as the limits of thought, and for his skepticism about infinity. And despite his denigration of paradoxes, he cannot stop inventing puzzles about infinity and rule following.

Wittgenstein "once remarked that the only work of Moore's that greatly impressed him was his discovery of the peculiar kind of nonsense involved in such a sentence as 'It is raining but I don't believe it.'" (Malcolm 1958, 56) Is this a slight against the founder of analytic philosophy? Or is it the confession of a paradox addict?

Wittgenstein's runaway rumination brings to mind a passage from *Paradise Lost.* John Milton is describing hell as a varied terrain in which some fallen angels fight, others mournfully sing, and yet

> Others apart sat on a hill retired,
> In thoughts more elevate, and reasoned high
> Of Providence, Foreknowledge, Will, and Fate—
> Fixed fate, free will, foreknowledge absolute—
> And found no end, in wandering mazes lost. (II, 557-61)

The poor devils on the hill are tormented by the futility of their inquiry but cannot control their inquisitiveness. The more they think about why they must not think, the more deeply they wear the grooves of thought.

TWENTY-FOUR

# Quine's Question Mark

Logic chases truth up the tree of grammar.

(W. V. Quine, 70, 35)

Willard Van Orman Quine was born in Akron, Ohio, on "anti-Christmas," June 25, 1908. He died on Christmas 2000. Beginning a lifelong affiliation with Harvard University, Quine wrote a dissertation on *Principia Mathematica* under the supervision of Alfred North Whitehead. Although Quine made contributions to computer science, he continued to use his 1927 Remington typewriter. As a logician, he "had an operation on it" to change a few keys to accommodate special symbols. "I found I could do without the second period, the second comma—and the question mark." A reporter asked, "You don't miss the question mark?" to which Quine answered, "Well, you see, I deal in certainties."

I think paradoxes are riddles that overload the audience with good answers. Since a riddle adopts the form of a question, I doubt that Quine's modified typewriter can fluently formulate paradoxes. However, Quine is responsible for the most influential definition of "paradox."

## CARTER'S DOOMSDAY ARGUMENT

The first sense of "paradox" listed by the Oxford English Dictionary is "A statement or tenet contrary to received opinion or expectation." Quine thinks this overlooks the central role of argument. In "The Ways of Paradox," Quine develops the idea that "a paradox is just any conclusion that at first sounds absurd but that has an argument to sustain it." (1976, 1) The doomsdayer's "The end is near!" is a "tenet contrary to received opinion." But it is a paradox only if backed with a good argument.

Surprisingly, such an argument has arisen from the interaction between science and philosophy encouraged by Quine. The cosmologist Brandon Carter (1974) notes that in the absence of any evidence that I am special, I should regard myself as being located in the same segment of history as the average man. Since the population has been growing exponentially, most people have recent birth dates. Therefore, I should assign a surprisingly high probability to the hypothesis that I am writing near the end of human history.

Does Carter's argument "sustain" the surprising conclusion? The philosopher John Leslie defends Carter's argument at book-length. In *The End of the World*, Leslie contends that the doomsday argument gives us extra reason to respond to threats of human extinction.

I used to think the doomsday argument commits a fallacy that I could diagnose on a Sunday afternoon. But each apparent refutation was followed by a reply that left the doomsday argument essentially intact. After a month of Sundays, the resilient doomsday argument earned my grudging respect (though not my assent). I think this robustness is what Quine is driving at when he talks of an argument *sustaining* a surprising conclusion.

## VERIDICAL AND FALSIDICAL PARADOXES

As may be surmised from the positive associations of "sustain," Quine believes some paradoxical arguments have true conclusions. His illustration of a *veridical* paradox is drawn from *The Pirates of Penzance*. The protagonist, Frederic, is 21 years old and yet has had only five birthdays. Although this seems like a contradiction, we see how it must be true after being informed that Frederic was born on February 29. Leap years make it possible to be age $4n$ on one's $n$-th birthday. Quine pictures veridical paradoxes as lines of reasoning that are eventually vindicated.

Quine does not mean that all sustaining arguments are *sound*, for he thinks many paradoxes are false conclusions. He calls these "falsidical paradoxes." Nor does Quine think that a sustaining argument must be deductively valid. For Quine thinks that all sustaining arguments for falsidical paradoxes are fallacious.

Quine thinks antinomies differ by producing "a self-contradiction by accepted ways of reasoning." (1976, 5) Recall Russell's antinomy about the set that contains all and only those sets that do not contain themselves. Is this set a member of itself? Quine says this paradox "establishes that some tacit and trusted pattern of reasoning must be made explicit and henceforward avoided or revised." Quine recommends that we "inactivate" the antinomy by adopting grammatical rules that prevent it from being formulated. He extends this proposed ban to semantic paradoxes such as the liar by requiring all uses of "true" to be relativized to a language. "Violations of this restriction would be treated as meaningless, or ungrammatical, rather than as true or false sentences." (1976, 8) Quine admits that it seems repressive to ban talk of simple "truth." But he predicts that, in time, the sense of artificiality will disappear and the self-referential antinomies will become falsidical paradoxes. Set theorists will think Russell's antinomy commits a fallacy just as mathematicians now think Zeno's bisection paradox simply mishandles the concept of a convergent series.

But hold on Professor Quine! Weren't falsidical paradoxes supposed to have false conclusions? If the endpoints of Russell's antinomy are meaningless, then they cannot be false; nor can they even be *conclusions* that are sustained by arguments. All conclusions are meaningful statements. Quine's definition would therefore imply that the antinomies of self-reference are not genuine paradoxes.

Recall that Jean Buridan studied *contingent* liar paradoxes: Mr. Straight asserts "The next thing Mr. Crooked says is true" and Mr. Crooked says "What Straight said is false." If Crooked said, "118 countries received a visit from Quine," then both statements would have been true. If the liar paradox is meaningless (as I believe Quine is correct in contending), then the contingent liars show that meaninglessness is sometimes undetectable by the speaker. The internal rationality of the speaker is not enough to guarantee that his utterances are meaningful.

If all sustaining arguments had to be deductively valid, then there would be no *inductive* paradoxes. But Quine must concede that there are paradoxes in which the surprising conclusion only purports to be probable. Consider the following instance of the birthday paradox. Professor Statistics predicts that two of his students share a birthday from the premise that there are forty students in the class. At first, the professor's conclusion merely seems rash. The paradox emerges when Professor Statistics divulges his reasoning: "'There are forty students' gives my conclusion a probability of 89.1 percent. To see why, picture a calendar with 365 days on it. Mark your birthday. A second student now marks his birthday. She has a probability 364/365 of marking an empty day. The third person to mark the calendar has a 363/365 chance of marking an empty day. The chance that N people manage to mark an empty day is $1 - (365 \times (365 - 1) \times (365 - 2) \ldots \times (365 - (N-1)/(365N)$. So when there are 23 people there is a 50.7 percent chance of a shared birthday. When $N = 40$, the formula implies that the probability of a shared birthday is 89.1 percent."

But having gone through all this, further suppose Professor Statistics has been unlucky: none of the forty students shares a birthday. His paradoxical prediction turns out to be false even though it was backed by a true premise and an appropriate rule of inference.

What makes the professor's prediction paradoxical is the reasoning behind it. The reasoning does not need to be perfect. Like most purveyors of the birthday paradox, Professor Statistics skated over the fact that some years have more than 365 days. Nor does he consider travelers who lost their birthdays while crossing the International Date Line. (An old man could die without having any birthdays.) The paradox survives because these omissions are insignificant.

We could try to force each paradoxical induction into the deductive mold by treating it as an enthymeme (an argument with an unstated premise or conclusion). Each induction would have the tacit premise "If the stated premises are true, then the conclusion is true." This ploy renders *all* inductions, both good and bad, deductively valid. Questions about reasoning are turned into questions about the truth of this postulated conditional. This maneuver does not resolve the narrowness of a purely deductive definition of "paradox." For consider the original inductive arguments that are not treated as disguised deductions. All of them remain paradoxical.

## THE NEW RIDDLE OF INDUCTION

Formulations of inductive paradoxes are more likely to become outdated. A valid deductive argument remains valid whatever new information comes along. But the cogency of inductive reasoning is affected by the addition of new premises. I was taught Nelson Goodman's (1906-1998) "new riddle of induction" from Brian Skyrms's *Choice and Chance*. Skyrms reviews how John Stuart Mill inaugurated the formal study of induction by codifying the sort of inference patterns experimentalists love. Just as Aristotle codified argument patterns that ensure deductive validity, Mill searches for argument patterns that make the conclusion probable given the premises. Here is a simple example: "All past *F*s are *G*s, therefore, the next *F* will be *G*." In 1946 Goodman published an objection to the whole enterprise of inductive logic. It attracted scant attention. In 1954, he repackaged the idea. Goodman's new presentation borrowed "gruebleen" from James Joyce's novel *Finnegans Wake*. In Skyrms's formulation, "grue" means "is green and observed before time 2000 or is blue and observed during or after 2000." Suppose all the examined emeralds before 2000 are green. What should the "grue" speaker expect in the year 2000? Given the rule "All past *F*s are *G*s, therefore, the next *F* will be *G*," he should predict that the next observed emerald will be grue. This means the "grue" speaker is predicting that the emerald will be blue! Goodman's riddle is an *inductive* antinomy:

| *Green thesis* | *Grue antithesis* |
|---|---|
| All emeralds before 2000 have been green. | All emeralds before 2000 have been grue. |
| So, the emerald seen in 2000 will be green. | So, the emerald seen in 2000 will be grue. |

The opposed predictions share the same argument form and are based on the same data.

My first thought was that the grue thesis prevails because "green" is the more basic predicate. After all, green was used to define grue. But Goodman points out that green can be defined in terms of grue and another term, bleen. Let "bleen" mean "green and observed before 2000 or blue and observed during or after 2000." Goodman can then define "green" as "grue and observed before 2000 or bleen and observed at sometime thereafter."

My second thought was that the green thesis prevails because it did not require a change in the course of nature. But a classmate argued that change was relative. From the perspective of the grue speakers, *I* was the one postulating a mysterious discontinuity in the year 2000. The grue speakers were expecting grue things to stay grue.

Quieted, I resolved to wait out the antinomy. If, in 2000, the grass came up blue and the bluebell flowers came up green, then I would desert the green party. But if 2000 conformed to my expectations, I would consider the antithesis defeated.

My patience was vindicated. But this disconfirmation of the antithesis is only an insignificant dent in the argument sustaining the new riddle of induction. The antithesis is still a good argument even though I know its conclusion is false. The value of the induction lies in its process of reasoning, not its product. The technique of concocting "gruesome" predicates is readily adapted to arguments that will elude the strategy of patience. Indeed, Goodman never actually specifies the year 2000 in his "definition" of a grue. He only provides a definition *schema* that employs the temporal variable $x$.

Quine offers a diagnosis of Goodman's paradox: induction only works for predicates that correspond to natural kinds. Aristotle believed that just as a butcher cuts at the joints, a scientist classifies in accordance with preexisting divisions. Contrary to a purely conventional view of language, Aristotle thought that some of our vocabulary refers to these natural kinds. Quine thinks this is especially plausible in light of evolutionary theory. Reasoners who sort objects into categories that correspond to natural boundaries will enjoy greater reproductive success. Their predictive success is enhanced artificially by scientific investigation. Part of scientific progress is devising a vocabulary that more closely matches natural divisions. We instinctively prefer "green" over "grue" because "green" comes closer to cutting nature at the joint.

Quine says his solution also solves Carl Hempel's (1945) raven paradox. Hempel notes that the observation of a black raven is some evidence in favor of "All ravens are black." Does the observation of a white handkerchief also confirm "All ravens are black"? Here is the case for indoor ornithology:

1. Nicod's criterion: A universal generalization "All *F*s are *G*s" is confirmed by "$x$ is an $F$ and a $G$."
2. Equivalence condition: Whatever confirms a statement confirms a logically equivalent statement.
3. Therefore, a white handkerchief confirms "All ravens are black."

"All ravens are black" is equivalent to "All nonblack things are nonravens." Nicod's criterion implies that "This is a raven and is black" confirms "All ravens are black." It also implies that a white handkerchief confirms "All nonblack things are nonwhite." So by the equivalence condition, the white handkerchief must also confirm "All ravens are black."

Quine rejects Nicod's criterion. He restricts confirmation to hypotheses employing natural-kind terms. Therefore, he denies that a white handkerchief confirms "All nonblack things are nonravens."

## THE ANALYTIC/SYNTHETIC DISTINCTION

Daniel Dennett's *The Philosophical Lexicon* defines "quine" as a verb: "To deny resolutely the existence of importance of something real or significant." Quine has quined names, intentions, and the distinction between psychology and epistemology. In 1951 Quine quined the distinction between analytic and synthetic statements. An analytic statement owes its truth-value to the meanings of its words. For instance, "You can receive an unbirthday present on most days of the year" is made true by Humpty Dumpty's definition of an unbirthday present in Lewis Carroll's *Through the Looking Glass.* In contrast, synthetic statements owe their truth-values to the world. "About nine million people share your birthday" is made true by the present population and the law of averages. The analytic/synthetic distinction was first explicitly drawn by Kant. It was almost universally accepted by philosophers until Quine's article "Two dogmas of empiricism." He made the distinction controversial by dwelling on the unclarities of the boundary between what is made true by meaning and what is made true by contingent facts.

Some readers may suspect that my riddle theory of paradoxes quines Quine's distinction between veridical and falsidical paradoxes. If paradoxes are questions, they cannot be true or false. They cannot be proved or refuted. After all, riddles can be neither believed nor disbelieved. The only direct kind of absurdity these riddles manifest is their overabundance of good answers. But remember that on my question-based account, *answers* to paradoxes can be true or false.

Quine's definition of paradox implies that wherever there is a paradox, there is an argument for an *absurd* conclusion. The next two sections present counterexamples to Quine's implication that all paradoxes are absurdities.

## RADICAL TRANSLATION

After the United States entered World War II, Quine left his fellowship at Harvard to become a Navy code breaker. He became intrigued by the problem of translation under adverse circumstances. Consider explorers who had to communicate with aborigines:

> On their voyage of discovery to Australia a group of Captain Cook's sailors captured a young kangaroo and brought the strange creature back on board their ship. No one knew what it was, so some men were sent ashore to ask the natives. When the sailors returned they told their mates, "It's a kangaroo." Many years later it was discovered that when the aborigines said "kangaroo" they were not in fact naming the animal, but replying to their questioners, "What did you say?"
>
> (*The Observer* magazine supplement, November 25, 1973)

Even if apocryphal, anecdotes about radical mistranslations raise the issue of whether we can ever know that a translation is correct. If the mistranslation were systematic enough, no amount of speech or behavior could reveal the error.

Quine (1960) conjugates this skeptical challenge into a semantic paradox. Suppose an anthropologist sees a rabbit run by and the native says, "Gavagai!" The utterance could be translated as (a) Lo, a rabbit; (b) Lo, an undetached rabbit-part; (c) Lo, an instantiation of the universal rabbithood; (d) Lo, a temporal stage of a rabbit. The anthropologist is free to choose any of (a) to (d) as long as he makes adjustments elsewhere in his translation manual. Quine maintains that there are infinitely many translation manuals that account for all the speech and behavior of the natives.

Is the skeptic right about us being ignorant of the correct translation? Not quite, says Quine. He thinks that when there is no possible empirical difference between the manuals, the issue of correctness does not arise. The underdetermination of the hypotheses by the data renders them indeterminate.

This indeterminacy of translation extends to the problem of interpreting the world. There are infinitely many theories that accommodate all the data we will ever possess. Galileo said that nature is a book written in the language of mathematics. Even if this were true, there are infinitely many mathematical functions that can summarize all the data we could ever acquire.

"What is the translation of 'Gavagai!'?" has infinitely many rival answers. According to Quine, the problem is that infinitely many of these are equally good answers. Quine's paradox of radical translation is a counterexample to his own definition of paradox. In addition to showing that absurdity is inessential to paradox, the paradox of radical translation shows that the paradox can be free of arguments and conclusions. "What is the translation of 'Gavagai'?" has answers obtained by translation, not conclusions derived by arguments.

## THE ODD UNIVERSE

Like most logicians, Quine treasures simplicity. He hates to postulate anything more than is needed to explain the data. Quine politely characterizes his preference as a "taste for desert landscapes." But more outspoken lovers of simplicity warn that you take a risk whenever you postulate a new entity. Minimizing postulates minimizes error. This is especially plausible when unprecedented entities are in question. Abstract objects are discontinuous with what we know best. Safety would be served by avoiding them. Indeed, Quine once co-authored a defense of nominalism with Nelson Goodman. Nominalists reject abstract entities—they think that everything has a position in space or time. Their diet is aimed against philosophical excesses such as Plato's forms. However, nominalism also winds up prohibiting entities that scientists help themselves to—numbers, geometrical points, sets, etc.

Quine soon felt the pinch. He became persuaded that sets are indispensable for mathematics. To retain mathematics, he relented and swallowed sets. Quine is a pragmatist. Sets earned their way into Quine's metaphysics by being useful. *Principia Mathematica* teaches that sets plus logic are enough to reconstruct all of mathematics. In turn, mathematics is essential to theoretical physics. Science and mathematics set the standard for rationality, so Quine feels entitled to believe in whatever is indispensably postulated by scientists. For Quine, metaphysics is an afterthought of science.

Meanwhile, Nelson Goodman kept sharpening the knife of nominalism. In 1951 he published *The Structure of Appearances.* This book contains a logic of parts and wholes. Goodman denies that there are sets. Instead, there are *fusions* built up from smaller things. Unlike a set, a fusion has a position in space and time. You can touch a fusion. I'm a fusion. So are you. Goodman's "calculus of individuals" says that there are only finitely many atomic individuals and that any combination of atoms is an individual. Objects do not need to have all their parts connected, for instance, Alaska and Hawaii are parts of the United States of America. Goodman does not let human intuition dictate what counts as an object; he also thinks that there is the fusion of his ear and the moon.

In a seminar Goodman taught at the University of Pennsylvania around 1965, John Robison pointed out that

*The Structure of Appearances* implies an answer to "Is the number of individuals in the universe odd or even?" Since there are only finitely many atoms and each individual is identical to a combination of atoms, there are exactly as many individuals as there are combinations of atoms. If there are $n$ atoms, there are $2^{n-1}$ combinations of individuals. No matter which number we choose for $n$, $2^{n-1}$ is an odd number. Therefore, the number of individuals in the universe is odd!

The exclamation point is not for the oddness per se. Aside from those who think the universe is infinite, people agree that the universe contains either an odd number of individuals or an even number of individuals. What they find absurd is that there could be a *proof* that the number of individuals is odd.

"Is the number of individuals in the universe odd or even?" illustrates the possibility of *one* good answer being too many. Our expectation is that this question is unanswerable. The lone good answer confounds beliefs about what arguments can accomplish. Here the excess is a top-down judgment. (More commonly, the overabundance is a bottom-up verdict: a good answer clashes with another good answer.)

## INTERESTING NUMBERS

Our meta-argumentative expectations can also be frustrated by *how* something is proved rather than the sheer fact that it is proved. Consider the question of whether all natural numbers are interesting. When G. H. Hardy visited the mathematical genius Ramanujan as he lay dying in a sanitarium, he was at a loss for what to say. So Hardy mentioned that the taxi that he had hired to take him to the sanitarium had the rather dull number 1729. "Oh no, Hardy. It is a captivating one. It is the smallest number that can be expressed in two different ways as a sum of two cubes," replied Ramanujan. ($1{,}729 = 1^3 + 12^3 = 10^3 + 9^3$). Francois Le Lionnais's *Nombres remarguables* shows that many apparently dull numbers are interesting. The first integer for which he can find no remarkable property is 39. Le Lionnais muses that this lack of a remarkable property makes 39 interesting after all. Just as 81 is interesting because it is the smallest square that can be decomposed into a sum of three squares ($9^2 = 1^2 + 4^2 + 8^2$), the number 39 is interesting because it is the smallest uninteresting integer.

Mathematicians have generalized Le Lionnais's comment into a proof that all natural numbers are interesting. If there is an uninteresting number, then there must be a first uninteresting number. But being the first uninteresting number would itself be an interesting property. Therefore, all numbers are interesting.

Maybe each natural number could have some surprising feature that makes it interesting. Often, what appears to be a dull number has proven to be "captivating." Maybe that is how it always is. There might even be some fancy proof to show that all appearances of dullness are illusory. But it seems strange that we could prove that each and every natural number is interesting by virtue of the least number theorem (which says that if any natural number has a property, then there is a least number that has that property). The argument seems too simple.

Consider the plight of ambivalent mathematicians who independently believe the conclusion of the simple argument. Since the conclusion implies each of the premises, they think the simple argument is valid and believe the premises and the conclusion. Despite granting that the argument is sound, they have difficulty believing that the premises give them extra warrant for the conclusion.

## ARE PARADOXES SETS?

At least since Epictetus, many philosophers have said that a paradox is a *set* of propositions that are individually plausible and yet jointly inconsistent. Notice that this set-based definition of paradox gives us a lower count of paradoxes than definitions that identify paradoxes with arguments or conclusions. Corresponding to a set with $n$ members will be $n$ arguments with the properties that Quine deems sufficient for paradox. For the negation of any member of the set is the conclusion of an argument containing the remaining members as premises. Since members of the original set are jointly inconsistent, the argument will be valid. And since the members are individually plausible, the audience will also find each premise of the argument persuasive.

This convertibility from sets to arguments only holds when the set is finite. If a set contains infinitely many propositions, then an argument does *not* result when one proposition is negated and the rest are used as premises. For an argument can only have finitely many premises.

The considerations lying behind the jumble arguments of chapter 8 show that even finitely large sets create a problem for the set-based definition of paradox. Each of the first 10,000 assertions in this book are believed by me but I also think they are jointly inconsistent. Yet that set is not really a paradox.

Nicholas Rescher has developed the set-theoretic conception of paradox with encyclopedic systematicity. He packs all of philosophy into the briefcases of paradox resolution.

To meet this corporate goal, Rescher imposes further requirements on the structure of paradoxes. He says that each member of the paradox must be self-consistent. (2001, 8) That way, the rejection of any member of the set is enough to restore consistency. Rescher defends this principle of self-consistency with the generalization that no contradiction is plausible.

The plausibility of contradictions is made poignant by Rescher's own violation of the consistency requirement. Consider a barber who shaves all and only those who do not shave themselves. Does the barber shave himself? Rescher formulates the set with the following as its first element: "There is—or can be—a barber who answers the specifications of the narrative." (2001, 144) Rescher says that this member of the set should be rejected: "there is not and cannot be a barber who answers to the specified conditions." Rescher is definitely correct; it is a theorem of logic that nothing can a bear a relation to all and only the things that do not bear it to themselves. (Thomson 1962, 104) But this means that the Barber paradox's "aporetic cluster" contains a contradiction (not a mere joint inconsistency as Rescher requires).

All of the direct answers to "Does the barber shave himself?" are strict contradictions. Furthermore, they are *indivisible* contradictions. The contradiction cannot be divided into self-consistent propositional components in the way "*P* and not *P*" can be segregated into a self-consistent *P* and a self-consistent not *P*.

Logical paradoxes are counterexamples to the principle that logic alone never implies a solution to a paradox. When a member of the paradox is a logical falsehood, logic *does* dictate what must be rejected. Since the inference to a logical truth is premiseless, the conclusion cannot be avoided by rejecting a premise. These paradoxes can be solved individualistically, without regard for the larger context of other beliefs. Holism about paradoxes does not hold universally.

## PARADOXES WITHOUT PREMISES

Unlike Rescher, Quine can allow for the possibility of paradoxes that are composed of a single proposition. As evident from the argument forms of *reductio ad absurdum* and conditional proof, there are arguments that support their conclusions solely through inference rules. The need to distinguish between inference rules and premises was made vivid by a dialogue published by Lewis Carroll (1895). Achilles tries to persuade the Tortoise with a syllogism:

(A) Things that are equal to the same are equal to each other.
(B) The two sides of this Triangle are things that are equal to the same.
(Z) The two sides of this Triangle are equal to each other.

The affable Tortoise will grant Achilles any premise he wishes. But the Tortoise insists that Achilles securely link the premises to the conclusion via a further premise:

(C) If A and B are true, Z must be true.

When Achilles adds (C) as an extra premise to (A) and (B), he finds that the Tortoise is still not willing to grant (Z). The Tortoise does not doubt the premises but wants a guarantee that the new set of premises really implies (Z). Accordingly, Achilles adds a second supplementary premise:

(D) If A and B and C are true, Z must be true.

Once again, the Tortoise grants all the premises but insists on a guarantee that the expanded set really implies the conclusion. And once again, Achilles bestows the desired premise: "If A and B and C and D are true, Z must be true." Achilles will never catch up to the Tortoise's incremental requests for extra premises.

Notice that what is puzzling here is the *sequence* of arguments, not any particular argument in the sequence. Why is the Tortoise being unreasonable when he cautiously asks for an extra premise to cement the relationship between the previous premise set and the conclusion? The common solution is to deny that any extra premises are needed to link the premises and the conclusion. They are instead linked by an inference rule.

The need to distinguish between premises and inference rules is compatible with their interchangeability. An axiom that states *P* is the case can be considered as an inference rule lets us introduce *P* into a proof without any premises. Carroll's puzzle does show that a system that contains just axioms cannot have any deductions. A proof system must have *some* inference rules. However, a system need not have any axioms. Indeed, systems of natural deductions are practical alternatives in logic instruction.

Formally, premiseless paradoxes are surprises deduced from the empty set. If validly deduced, they are veridical paradoxes. The most celebrated example is Kurt Godel's second incompleteness theorem: a consistent proof system that is strong enough to generate elementary number theory must be incomplete. There could be premiseless antinomies: two accepted inference rules might lead to opposite conclusions. (This would elegantly demonstrate that at least one of the accepted rules must actually be invalid.)

The interchangeability of inference rules and premises shows that the distinction between a substantive mistake and a mistake in reasoning is flexible. Rescher is being arbitrary when he says "Paradox is the product not of a mistake in *reasoning* but of a defect of substance: a dissonance of endorsements." (2001, 6-7) Quine is being equally arbitrary when he says that all falsidical paradoxes involve fallacious rules of inference. Often, a mistake that is characterized as a myth (a commonly believed falsehood) can be equally well characterized as a fallacy (an illegitimate but commonly applied inference rule).

As a logician, Quine was the victim of several unpremised paradoxes. In 1937 he published a new foundation of mathematical logic. His system was widely regarded as having advantages over previous systems. However, it was soon discovered to be too weak—in particular, there was no way to derive the axiom of infinity (which affirms the existence of infinite collections). In 1940 Quine strengthened the foundations in his book *Mathematical Logic*. But Barkley Rosser (1942) proved that Quine's supplemented system implies the Burali-Forti paradox. This demonstrated that Quine's book had jointly inconsistent axioms. When *logical* axioms are jointly inconsistent, then at least one of them is a contradiction. Since Quine chose only plausible axioms, Quine knew firsthand that there are plausible contradictions. (Quine was rescued from the quandary by Hao Wang [1950]. Wang surgically replaces a cancerous axiom with a consistent but industrious alternative.)

## GRADUALISM ABOUT PARADOXES

Before Quine challenged the analytic-synthetic distinction, there was a tendency to regard philosophy as being qualitatively different from the sciences. Scientists focus on synthetic statements whereas philosophers focus on analytic statements. Scientists explore reality with observations and experiments. Philosophers map our conceptual scheme through a logical study of semantics.

Quine agreed that philosophers are more apt to use the strategy of semantic ascent: they love to switch the topic from the things that puzzle us to the words we use in describing those puzzling things. "Don't talk about Truth! Talk about 'true'!" This strategy works when the words are better understood than the things. Such will be the case when we lack the standard techniques for solving problems that constitute each science. But Quine thinks that the use of semantic ascent is only a rough mark of philosophy. The physicist Albert Einstein engaged in semantic ascent when trying to resolve anomalies about the nature of simultaneity. And metaphysicians sometimes appeal to empirical results to solve philosophical problems.

Quine has fostered this naturalistic turn in philosophy. He maintains that philosophy differs from science in degree rather than kind. Philosophy should heed biology just as biology heeds physics and vice versa. Philosophy takes the further step of trying to organize the results of science into an overall view of the universe. But as we have seen with Brandon Carter's case for human extinction, cosmologists also take a wide perspective.

Lord Kelvin contrasted the unclarity of metaphysics with the rigor of physics by claiming that "In science there are no paradoxes." But if you enter "paradox" in a search engine for scientific journals, you get many references to scientific paradoxes. Many of the scientific paradoxes have been solved. But the same can be said about philosophical paradoxes such as those made famous by Zeno. Philosophical progress tends to be self-effacing because, over time, its solutions are incorporated as results in other fields. "Philosophy" is an indexical term akin to "here," "yesterday," "news." Its meaning shifts to cover issues that cannot (yet) be profitably delegated to the sciences.

Philosophy is like an expedition to the horizon. Under one interpretation, the venture is hopeless. We cannot reach the destination because what counts as the horizon constantly shifts. But becoming a pessimist on the basis of this tautology is like adopting a here-and-now philosophy on the strength of "Tomorrow never comes."

We can reach the horizon when the meaning of philosophy is rooted. Understandably, we look at the history of philosophy from the vantage point of the present. We are impressed by the resiliency of its issues and the broken ambitions of past thinkers. But an accurate measure of progress requires the adoption of an historical perspective. By this, I do not mean simply looking at the past. I mean looking *from* the past.

The twenty-first-century conception of philosophy will itself become a tonic to the vacuous pessimism of future generations. Given that I have correctly gauged the merits of Carter's doomsday argument, some philosopher in the distant future will find this book aging away in the remote corner of a library. As he browses, he will be amazed by what philosophers back in 2003 regarded as philosophy. He will know that many of the "paradoxes" discussed in this book are now definitively answered by physics or mathematics (or by some hitherto unconceived field). This future reader will wonder why *philosophers* tried to answer those questions. As he reads this final sentence, I remind him that he stands at a new horizon, inaccessible to the author of this book.

# Bibliography

Anscombe, G. E. M. (1956). "Aristotle and the Sea Battle." *Mind* 64:1–15.

Aquinas, Thomas (1929). *Summa contra gentiles*. Trans. The English Dominican Fathers. London: Burns, Oates & Washbourne, Ltd.

Aristotle (1941). *The Basic Works of Aristotle*. Ed. Richard McKeon. New York: Random House.

——— (1955). *Fragmenta Selecta*. Ed. W. D. Ross. Oxford: Oxford University Press.

Ashworth, E. J. (1984). "Inconsistency and Paradox in Medieval Disputations." *Franciscan Studies* 44:129–39.

Augustine (1872). *City of God*. Trans. M. Dods. Edinburgh: T. & T. Clark.

——— (1963). *The Trinity*, in *Fathers of the Church*, vol. 45. Trans. Stephen McKenna. Washington, D.C: Catholic University of American Press.

Beckmann, Peter (1970). *A History of Pi*. Boulder, Colo.: Golem Press.

Bennacerraf, P. (1970). "Task, Super-Tasks, and the Modern Eleatics," in *Zeno's Paradoxes*. Ed. Wesley C. Salmon. New York: Bobbs-Merrill.

Berkeley, G. (1944). *Philosophical Commentaries, Generally Called the Commonplace Book*. Ed. A. A. Luce. London: Kegan Paul, Trench.

——— (1986). *A Treatise Concerning the Principles of Human Knowledge*. La Salle, Ill.: Open Court.

Bernardete, José (1964). *Infinity: An Essay in Metaphysics*. Oxford: Clarendon Press.

Bertrand, Joseph (1889). *Calcul des probabilités*. Paris: Gauthier-Villars.

Boethius (2000). *The Consolation of Philosophy*. Trans. P. G. Walsh. Oxford: Oxford University Press.

Burke, Michael (1994). "Dion and Theon: An Essentialist Solution to an Ancient Puzzle." *Journal of Philosophy* 91: 129–39.

Canfield, John, and Don Gustavson (1962). "Self-Deception." *Analysis* 23:32–36.

Carroll, Lewis (1850). *The Rectory Umbrella and Mischmasch*. New York: Dover, reprinted 1971.

——— (1895). "What the Tortoise Said To Achilles." *Mind* 4:278–80.

Carter, Brandon (1974). "Large Number Coincidences and the Anthropic Principle in Cosmology," in *Confrontation of Cosmological Theories with Observational Data.* Ed. M. S. Longair. Dordrecht: Reidel.

Chisholm, Roderick (1979). *Person and Object.* La Salle, Ill.: Open Court.

Chroust, A. H. (1973). *Aristotle: New Light on His Life and on Some of His Lost Works.* Notre Dame, Ind.: Notre Dame University Press.

Cicero (1960). *De Fato.* Trans. H. Rackham. Cambridge: Harvard University Press.

Cole, John R. (1995). *Pascal.* New York: New York University Press.

Coleman, Francois (1986). *Neither Angel nor Beast.* London: Routledge & Kegan Paul.

Copleston, Frederick (1962). *A History of Philosophy*, vol. 1. Garden City, N.Y.: Image Books.

Darrow, Clarence (1957). *Attorney for the Damned.* Ed. Arthur Weinberg. New York: Simon & Schuster.

Diogenes Laertius (1925). *Lives of Eminent Philosophers*, 2 vols. Trans. R. D. Hicks. Cambridge: Harvard University Press.

Epictetus (1916). *The Discourses and Manual.* Trans. P. E. Matheson. Oxford: Clarendon Press.

Fadiman, Clifton (1985). *The Little, Brown Book of Anecdotes.* Boston: Little, Brown.

Findlay, J. N. (1958). *Hegel: A Reexamination.* London: Allen & Unwin.

Frege, Gottlob (1980). *Philosophical and Mathematical Correspondence.* Trans. H. Kaal. Chicago: Chicago University Press.

Gazzaniga, Michael S. (1998). *The Mind's Past.* Berkeley: University of California Press.

Geach, Peter (1948). "Mr. Ill-Named." *Analysis* 9:14–16.

Gibbard, Allan (1975). "Contingent Identity." *Journal of Philosophical Logic* 4:187–221.

Goodman, Nelson (1954). *Fact, Fiction and Forecast.* Cambridge: Harvard University Press.

Hall, Roland (1967). "Dialectic." *Encyclopedia of Philosophy.* Ed. Paul Edwards. Vol. 2: 385–88. New York: Macmillann.

Hallett, Michael (1984). *Cantorian Set Theory and Limitation of Size.* Oxford: Oxford University Press.

Harman, Gilbert, (1973). *Thought.* Princeton: Princeton University Press.

Heath, Thomas L. (1921). *A History of Greek Mathematics.* Oxford: Clarendon Press.

Hegel, G. W. F. (1880). *Hegel's Logic; being Part One of the Encyclopedia of the Philosophical Sciences*. Trans. W. Wallace. Oxford: Oxford University Press, 1975.

——— (1892). *Lectures on the History of Philosophy*, Vol. 1. Trans. E. S. Haldane. London: Kegan Paul, Trench, Trubner.

——— (1959). *Encyclopedia of philosophy*. Trans. and annotated Gustav Emil Mueller. New York: Philosophical Library.

——— (1969). *The Science of Logic*. Trans. A. V. Miller. London: Allen & Unwin.

——— (1970). *Vorlesungen ueber die Aesthetik*. 3 vols. Ed. E. Moldenauer and M. Michel Trans. Allegra De Laurentiis. Frankfurt: Suhrkamp.

——— (1973). *The Philosophy of Right*. London: Oxford University Press.

Hempel, Carl G. (1945). "Studies in the Logic of Confirmation." *Mind* 54:1–26, 97–121.

Herodotus (1920). *The Histories*. Trans. A. D. Godley. Cambridge: Harvard University Press.

Hume, David (1739). *A Treatise of Human Nature*. Ed. L. A. Selby-Bigge. Oxford: Clarendon Press, 1978.

——— (1951). *Enquiries*. Ed. L. A. Selby-Bigge. Oxford: Oxford University Press.

Jacquette, Dale (1991). "Buridan's Bridge." *Philosophy* 66/256: 455–71.

Jaynes, E. T. (1973). "The Well-Posed Problem." *Foundations of Physics* 3:477–92.

Johnston, L. S. (1940). "Another Form of the Russell Paradox." *American Mathematical Monthly* 7:474.

Kant, Immanuel (1950). *Prolegomena to Any Future Metaphysics*. Trans. Lewis White Beck. Indianapolis: Bobbs-Merrill.

——— (1965). *Critique of Pure Reason*. Trans. N. K. Smith. London: Macmillan.

Kelsen, H. (1937). "The Philosophy of Aristotle and the Hellenic-Macedonian Policy." *International Journal of Ethics* 48(1):1–64.

Kneale, William and Kneale, Martha (1962). *The Development of Logic*. Oxford: Clarendon Press.

Kraitchik, Maurice (1930). *La mathématique des jeux, ou Récréations mathématiques*. Bruxelles: Stevens Frères.

Kretzmann, Norman (1990). "Faith Seeks, Understanding Finds," in *Christian Philosophy*. Ed. Thomas P. Flint. Notre Dame, Ind.: University of Notre Dame Press.

Kripke, Saul (1972). *Naming and Necessity*. Cambridge: Harvard University Press.

——— (1982). *Wittgenstein on Rules and Private Language*. Cambridge: Harvard University Press.

Kuehn, Manfred (2001). *Kant: A Biography*. New York: Cambridge University Press.

Langford, C. H. (1968). "The Notion of Analysis in Moore's Philosophy," in *The Philosophy of G. E. Moore*. Ed. P. A. Schlipp. La Salle, Ill.: Open Court.

Leibniz, G. W. (1989). *Philosophical Essays*. Trans. and ed. Roger Ariew and Daniel Garber. Indianapolis: Hackett Publishing.

Le Lionnais, Francois (1983). *Nombres remarquables*. Paris: Hermann.

Leslie, John (1996). *The End of the World*. London: Routledge.

Littlewood, J. E. (1953). *Littlewood's Miscellany*. Ed. Bela Bollobas. Cambridge: Cambridge University Press.

Locke, J. (1975). *An Essay Concerning Human Understanding*. Ed. P. H. Nidditch. Oxford: Clarendon Press.

Long, A., and D. Sedley, trans. (1987). *The Hellenistic Philosophers*, vol. 1. Cambridge: Cambridge University Press.

Lucian (1901). *Dialogues and Stories from Lucian of Samosata*. Trans. Winthrop Dudley Sheldon. Philadelphia: Drexel Biddle.

Lutz, Cora E. (1975). "A Fourteenth-Century Argument for an International Date Line." *Essays on Manuscripts and Rare Books*. Hamden, Conn: Archon Books.

Mackie, J. L. (1973). *Truth, Probability, and Paradox*. Oxford: Oxford University Press.

Mackinson, D. C. (1965). "The Paradox of the Preface." *Analysis* 25:205–207.

Malcolm, Norman (1958). *Ludwig Wittgenstein*. New York: Oxford University Press.

Mann, Thomas (1955). *The Magic Mountain*. Trans. by Helen T. Lowe-Porter. New York: McGraw-Hill.

Matthews, Gareth (1974). "Paradoxical Statements." *American Philosophical Quarterly* 11:133–39.

McCarthy, John and Patrick Hayes (1969). "Some Philosophical Problems from the Standpoint of Artificial Intelligence." *Machine Intelligence*, 4. Ed. B. Metzer and D. Michie. Edinburgh: Edinburgh University Press.

McTaggert, John M. E. (1908). "The unreality of time." *Mind* 17:457–74.

——— (1921). *The Nature of Existence*, 2 vols. Ed. C. D. Broad. Cambridge: Cambridge University Press.

Miles, Jack (1995). *God: A Biography*. New York: Alfred A. Knopf.

Mill, John Stuart (1979). *An Examination of Sir William Hamilton's Philosophy*. Ed. J. Robeson. Toronto: University of Toronto Press.

Miller, J. (1998). "Aristotle's Paradox of Monarchy and the Biographical Tradition." *History of Political Thought* 19/4:501–16.

Moline, Jon (1969). "Aristotle, Eubulides and the Sorites." *Mind* 78/311: 293–407.

Moore, G. E. (1922). *Philosophical Studies*. London: Kegan Paul.

———(1939). "Proof of an External World." *Proceedings of the British Academy* 25:273–300.

Pascal, Blaise (1966). *Pensées*. Trans. A. J. Krailsheimer. London: Penguin.

Pausanias (1971). *Description of Greece*. Trans. Peter Levi. Harmondsworth: Penguin.

Pigafetta, Antonio (1969). *Magellan's Voyage: A Narrative Account of the First Circumnavigation*, 2 vols. Ed. and trans. R. A. Skelton. New Haven: Yale University Press.

Plato (1892). *The Dialogues of Plato*. Trans. B. Jowett. New York: Random House.

Plutarch (1880). *Plutarch's Lives of Illustrious Men*. Trans. John Dryden, revised by A. H. Clough. Boston: Little, Brown.

Pollock, John (1983). "How Do You Maximize Expectation Value." *Nous* 17/3:409–21.

Priest, Graham (1987). *In Contradiction*. Dordrecht: Martinus Nijhoff.

Quine, W. V. (1940). *Mathematical Logic*. New York: W. W. Norton.

——— (1960). *Word and Object*. Cambridge: MIT Press.

——— (1969). "Natural Kinds," in *Ontological Relativity and Other Essays*. New York: Columbia University Press.

——— (1970). *Philosophy of Logic*. Englewood Cliffs, N.J.: Prentice-Hall.

——— (1976). "The Ways of Paradox," in *The Ways of Paradox and Other Essays*. Cambridge: Harvard University Press.

Rea, Michael (1995). "The Problem of Material Constitution." *Philosophical Review* 104/4:525–52.

Read, Stephen (1979). "Self-Reference and Validity." *Synthese* 42/2 :265–74.

Reid, Thomas (1974). *An Inquiry into the Human Mind: On the Principle of Common Sense*. Ed. Derek R. Brooks. University Park, Penn.: Pennsylvania State University Press, 1997.

——— (1785). *Essays on the Intellectual Powers of Man*. Ed. Derek R. Brooks. University Park, Penn.: Pennsylvania State University Press, 2002.

Rescher, Nicholas (2001). *Paradoxes: Their Roots, Range, and Resolution*. Chicago: Open Court.

Rosser, Berkeley (1942). "The Burali-Forti Paradox." *Journal of Symbolic Logic* 7:1–17.

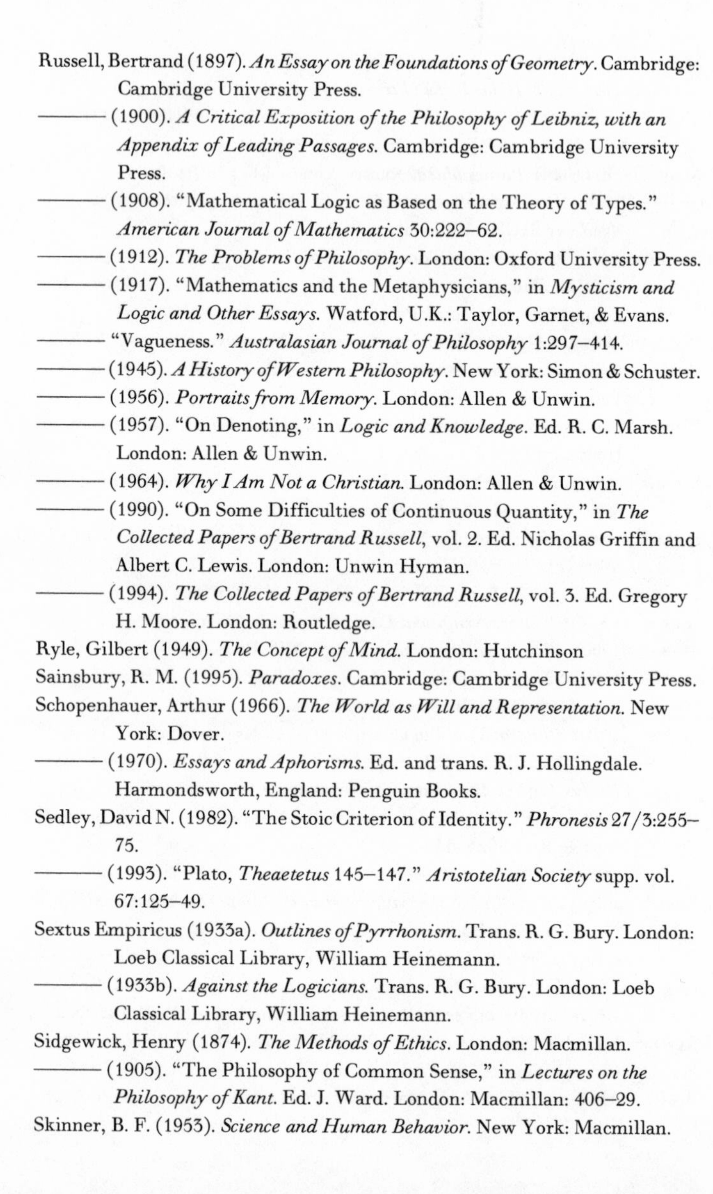


Russell, Bertrand (1897). *An Essay on the Foundations of Geometry*. Cambridge: Cambridge University Press.

——— (1900). *A Critical Exposition of the Philosophy of Leibniz, with an Appendix of Leading Passages*. Cambridge: Cambridge University Press.

——— (1908). "Mathematical Logic as Based on the Theory of Types." *American Journal of Mathematics* 30:222–62.

——— (1912). *The Problems of Philosophy*. London: Oxford University Press.

——— (1917). "Mathematics and the Metaphysicians," in *Mysticism and Logic and Other Essays*. Watford, U.K.: Taylor, Garnet, & Evans.

——— "Vagueness." *Australasian Journal of Philosophy* 1:297–414.

——— (1945). *A History of Western Philosophy*. New York: Simon & Schuster.

——— (1956). *Portraits from Memory*. London: Allen & Unwin.

——— (1957). "On Denoting," in *Logic and Knowledge*. Ed. R. C. Marsh. London: Allen & Unwin.

——— (1964). *Why I Am Not a Christian*. London: Allen & Unwin.

——— (1990). "On Some Difficulties of Continuous Quantity," in *The Collected Papers of Bertrand Russell*, vol. 2. Ed. Nicholas Griffin and Albert C. Lewis. London: Unwin Hyman.

——— (1994). *The Collected Papers of Bertrand Russell*, vol. 3. Ed. Gregory H. Moore. London: Routledge.

Ryle, Gilbert (1949). *The Concept of Mind*. London: Hutchinson

Sainsbury, R. M. (1995). *Paradoxes*. Cambridge: Cambridge University Press.

Schopenhauer, Arthur (1966). *The World as Will and Representation*. New York: Dover.

——— (1970). *Essays and Aphorisms*. Ed. and trans. R. J. Hollingdale. Harmondsworth, England: Penguin Books.

Sedley, David N. (1982). "The Stoic Criterion of Identity." *Phronesis* 27/3:255–75.

——— (1993). "Plato, *Theaetetus* 145–147." *Aristotelian Society* supp. vol. 67:125–49.

Sextus Empiricus (1933a). *Outlines of Pyrrhonism*. Trans. R. G. Bury. London: Loeb Classical Library, William Heinemann.

——— (1933b). *Against the Logicians*. Trans. R. G. Bury. London: Loeb Classical Library, William Heinemann.

Sidgewick, Henry (1874). *The Methods of Ethics*. London: Macmillan.

——— (1905). "The Philosophy of Common Sense," in *Lectures on the Philosophy of Kant*. Ed. J. Ward. London: Macmillan: 406–29.

Skinner, B. F. (1953). *Science and Human Behavior*. New York: Macmillan.

Skyrms, Brian (1975). *Choice and Chance*. Encino, Cal.: Dickenson Publishing.

Smullyan, R. (1978). *What Is the Name of This Book?* Englewood Cliffs, N.J.: Prentice-Hall.

Spade, Paul Vincent (1973). "The Origins of the Medieval 'insolubilia.'" *Franciscan Studies* 33:292–309.

Strabo (1929). *The Geography of Strabo*. Trans. Horace L. Jones. Cambridge, Mass.: Loeb Classical Library.

Thomas, Henry (1965). *Biographical Encyclopedia of Philosophy*. Garden City, N.Y.: Doubleday.

Thomson, J. F. (1962). "On Some Paradoxes," in *Analytical Philosophy*. Ed. R. J. Butler. New York: Barnes & Noble: 104–19.

——— (1970). "Tasks and Super-tasks," in *Zeno's Paradoxes*. Ed. Wesley C. Salmon. New York: Bobbs-Merrill.

Thorndike, Lynn (1944). *University Records and Life in the Middle Ages*. New York: Columbia University Press.

Turing, Alan (1936). "On Computable Numbers with an Application to the Entscheidungsproblem." *Proceedings of the London Mathematical Society*, Series 2, vol. 42: 230–65.

Unger, Peter (1979a). "I Do Not Exist," in *Perception and Identity*. Ed. G. F. MacDonald. Ithaca, N.Y.: Cornell University Press.

——— (1979b). "There Are No Ordinary Things." *Synthese* 4:117–54.

——— (1980) "The Problem of the Many." *Midwest Studies in Philosophy* 6:411–67.

Van Fraassen, Bas (1989). *Laws and Symmetry*. Oxford: Clarendon Press.

Van Inwagen, Peter (1981). "The Doctrine of Arbitrary Undetached Parts." *Pacific Philosophical Quarterly* 62:123–37.

Vlastos, Gregory (1983). "The Socratic Elenchus." *Oxford Studies in Ancient Philosophy* 1:27–58.

Wang, Hao (1950). "A Formal System of Logic." *Journal of Symbolic Logic* 15/1:25–32.

Wheeler, Samuel C. (1983). "Megarian Paradoxes as Eleatic Arguments." *American Philosophical Quarterly* 20/3:287–95.

Whitehead, Alfred North (1929). *Process and Reality*. Cambridge: Cambridge University Press.

——— (1947). *Essays in Science and Philosophy*. New York: Philosophical Library.

Wittgenstein, Ludwig (1958). *Philosophical Investigations*. Trans. G. E. M. Anscombe. New York: Macmillan.

——— (1964). *Philosophical Remarks.* Ed. R. Rhees. Trans. R. Hargreaves and R. White. Oxford: Basil Blackwell.

——— (1969a). *Tractatus Logico-Philosophicus.* Oxford: Basil Blackwell.

——— (1969b). *On Certainty.* Ed. G. E. M. Anscombe and G. H. von Wright, trans. D. Paul and G. E. M. Anscombe. Oxford: Basil Blackwell.

——— (1975). *Lectures and Conversations on Aesthetics, Psychology and Religious Belief.* Ed. C. Barrett. Berkeley: University of California Press.

——— (1976). *Wittgenstein's Lectures on the Foundations of Mathematics, Cambridge, 1939.* Ithaca, N.Y.: Cornell University Press.

——— (1978). *Remarks on the Foundations of Mathematics.* Oxford: Basil Blackwell, 3rd edition

Yablo, Stephen (2000). "A Reply to the New Zeno." *Analysis* 60/2:148–51.

# Index

Note: Page numbers in **bold** refer to the primary treatment of a specific philosopher. Page numbers in *italics* refer to concept definitions. Page numbers with *(fig)* refer to illustrations.